Faith, Mission and Challenge in Catholic Education

D1448470

In the **World Library of Educationalists**, international experts compile career-long collections of what they judge to be their finest pieces – extracts from books, key articles, salient research findings, major theoretical and practical contributions – so the world can read them in a single manageable volume. Readers will be able to follow the themes and strands and see how their work contributes to the development of the field.

Gerald Grace is renowned internationally for his research and teaching in the areas of Catholic education, spirituality, leadership and effectiveness in faith schooling, and educational policy. In *Faith, Mission and Challenge in Catholic Education*, Gerald Grace brings together 16 of his key writings in one place. Starting with a specially written Introduction, which gives an overview of his career and contextualises his selection within the development of the field, the chapters cover:

- the interactions of faith, mission and spirituality in the development of Catholic education, with special reference to the concept of spiritual capital
- how to replace ideology, polemic and prejudice in discussions about faith-based schooling with evidence-based argument
- understanding the distinctive nature of concepts such as 'leadership' and 'effectiveness' in faith-based education
- using 'mission integrity' as a key concept for the evaluation of contemporary Catholic schooling
- examining the interactions of Catholic values, Catholic curriculum and educational policy developments.

This book not only shows how Gerald Grace's thinking developed during his career, it also gives an insight into the development of the fields to which he contributed.

Gerald Grace was Visiting Professor and Founding Director of the Centre for Research and Development in Catholic Education (CRDCE) from 1997 to 2015 at the University of London Institute of Education, UK. He is currently Visiting Professor at St Mary's University, London's Catholic university.

Faith, Mission and Challenge in Catholic Education

The selected works of Gerald Grace

Taylor & Francis Group

LONDON AND NEW YORK

First published 2016 by Routledge

2 Park Square, Milton Park, Abingdon, Oxon OX14 4RN
711 Third Avenue, New York, NY 10017, USA

Routledge is an imprint of the Taylor & Francis Group, an Informa business.

First issued in paperback 2017

British Library Cataloguing in Publication Data
A catalogue record for this book is available from the British
Library

Library of Congress Cataloging-in-Publication Data
A catalog record for this book has been requested

ISBN: 978-1-138-83378-4 (hbk)
ISBN: 978-1-138-29653-4 (pbk)

Typeset in Sabon
by Apex CoVantage, LLC

Contents

Acknowledgements

In 1993, when I was Head of the School of Education at the University of Durham I attended a seminar organised by Dr Terry McLaughlin and Dr Bernadette O'Keeffe at St. Edmund's College, University of Cambridge. We had all gathered to discuss a recently published research study, *Catholic Schools and the Common Good* (1993) written by Professor Tony Bryk and his colleagues at Chicago University. This meeting with a number of Catholic scholars and researchers, including Tony Bryk, Joseph O'Keefe SJ, John Haldane, Richard Pring, James Arthur, Bernadette and Terry, caused a major change in my academic life and research interests. I was so impressed by the scholarly and research excellence of Bryk's study and so dismayed by the relatively undeveloped state of Catholic education research in the UK and Europe at the time, that I felt impelled – or as Catholics would say – 'called' to do something about it.

In 1996, I was invited to write a chapter on 'Leadership in Catholic Schools' in a collection of papers arising from the seminar and published as *The Contemporary Catholic School: context, identity and diversity*, edited by T. McLaughlin, J. O'Keefe SJ and B. O'Keeffe.

Following my retirement from Durham in September 1996, I formed the idea that what was required was a dedicated Centre for Research and Development in Catholic Education (CRDCE) to be established in a world-class centre for educational scholarship and research, with a remit to investigate Catholic education not only in the UK but internationally. In 1997, I approached Professor Peter Mortimore, the Director of the Institute of Education in the University of London, and put these ideas to him. As a leading educational researcher, Peter recognised that the whole field of Catholic education and of faith school education needed to be opened up to systematic enquiry and investigation. He supported the concept of CRDCE, assigned a room in the Institute for its use and arranged that I, as a Visiting Professor at the IOE, should be its first Director. He explained, however, that as a secular institution the IOE could not provide any funding for the Centre and that my first challenge would be to obtain such funding. This funding was subsequently provided with an initial grant from the Society of Jesus (British

Province) and further donations from 37 other religious congregations with missions in education, 3 charitable trusts and 2 Catholic teachers' associations. CRDCE, housed in the Institute of Education and supported by these voluntary contributions, has been the creative location which has facilitated all my research and publications in the period 1997–2015. I thank all these co-creators of CRDCE.

These acknowledgements witness that, in keeping with Catholic tradition, this book is the outcome of a communal effort and not simply of an individual; a communal effort and inspiration of the people and organisations named above. The support of Dr Paddy Walsh (Deputy Director: CRDCE) is especially acknowledged.

On a personal level, I wish to thank my family for their constant support, my friends, professional and academic colleagues and those who have acted as research assistants, secretarial and administration staff from 1997 to 2015: Mary Atherton, Alex Mermikides, Katja Hilevaara, Kate Punnachet, Sister Maria Supavai, SPC, Matthew Urmenyi, Sister Ugonna Igbo, DDL and Sister Leona Umeh, DDL.

The book would never have appeared without the encouraging and hospitable mentoring of the project by Anna Clarkson of Taylor and Francis/Routledge and I thank her for sustained support.

The following articles have been reproduced with the kind permission of the respective journals

'Renewing spiritual capital: An urgent priority for the future of Catholic education internationally', *International Studies in Catholic Education*, 2010, 2(2), 117–128.

'"First and foremost the Church offers its educational service to the poor": Class, inequality and Catholic schooling in contemporary contexts', *International Studies in Sociology of Education*, 2003, 13(1), 35–55.

'Making connections for future directions: Taking religion seriously in the sociology of education', *International Studies in Sociology of Education*, 2004, 14(1), 47–56.

'Educational studies and faith-based schooling: Moving from prejudice to evidence-based argument', *British Journal of Educational Studies*, 2003, 51(2), 149–167.

'On the international study of Catholic education: Why we need more systematic scholarship and research', *International Studies in Catholic Education*, 2009 1(1), 6–14.

'Faith school leadership: A neglected sector of in-service education in the United Kingdom', *Professional Development in Education*, 2009, 35(3), 485–494.

'The State and Catholic schooling in England and Wales: politics, ideology and mission integrity', *Oxford Review of Education*, 2001, 27(4), 489–500.

'Catholic social teaching should permeate the Catholic secondary school curriculum: an agenda for reform' *International Studies in Catholic Education*, 2013, 5(1), 99–109.

The following chapter extracts have been reproduced with kind permission of the respective publishers

'The Catholic school: the sacred and the secular' in G. Grace 'Catholic Schools: Mission, Markets and Morality, 2002, 3–17, Routledge Falmer.

'Catholic schools: The renewal of spiritual capital and the critique of the secular world' in G. Grace, *Catholic Schools: Mission, Markets and Morality*, 2002, 236–240, Routledge Falmer.

'Catholic schools and the common good: what this means in educational practice' from *Professional Focus Series* No. 2, 2000 2–10, Institute of Education, CRDCE.

'The dilemmas of Catholic headteachers', in G. Grace, *School Leadership: Beyond Educational Management*, 1995, 159–179, Falmer Press.

'Realising the mission: Catholic approaches to school effectiveness', in R. Slee, G. Weiner, S. Tomlinson (eds), *School Effectiveness for Whom?*, 1998, 117–127, Falmer Press.

'Mission integrity: contemporary challenges for Catholic school leaders: beyond the stereotypes of Catholic schooling', in K. Leithwood & P. Hallinger (eds)., *Second International Handbook of Educational Leadership and Administration*, Part 1, 2002, 427–440, Kluwer Academic Press.

'Christianity, modernities and knowledge', in R. Cowen, A. Kazamias & E. Unterhalter (eds), *International Handbook of Comparative Education*, Part 2, 2009, 907–922, Springer Publications.

'Catholic values and education policy', in J. Arthur & T. Lovat (eds) *Routledge International Handbook of Education, Religion and Values*, 2013, 84–99, Routledge.

Acknowledgement to the Benefactors of CRDCE, 1997–2015

Benefactors: The Society of Jesus (British Province); De La Salle Brothers; Christian Brothers; Faithful Companions of Jesus; Sisters of Charity of St Paul; Salesians of Don Bosco; Benedictines of Ampleforth; Sisters of Notre Dame; Society of the Holy Child Jesus; Missionaries of the Sacred Heart

(Dublin); Sisters of Mercy (England, N. Ireland and Ireland); Institute of the Blessed Virgin Mary; La Retraite Sisters; Servite Sisters; Congregation of Our Lady of the Missions; Order of the Holy Sepulchre; Loreto Sisters; The Daughters of the Cross of Liege; Daughters of Wisdom; Sisters of the Holy Family of Nazareth; Sisters of the Cross and Passion; Sisters of Charity of St. Louis; Presentation Brothers (Cork); Sisters of St. Joseph of the Apparition; Sisters of the Holy Family; Benedictines of Worth; Daughters of the Holy Spirit; Salesians of Don Bosco (Dublin); Ursulines of the Roman Union; Sisters of St. Paul of Chartres (Bangkok); Sisters of La Sainte Union; Marist Brothers (Melbourne); Daughters of Jesus; Malta Church Schools Association; Dominican Sisters of Cabra (Dublin); Xaverian Brothers; Archdiocese of Westminster; Archdiocese of Sydney; Jane Hodge Foundation; Catholic Association of Teachers, Schools and Colleges; Salesian Sisters; Benedictines of Ealing; Sisters of St. Joseph of Cluny (Dublin).

Foreword

Professor Grace has been very engaged in the longstanding debate about the distinctive mission of Catholic schools and universities which has been very much to the fore since the Second Vatican Council when Catholic schools were challenged to not only "develop with special care the intellectual faculties but also to form the ability . . . to foster a sense of values, to prepare for professional life" (Gravissimum Educationis 1965:5). This book marks Professor Grace's outstanding contribution to the Catholic Church's education mission, as teacher, university lecturer and professor and latterly as the Director of the Centre for Research and Development in Catholic Education, particularly in this significant year of the 50th anniversary of the Promulgation of Gravissimum Educationis.

The challenge to promote a holistic approach to Catholic education, implicit in the above quotation, encapsulates the substantial contribution of Professor Gerald Grace to the debate about the distinctive nature of Catholic education. As he indicates in the introduction to this collection of his writing on Catholic education Professor Grace was inspired by the seminal work of Anthony Bryk, *Catholic Schools and the Common Good*, published in 1993 which motivated him to found the Centre for Research and Development in Catholic Education and later to institute *International Studies in Catholic Education*, the first ever interdisciplinary and international journal devoted to the systematic study of Catholic education, in all its forms, across the world. Professor Grace has addressed a wide range of educational constituencies across the world including universities, international congresses and gatherings of Catholic headteachers among many others about the challenge to maintain a balance between school or university academic success and Catholic distinctiveness, warning constantly about the dangers of the hegemony of school effectiveness research in the educational discourse. In this context Professor Grace often acknowledges the influence of Basil Bernstein, his doctoral supervisor at the Institute of Education.

This collection of Professor Grace's writings ranges over six major fields of academic and research enquiry. The first part focuses on the challenge to build and promote spiritual capital, particularly among those charged with leading Catholic educational institutions in the 21st century. In this context Professor Grace often acknowledges the influence of Pierre Bourdieu. Grace builds on his paradigmatic definition of spiritual capital as "resources of faith and values derived from commitment to a religious tradition" (Grace 2002:232) to exhort Church and school leaders to ensure that such capital is constantly renewed in order to secure the future of Catholic education in an era marked by a precipitous decline in the number of teaching religious.

The second part underlines the Professor's best rehearsed theme of the primacy of the Church's educational mission to the poor, canonised in the records of the Westminster Synod and in the conciliar and post-conciliar Vatican documents on Catholic education. In the *International Handbook of Catholic Education*, which many regard as the apogee of his writings, the challenge of being faithful to the preferential option for the poor in an educational context stands out as *the* most crucial challenge, echoing the radical commitment to the service of the poor which stands at the heart of *The Catholic School* (1977).

In the third and fourth parts of this collection Professor Grace outlines arguments in support of schools with a religious character and the challenges faced by school leaders in an educational milieu dominated by market forces alluded to previously. This section of his writings is of particular significance in an era described recently by Cardinal Parolin as an "epochal transition" (UNESCO June 2015), marked by an almost exclusive tendency particularly in the West to focus on "having more as opposed to being more." This is reflected in the propensity of educational institutions to concentrate predominantly on measurable outcomes and their market position in relation to similar institutions. Professor Grace addresses this issue in the fifth part by speaking about mission integrity. In a definition close to the hearts of generations of Catholic leaders, "fidelity in practice and not just in public rhetoric to the distinctive and authentic principles of a Catholic education" (Grace 2002:8) is encapsulated in mission statements worldwide.

The final part of this collection focuses on Catholic Values, Catholic Curriculum and Educational Policies. The Professor states his admiration for Pope Benedict XVI's encyclical *Caritatis in Veritate* (2008) which he regards as a foundational text for post-16 students, particularly in regard to its exposition of the theological foundations for the Catholic Church's social teaching. Special mention is made to the contribution of the Jesuits in providing a model for the missions of subsequent religious orders dedicated to teaching many of whom flowered in the 19th century and whose charisms are often derivative to an extent of that of the Jesuits.

In inviting Professor Grace to contribute to their distinguished series World Library of Educationalists, Routledge have honoured him. It is, however, not alone. Alongside his many academic accolades, the Catholic Church has recognised Professor Grace's contribution to the Catholic educational mission. In 2010 he was invested as a Knight of the Equestrian Order of the Holy Sepulchre of Jerusalem (KHS) and in 2014 he was appointed by His Holiness Pope Francis as a Knight of the Order of St Gregory the Great. (KSG)

This book constitutes a valuable compendium for all involved in the Catholic Church's educational mission. It will feature prominently in the new Education Library being built here in St Mary's University, Twickenham, and London and across the world. St Mary's University wishes to congratulate wholeheartedly Professor Grace who has worked collegially and with a great generosity of spirit with colleagues from this University. I acknowledge in particular his outstanding contribution to the MA in Catholic School Leadership, this University's flagship Masters programme.

Ad Multos Annos!
Francis Campbell
Vice Chancellor
St Mary's University, Twickenham, London

Introduction

The international academic and research field of Catholic Education Studies is still in its early phase of development and my intention in assembling this collection of writings is to assist its further progress. On the basis of my own work (with others) I suggest that there are at least six major fields of scholarly enquiry and research investigation which provide a coherent and interrelated framework for future studies. The intention of this work is to stimulate such studies.

Part 1 addresses the first of these under the heading, 'Mission, spirituality and spiritual capital'. It may be said that one of the prime purposes of Catholic education, and perhaps its fundamental rationale, is to keep alive and to renew the culture of the Christian sacred in a profane and secular world. This, in itself, is a massive and daunting educational challenge, since the nature of the sacred is not easily articulated and represents as Emile Durkheim put it 'a struggle to conceive the inconceivable, to utter the unutterable and a longing for the Infinite' (1971, pp. 24–25).

Durkheim, in his classic study, *The Elementary Forms of the Religious Life* (1971),[1] made a sustained attempt, from the standpoint of religious anthropology and sociology, to understand the nature of the sacred and of its relation to the profane in human societies. For Durkheim, that which is sacred in a society refers to things which are superior in dignity and power to the elements of mundane life, to things 'set apart', to concepts of the transcendent and divine, of souls and of spirits and of the ultimate destiny of persons. The sacred is holy, ineffable and mysterious.

Religion, for Durkheim, was the social and cultural form which regulated relations with the sacred and prescribed the necessary rites 'of oblation and communion' in which believers must participate.

But religion also had other profound social and intellectual functions in that it was constitutive of categories of thought, of the nature of society and of constructs of an ideal world. Thus Durkheim concluded in a powerful and evocative passage:

> We have established the fact that the fundamental categories of thought . . .
> are of religious origin . . . Nearly all of the great social institutions have

been born in religion . . . If religion has given birth to all that is essential in society, it is because the idea of society is the soul of religion.

(p.419)

Catholic education in its various forms of school, college, university, parish and seminary is faced with the challenge of attempting to mediate to children, youth and adults some understanding of and some engagement with the power and nature of the sacred. For the Catholic Christian tradition this means in practice engagement with the life and teachings of Jesus Christ and of the saints, participation in the Holy Mass, the spiritual and moral teachings of the Church and the study and practice of the social teachings of the Church. It is a mission[2] and not just a social enterprise.

The three readings in Part 1 are my first attempts to think about these profound and foundational issues. Influenced by my own faith, study and empirical research and also by the writings of Pierre Bourdieu (1986) on the forms of capital, I suggested in *Catholic Schools: Mission, Markets and Morality* (2002) that 'spiritual capital' was the individual and collective inspiration and dynamic at the heart of Catholic education. What sustained the 60 Catholic headteachers in the inner-city schools which I had investigated in London, Birmingham and Liverpool was spiritual capital, which I defined initially as 'resources of faith and values derived from commitment to a religious tradition' (p. 236). I later elaborated and developed this central concept as:

- a source of vocational empowerment because it provides a transcendent awareness that can guide judgement and action in the mundane world, so that those whose own formation has involved the acquisition of spiritual capital do not act in education simply as professionals, but as professionals and witnesses.
- a form of spirituality in which the whole of human life is viewed in terms of a conscious relationship with God, in Jesus Christ and the saints, through the indwelling of the Spirit.
- a form of spirituality which has been the animating, inspirational and dynamic spirit which has empowered the mission of Catholic education internationally largely (although not exclusively) through the work of religious congregations with missions in education.

(2010 p. 125)

The argument of the first Part of this book suggests that it is spiritual capital which has sustained and inspired the worldwide Catholic educational mission in every country and it is the renewal of this spiritual capital in contemporary conditions that is essential for its future vitality and integrity.

If Part 1 is concerned with the spiritual foundations of Catholic education. Part 2, under the title 'The preferential option for the poor', is an exercise in clarifying the nature of the Church's commitment to the poor in its provision of educational services. In the absence of a fully articulated philosophy of Catholic education,[3] Catholic educators have in practice used as a resource the formal publications and declarations on Catholic education of the institutional Church. These publications, mediated by the Sacred Congregation for Catholic Education (later renamed the Congregation for Catholic Education), have provided the main source of theological, philosophical and educational guidance for lay Catholic educators. Of all the publications emanating from the Congregation, the 1977 document *The Catholic School* is, in my view, the most accessible and powerfully argued presentation of a new spirit of openness[4] and service to the wider world – the 'aggiornamento'[5] called for by the Second Vatican Council (1962–65) – and in this case applied to education. It marks the beginning of a new paradigm for Catholic education, with radical implications for policy and practice.

What should be called 'the foundation charter' for contemporary international Catholic education proclaimed three regulative principles for the future development of Catholic schooling, i.e. a commitment to the service of the common good in education, a commitment to solidarity and community in educational practice and a commitment to the service of the poor. The first of these was expressed as theology of praxis:

> For the Catholic school, mutual respect means service to the Person of Christ. Cooperation is between brothers and sisters in Christ. A policy of working for the common good is undertaken seriously as a working for the building up of the kingdom of God.
>
> (para 60)

The second represented a counter-cultural and oppositional stance to new ideological forms of aggressive individualism in public and economic policy in various contexts, the so-called 'New Right' syndrome.

> Today one sees a world which clamours for solidarity and yet experiences the rise of new forms of individualism. Society can take note from the Catholic school that it is possible to create true communities out of a common effort for the common good.
>
> (para 62)

The third involved a radical commitment to the poor (comprehensively defined): the 'poor' understood in economic terms, family terms and faith terms:

> First and foremost, the Church offers its educational service to the poor, or those who are deprived of family help and affection, or those who are far from the faith. Since education is an important means of improving

the social and economic condition of the individual and of peoples, if the Catholic school was to turn attention exclusively or predominantly to those from the wealthier social classes, it would be contributing towards maintaining their privileged position and could thereby continue to favour a society which is unjust.

(para 58)

The readings in Part 2 are my responses to taking these principles and commitments seriously. 'Catholic schools and the common good' was a paper delivered to a conference in South Africa in 2000 on what these commitments should mean in actual educational policy and practice, particularly in a country seeking a new vision after the fall of Apartheid.

The 'First and foremost' article arose from a presentation to the International Conference on Sociology of Education held in London in 2002 where the study theme was 'class, inequality and schooling in contemporary contexts'. I was attempting to persuade a very sceptical audience of sociologists (I think rather unsuccessfully!) that the Catholic Church was not part of the problem of class and inequality in schooling but potentially (post-Vatican II) part of the solution.

These papers and subsequent writings on the same theme were also designed to remind all Catholic educators that these are the proclaimed principles of modern Catholic educational policy and practice. In organising and editing the later publications, *International Handbook of Catholic Education* (2007) and the journal, *International Studies in Catholic Education* (2009–2015), I encouraged contributors to engage in empirical research to monitor the extent to which these principles were being realised in educational practice. For a variety of complex reasons,[6] it has to be said that the realisation of these social principles in Catholic educational practice is still a work in progress.

Part 3, 'Faith-based schools, religion and academe', is represented by three papers addressed to three different audiences. The 'Educational Studies and Faith-based Schooling' article of 2003 was a response to growing political and public debate about faith-based schooling conducted at a level of generalised assertion and ideological advocacy, with little reference to educational scholarship or research.

In 2001, the Humanist Philosophers' Group in their publication *Religious Schools: the case against* had claimed: 'We have clear evidence . . . from Northern Ireland where the separation of Catholic and Protestant schools has played a significant part in perpetuating the sectarian divide' (p. 35). No sources to substantiate this claim of 'clear evidence' were cited. Such disregard for the conventions of academic argument by university-based philosophers was, to say the least, disappointing.

In the same year, Professor Richard Dawkins of Oxford University writing in the *Times Educational Supplement* (23 February) asked the question,

'Why do people in Northern Ireland kill each other?' His answer was 'It is fashionable to say that the sectarian feuds are not about religion, the deep divides in that province are not religious, they are cultural, historical, economic. Well, no doubt they are . . . (but) . . . if Protestant and Catholic children ceased to be segregated throughout their school days, the troubles in Northern Ireland would largely disappear . . .'

This was a classic example of ideological, as opposed to scholarly, argument. Potentially significant structural causes of the troubles in Northern Ireland were described as 'fashionable' explanations, while the thrust of the article claimed that faith-based schooling was the fundamental cause of the problem – a massive over-simplification.

Provoked by these two examples of 'trahison des clercs', I felt I had to respond with a paper which argued that 'it is time to move on from prejudiced or ideological assertions about faith-based schooling to evidence-based argument' (p. 164) and I suggested a 'Research Agenda for Faith-based Schooling' so that such evidence could be realised.

My 'Taking Religion Seriously' article of 2004 was a second attempt to persuade one of the most sceptical of academic audiences, i.e. international sociologists of education, that their investigations of the social and cultural world of schooling needed to develop beyond a 'secularisation of consciousness paradigm'.[7] The paper argued that such a paradigm had limited the depth and scope of their intellectual enquiries: 'Sociological analysis which elides a religious dimension not only presents an over-simplified view of social relations in "the modern West", but it also fails to make an authentic engagement with many socio-cultural and educational situations internationally where God is far from dead'[8] (p. 47). I suggested that the mature work of one of the leading scholars in their field, Basil Bernstein, had in *Pedagogy, Symbolic Control and Identity* (1996) observed that in contemporary settings 'we are experiencing a truly secular concept of knowledge'[9] (p. 4). This secularised and marketised form of knowledge presented major dilemmas for all faith-based educational systems and an extensive research field which needed investigation. Michael Apple in his important book, *Educating the 'Right' Way: markets, standards, God and inequality* (2001) had given a lead but much more research of this type was required.

While the first two of these articles had been largely aimed at researchers and academics beyond the Catholic community, the third, 'On the international study of Catholic education', in 2009, was more explicitly directed to researchers and academics in Catholic higher education institutions. I had discovered during my preliminary researches to find qualified contributors to write for the research-based *International Handbook of Catholic Education* (2007) that a disturbingly large number of Catholic universities had nothing to contribute, because no research on Catholic education was being undertaken in their institutions. There existed therefore a major contradiction in the field of Catholic education. The educational system was the largest faith-based educational mission in the world, having almost 200,000 schools and 1,000 universities and colleges and yet very little systematic scholarship and research existed[10] to assist, evaluate and professionally develop this great mission as it faced the many challenges of the contemporary world. With the launch of the journal *International Studies in Catholic Education* in March 2009, I hoped to provide a stimulus for more research activity.

Taken together the readings in Part 3 of this book are a call to researchers both external to and internal to the Catholic community to assist in the work of building a robust and well-evidenced field of Catholic and Faith School Studies.

Part 4 focuses on 'Concepts of educational leadership and concepts of educational "effectiveness" in Catholic schooling'. As part of the rising dominance of market culture in education during the 1980s I noted the remarkable growth of education management studies (EMS) within the wider field of education studies. Education was being recontextualised in the marketplace, along with explicit assertions that 'education shares the main characteristics of other commodities traded in the market place' (New Zealand Treasury 1987, p. 33). The growth of EMS was a predictable cultural outcome of these ideological developments.

Texts on education management had become a significant sector of educational publishing but, more pervasively, the language, assumptions and ideology of management has started to dominate the language, consciousness and actions of many of those working within the education sector. My concern was that the study and practice of school leadership risked being reduced to a branch of EMS, to a set of technical and logistical considerations about the school as 'a production-function centre',[11] a devolved budget centre or a value-adding centre. All of this threatened the historical associations of school leadership with vision, mission and values in education, and responsibilities for social, spiritual and moral formation.

In *School Leadership: Beyond Education Management* (1995) I argued that, while educational management *is* crucial for achieving organisational effectiveness, educational leadership has responsibilities for determining what 'effectiveness' actually means in any school situation and for constant monitoring that the school is actually living in practice the principles declared in its mission statement.

The extract 'The dilemmas of Catholic headteachers', taken from the 1995 book, reports my research with 35 school leaders in England where the analytical focus was to investigate how they understood educational leadership and how they were responding to the changing culture of English schooling in the 1980s and early 1990s.

As might be expected, this research demonstrated a range of opinions about the nature of leadership and about responses to the changing context of schooling. However, this sample of Catholic school leaders was largely in agreement that as leaders they faced a spectrum of moral, ethical and professional dilemmas of a kind not faced by their predecessors. These dilemmas included issues of moral behaviour relating to students, parents and teachers; problems of admissions and exclusions; how to respond to government policy initiatives[12]; and perceived tensions between Catholic values and market values in education.

Overall there was a clear sense that the role of a Catholic school leader was becoming much more demanding and they looked for much more professional support from their local diocese. This was not always forthcoming.[13]

What the research did establish was that there existed distinctive concepts of Catholic school leadership expressed in a language[14] that would not be found in the ubiquitous textbooks of education management studies. School leadership per se was not simply a secular and technical concept which could learn much from the corporate world of business (as EMS texts suggested); it had, at least in the faith school sector, distinctive associations with religious, spiritual and moral values. These had to be recognised and defended in a growing culture of market-place education.

Having argued this case in 1995, a further opportunity presented itself in 1997 when I was invited to contribute a chapter for a book entitled, *School Effectiveness for Whom? Challenges to the School Effectiveness and School Improvement Movements* which was published in 1998. This chapter argued that there was a distinctive Catholic approach to the concept of school effectiveness which worked from the commitments of the school's mission statement. As I expressed it in 'Realising the mission: Catholic approaches to school effectiveness':

> Mission statements have many catholic virtues. They constitute a principled and comprehensive articulation of what a school claims to be its distinctive educational, social and moral purposes . . . They are published to the community as a statement saying 'this is the basis upon which you can judge us' . . . School effectiveness research could then become a report to the community on 'realising the mission' and upon what aspects of the mission were being realised and what aspects were being impeded and why. This would be a catholic and Catholic approach to SER in the sense of being inclusive of the full range of school outcomes.
> (pp. 120–121)

Such an inclusive concept of 'effectiveness' would help to resist the contemporary tendency to evaluate schools predominantly upon their academic and test results by adding a serious evaluation of their spiritual, civic, moral and social outcomes to provide a more holistic picture.[15]

Part 4 concludes with a brief paper written for the journal *Professional Development in Education* in 2009. In 'Faith school leadership: a neglected sector of in-service education in the United Kingdom', I tried to encourage universities, professional development agencies and bodies such as the

National College for School Leadership (NCSL) to recognise the needs of the faith school sector and I outlined a possible research agenda to underpin such work.[16]

Part 5, 'Mission integrity', highlights a central concept in all my writing, research and conference presentations. Having always insisted that Catholic education was a mission and not just a social or business enterprise, and having emphasised the importance of mission statements as a condensed form of the theology of Catholic schooling, the issue of the status of mission integrity in contemporary Catholic education naturally followed.

I first used the concept of mission integrity in a paper written for the *Oxford Review of Education* in 2001 and published as 'The State and Catholic Schooling in England and Wales: politics, ideology and mission integrity'. This was a social-historical study which attempted to illustrate how the Catholic hierarchy struggled to preserve the mission integrity of their schools in the face of sometimes hostile policies of English government in the nineteenth and early twentieth centuries. In the 1980s and 1990s, a strong interventionist State was propagating an individualistic and market competitive culture in education which, in the view of the Catholic Bishops' Conference, threatened Catholic values in education and the relative autonomy of schools. In 1997, the Catholic hierarchy in a publication entitled *The Common Good in Education* gave a decisive rejection of State-sponsored policies of marketisation in education: '**Education is not a commodity to be offered for sale. The distribution of funding solely according to the dictates of market forces is contrary to the Catholic doctrine of the common good**' (p. 13).

Although the Catholic bishops did not use the language of mission integrity in this document, this was the concept which I used in interpreting their defence of the educational cultures of Catholic schools at this time. The concept of mission integrity was therefore first launched in the context of Church–State relations in the 1980 and 1990s in England, but it was one that could be clearly applied internationally.

Invited to write a chapter for the *Second International Handbook of Educational Leadership and Administration,* to be published in 2002, I decided to elaborate the brief definition of mission integrity[17] which I had given earlier and also to illustrate it by providing more empirical and research detail. This resulted in the chapter 'Mission integrity: contemporary challenges for Catholic school leaders'. The concept of mission integrity was now focused upon individual schools and upon the responsibilities of Catholic school leaders to be guardians of the integrity of their schools. Further development of the concept was given as a formal definition, i.e. 'fidelity in practice and not just in public rhetoric to the distinctive and authentic principles of a Catholic education' (p. 432), and it was fully recognised that mission integrity was a contested concept because different interpretation of it existed both internationally and in local contexts.[18] However, it was emphasised that any school which claimed the title 'Catholic' could not be seriously at odds with what the Congregation for Catholic Education suggested were the authentic principles for Catholic education.

In conference presentation in various parts of the world I have therefore encouraged leaders of schools, colleges and universities to regard the monitoring and defence of mission integrity as one of their prime responsibilities, possibly *the* prime responsibility.

Part 6, 'Catholic values, Catholic curriculum and education policy' represents three extracts from my most recent writings. I am aware that only the 2013 article, 'Catholic social teaching should permeate the Catholic secondary school curriculum: an agenda for reform' can claim any real originality. The 2009 and 2013 chapters for the *International Handbook of Comparative Education* and the *Routledge International Handbook of Education, Religion and Values* do repeat earlier themes in my writing. All I can say in my defence is that the titles of the chapters were specified by the editors of the handbooks. I must therefore confess (in Catholic tradition) that there is much repetition in these chapters, with perhaps a few new insights.

My thinking about Catholic social teaching was stimulated by an invitation to contribute a chapter to a proposed book, to be edited by Keith Chappell and Francis Davis, entitled *Catholic Social Conscience: reflection and action on Catholic social teaching* (2011). The book itself arose from a conference at Blackfriars Hall in Oxford and the paper I presented there was subsequently developed as the article, 'Catholic social teaching should permeate the Catholic secondary school curriculum: an agenda for reform' (2013).

The encyclical *Caritas in Veritate* (2009) of Pope Benedict XVI[19] had made a deep impression upon me. It presented an accessible survey of contemporary religious, moral and cultural issues, of economic, business and enterprise issues and of social, environmental and political issues for its readers to think about. At the same time, these issues were powerfully integrated with the theological and social teachings of the Church. All of this provided a rich resource for curriculum and pedagogic development in Catholic schools across the world, with implications for the teaching of all subject areas. In the article 'Catholic social teaching should permeate . . .', I suggested that here was a resource which would engage the interest of senior students in Catholic schools and at the same time strengthen the distinctive Catholicity of the curriculum programmes of the schools.

My contribution to the *International Handbook of Comparative Education, Part Two* (2009) had required me to write on the theme, 'Christianity, modernities and knowledge'. I was instructed by the editor, Professor Robert Cowen, that while my writing could concentrate mainly upon Catholic Christianity, some comparative analysis would have to be made relating to cultures of Reformed Christianity.

This chapter was based upon a socio-historical analysis of the educational responses of Catholic Christianity to the challenges of early Modernity in

Europe, particularly as constituted by the Protestant reformations in the six-teenth and seventeenth centuries and later by ideas generated by the Enlight-enment in the eighteenth and early nineteenth centuries.

The Catholic response to these challenges of early modernity was to gen-erate specially trained men and women in organised formations dedicated to the work of Catholic education to counter these threats to 'Catholic Truth'.[20] The Society of Jesus (the Jesuits) was the most powerful of these religious congregations working in education and provided a model for the missions of many subsequent religious congregations working in education in Europe and the wider world. Durkheim, in his classic study *The Evolution of Educational Thought* (1938/1977), assigned three chapters of his book to a close examination of Jesuit educational culture – its curriculum, pedagogy and assessment – and noted its considerable influence upon Catholic educa-tional culture in Europe.

In facing the challenges of late modernity for Catholic education an argu-ment was made that the Second Vatican Council (1962–1965) and especially the aggiornamento thinking propagated by the *Catholic School* document of 1977 was crucial. My analysis suggested that 'the foundation principles for Catholic education in the era of Late Modernity' could be summarised as:-

- a case for the distinctive and necessary role of the Catholic school in pluralism
- the relation of Catholic education to human formation in a holistic sense
- the integration of Faith and Life to be achieved by educational experience
- a distinctive conception of the nature and purposes of knowledge
- the role of teachers as witnesses
- a distinctive relation to concepts of the sacred
- a necessary relation to concepts of social justice and the common good
- an openness to the wider world.

A brief and inadequate section on 'The Educational Responses of Reformed Christianity', building upon the work of Karen Armstrong (2001) and of Michael Apple (2001) observed the growing influence of types of evangeli-cal Christianity in the field of international education.[21] These developments constituted a fundamentalist Christian response.

The last extract in Part 6 is taken from my chapter 'Catholic values and education policy', written for the *Routledge International Handbook* in 2013. Here I attempted to highlight to what extent the educational principles articulated by Rome had been responded to in policy and practice by Bish-ops' Conferences, Religious Congregations and by Catholic school leaders. This analysis identified that Bishops' Conferences (as executive agencies) had been particularly active in South Africa (against apartheid schooling); in England and Wales (in propagating common good educational ideas) in Latin America (in linking liberation theology, the preferential option for the poor and the educational ideas of Paulo Freire) and in India (with programmes for the marginalised). The analysis concluded with observing a contradiction in which many Catholic schools internationally are located:

> Many states in the contemporary globalised world want to benefit from the academic quality of Catholic schools but their counter-cultural tendencies can be politically problematic because they often constitute a religious, moral and social critique of some of policies that governments are pursuing. It is therefore in the interests of the State to maximise and reward the former, while seeking to ignore or marginalise the latter.
>
> (p. 97)

My conclusion to this chapter can also serve as the conclusion to this Introduction with these words 'The Catholic Church at various levels has to resist these strategies to compromise the mission integrity of its schools, colleges and universities. It has to hold fast to the teaching of Jesus Christ, "Render to Caesar that which is Caesar's, and to God that which is God's" (Mt. 22. 21)'.

Notes

1 Original publication in French (1912): first published in English in 1971.
2 Inspired by the imperative of Jesus Christ, 'Go and teach all nations' (Mt. 28. 19).
3 See contemporary attempts to articulate a philosophy of Catholic education in Carmody (2011), Whittle (2014) and Whittle (2015).
4 As *The Catholic School* document expressed it:

> In the certainty that the Spirit is at work in every person, the Catholic school offers itself to all, non-Christians included . . .
>
> (para 85)

5 Defined by Joseph Ratzinger (later Benedict XVI) as: 'bringing up to date' (1966. p. ix)
6 These include ideological, political and economic challenges in different countries and also slowness on the part of national Conferences of Catholic Bishops (the executive agencies) in some countries to act upon these principles.

 The relative fall in vocations to Religious Congregations (in the West) and the economic consequences of this for teacher employment has been a major factor in weakening services to the poor.
7 I developed this concept from the writings of Michael Paul Gallagher, SJ, who argued that contemporary intellectual culture in the West is characterised by 'secular marginalisation'. Gallagher claimed that, 'especially in the academic and media worlds, a secular culture reigns, with the result that religion is subtly ignored as unimportant' (1997, p. 23).
8 The use of this phrase was intended as a counter to Steve Bruce's book, *God is Dead: secularization in the West* (2002). A dramatic title, but at the cost of a considerable oversimplification of religious culture in the West.

9 Bernstein developed this observation to say:

> Of fundamental significance, there is a new concept of knowledge and of its relation to those who create it and use it. The new concept is a truly secular concept. Knowledge should flow like money to wherever it can create advantage and profit. Indeed Knowledge is not like money, it *is* money.
>
> (1996, p. 87)

10 The obvious exception to this situation was the USA, where considerable and sophisticated empirical work had been undertaken for several decades on various aspects of Catholic education studies. See Grace (2002, pp. 96–99).

11 Schools had been referred to in these terms in the New Zealand Treasury document (Vol 2. *Education Issues*, 1987; see Grace 1989, p. 213).

12 The particular policy issue at this time related to Grant Maintained School status, see Grace (1995, pp. 169–174).

13 In fairness, it must be stated that many Diocesan Education Offices in England operated with a relatively small number of professional staff, and this is still the case.

14 A typical example would be:

> To demonstrate that Christian values and beliefs are relevant and of use in the modern world. To help young people have a sense of justice, rights and responsibilities which transcends pragmatism. To help them towards a knowledge that there is a God who loves them and gives them worth.
>
> (p. 162)

15 Much more scholarly and research attention must be given to ways of making systematic evaluations and assessments of school outcomes related to spiritual, civic, moral and social developments of school students.

16 It is encouraging to report that the National College for Teachers and Leadership in the UK is taking this seriously, with the recent launch of a Module on 'Faith School Leadership'.

17 Stated at the time as 'fidelity in practise and not just in doctrine to the distinctive and authentic principles of Roman Catholic education' (p. 498).

18 External observers of the Catholic Church concentrate upon its monolithic characteristics but seem to be unaware of its internal differentiation characterised by some as 'Faithful Dissent'. See Curran (1986).

19 Pope Benedict XVI has often been represented as a 'conservative' thinker. Any serious reading of *Caritas in Veritate* (2009) makes some revision of this judgement necessary.

20 The Catholic Church at this time held an absolutist conception of Truth, i.e. the Truth (which was from God) was in the sole possession of the Church.

21 I noted the historical irony that the Catholic Church is now witnessing a serious reduction in its missionaries of education (i.e. the religious congregations), while the missionaries of Evangelical Christianity appear to be increasing rapidly across the world.

References

Apple, M. (2001) *Educating the 'Right' Way: markets, standards, God and inequality*, New York, RoutledgeFalmer.

Armstrong, K. (2001) *The Battle for God: A History of Fundamentalism*, New York, Ballantine.

Arthur, J. & Lovat, T. (eds) (2013) *Routledge International Handbook of Education, Religion and Values*, London, Routledge.

Bernstein, B. (1996) *Pedagogy, Symbolic Control and Identity,* London, Taylor & Francis.

Bishops' Conference of England & Wales. (1997) *The Common Good in Education,* London, CES.

Bourdieu, P. (1986) 'The Forms of Capital', in J. McPherson (ed.) *Handbook of Theory and Research for the Sociology of Education*, New York, Greenwood Press.

Bruce, S. (2002) *God is Dead: secularization in the West*, Oxford, Blackwell Publishing.

Carmody, B. (2011) 'Towards a Contemporary Catholic Philosophy of Education'. *International Studies in Catholic Education.* 3 (2) pp. 106–119.

Cowen, R., Kazamias, A. & Unterhalter, E. (eds) (2009) *International Handbook of Comparative Education*, Dordrecht, Springer.

Curran, C. (1986) *Faithful Dissent*, London, Sheed & Ward.

Dawkins, R. (2001) 'No faith in the Absurd', *Times Educational Supplement.* 23 February, London.

Durkheim, E. (1971) *The Elementary Forms of the Religious Life: a study in religious sociology*, London, Allen & Unwin.

Durkheim, E. (1977) *The Evolution of Educational Thought,* London, Routledge & Kegan Paul.

Gallagher, M. (1997) 'New Forms of Cultural Unbelief', in P. Hogan & K. Williams (eds), *The Future of Religion in Irish Education,* Dublin, Veritas.

Grace, G. (1989) 'Education: Commodity or Public Good?' *British Journal of Educational Studies* 37 (3), pp. 207–221.

Grace, G. (1995) *School Leadership: Beyond Education Management*, London, Falmer.

Grace, G. (2002) *Catholic Schools: Mission, Markets and Morality*, London, RoutledgeFalmer.

Grace, G. & O'Keefe, J. (eds). (2007) *International Handbook of Catholic Education*, 2 vols. Dordrecht, Springer Publications.

Humanist Philosophers' Group (2001) *Religious Schools: the case against*, London, British Humanist Association.

New Zealand Treasury, (1987) *Government Management: Brief to the in-coming government. Vol 2. Education Issues*, Wellington, Government Printer.

Pope Benedict XVI (2009) *Caritas in Veritate*, London, Catholic Truth Society.

Ratzinger, J. (1966/2009) *Theological Highlights of Vatican II*, New York, Paulist Press.

Sacred Congregation for Catholic Education (1977) *The Catholic School,* Vatican City, Liberia Editrice Vaticana.

Slee, R., Weiner G. & Tomlinson, S. (eds). (1998) *School Effectiveness for Whom?* London, Falmer.

Whittle, S. (2014) 'Towards a contemporary philosophy of Catholic education: moving the debate forward', *International Studies in Catholic Education* 6 (1), pp. 46–59.

Whittle, S. (2015) *A Theory of Catholic Education,* London, Bloomsbury Academic.

Part I

Mission, spirituality and spiritual capital

Chapter 1

The Catholic school

The sacred and the secular

Catholic Schools: Mission, Markets and Morality, 2002, 3–17,
RoutledgeFalmer.

The future of the Catholic voluntary-aided school in England and Wales looks bright and is, from one perception, an occasion for celebration. Catholic schools, both primary and secondary, have been well placed in the public league tables of academic and test results which are, in contemporary society, an important source of the making or breaking of a school's reputation and public image.[1] In addition to support from local Catholic communities, the schools are much sought after by parents of other Christian faith communities and by those of other faiths. In many areas therefore Catholic schools are filled to capacity and are in fact over-subscribed by parents attracted by the Catholic school's reputation for academic success, 'good' discipline and for taking spiritual and moral education seriously. Speaking of 'The Church's Mission in Education', Cardinal Hume argued that:

> Today, Catholic schools are increasingly popular, not only because of the good academic results they often achieve, but also because many parents sense that a Catholic school might help their children to develop the self-discipline, moral resilience and spiritual maturity so necessary in surviving exposure as young adults to the winds of secularism and materialism in our society.
>
> (1997, pp. 25–6)

The decision by the British Prime Minister (an Anglican) and his wife (a Catholic) to send their children to Catholic secondary schools in London appeared to confer public and political legitimacy upon a schooling system that has, even as late as the 1970s, been subject to ideological critique from some sections of the Left and to calls for its abolition on the grounds of social divisiveness, covert selection and a general undermining of the reputation and effectiveness of the state system of schooling.[2]

The contemporary 'success' and legitimacy of Catholic schools now appear to be assured. The schools have most of the surface and visible indicators of success and effectiveness and most of them enjoy a strong position in the competitive internal market for schooling which developed in the 1980s. In an educational culture and discourse in which 'improvement', 'quality assurance', 'stakeholder confidence', 'success', 'effectiveness' and 'excellence' are dominant categories for the making of public judgements, Catholic schools have moved from a previously marginal[3] to a currently centre-stage position of public and official endorsement.

While there is cause for celebration among the Catholic community in England and Wales for the present achievements of a schooling system which began with the efforts of the Catholic Poor-School Committee in 1847, the paradox is that this very evident success generates its own contemporary threats to the integrity of the holistic mission caused by undue emphasis upon part of the mission; the potential to become preoccupied by the visible and measurable in education to the detriment of the invisible and more intangible outcomes of schooling; the potential for Catholic schools to be incorporated into a secular market place for education which may weaken their relation with the sacred and the spiritual and the distinctive culture of Catholicity itself. As the Sacred Congregation for Catholic Education observed in 1977:

> Today, as in the past, some scholastic institutions which bear the name Catholic, do not appear to correspond fully to the principles of education which should be their distinguishing feature.
>
> (p. 50)

If this situation was perceived in 1977, it seems very likely that over two decades later, following the impact of instrumentalist and radical reforms in education, the gap between the theory and the practice of Catholic schooling may have increased. Part of the intention of this present study is to attempt to illuminate this issue by reference to contemporary fieldwork data. However, before this is attempted, the enterprise of Catholic schooling must be located in relation to its theoretical, historical and cultural contexts. From what I have called, in other places, a policy scholarship perspective,[4] there can be no significant understanding of contemporary Catholic schooling which does not involve some engagement with its theological–social rationale and some awareness of the historical and cultural contexts which have shaped and influenced its development. It seems evident that the analytical priority has to be given to what I have called the *theological–social rationale* of the Catholic school and in particular to the Catholic school's relation to concepts of the sacred, the profane and the secular; to its relation to contemporary educational principles and practice; and to its relation to the institutional Roman Catholic Church.

The Catholic school and the culture of the sacred

It may be said that one of the prime purposes of the Catholic school and perhaps its fundamental rationale is to keep alive and to renew the culture of the sacred in a profane and secular world. This, in itself, is a massive and daunting educational challenge since the nature of the sacred is not easily articulated and represents 'a struggle to conceive the inconceivable, to utter the unutterable and a longing for the Infinite'.[5] Durkheim, in his classic study *The Elementary Forms of the Religious Life* (1971), made a sustained attempt, from the standpoint of religious sociology, to understand the nature of the sacred and of its relation to the profane in human societies. For Durkheim, that which was sacred in a society referred to things which were superior in dignity and power to the elements of mundane life, to things 'set apart', to notions of the transcendent and divine, of souls and of spirits and of the ultimate destiny of persons. The sacred was a representation of the Other in human existence, 'something added to and above the real',[6] that which was holy, ineffable and mysterious. Religion, for Durkheim, was the social and cultural form which regulated relations with the sacred and prescribed the necessary rites 'of oblation and communion, imitative rites, commemorative rites and expiatory rites'.[7] But religion, in the societies which Durkheim studied, had other profound social and intellectual functions in that it was perceived to be constitutive of categories of thought, the nature of society and constructs of an ideal world. Thus Durkheim concluded in a powerful and evocative passage:

> We have established the fact that the fundamental categories of thought . . . are of religious origin . . . Nearly all of the great social institutions have been born in religion . . . If religion has given birth to all that is essential in society, it is because the idea of society is the soul of religion.[8]

Given Durkheim's conviction that 'the idea of society is the soul of religion', it is not surprising that he was opposed to forms of radical individualism and there can be little doubt about what his response to Mrs Thatcher's assertion that 'there is no such thing as society' would have been.[9] For Durkheim, religion constituted not only what society was but crucially also what it could be in a perfected and ideal form. While the concept of 'utopia' is not explicitly used in *The Elementary Forms of the Religious Life*, it is clear that Durkheim saw religion as contributing to the formation of an ideal world.[10]

In this analysis, religion is seen to be an essential cultural relay between the sacred and the profane but the categories themselves are sharply differentiated:

> In all the history of human thought there exists no other example of two categories of things so profoundly differentiated or so radically opposed to one another . . . The sacred and the profane have always and everywhere been conceived by the human mind as two distinct classes, as two worlds between which there is nothing in common. To move from one world to another requires initiation rites in a long series of ceremonies.
>
> (1971, pp. 38–9)

At the basis of this sharp distinction between the sacred and the profane is the notion that the profane, viewed as the mundane exigencies of everyday living, has the potential to pollute and devalue the purity and the integrity of that which is sacred. From this perspective the polluting potential of the mundane world has to be counteracted by the creation of social distance, ritual formulation, strong cultural insulators and physical structures designed to protect the integrity of the sacred. The forms of religious culture and practice are designed to connect the world of the sacred with the world of the profane while ensuring, through a whole array of cultural insulations and boundaries, that the sacred is not devalued by this connection.

This concept of the sacred and of its associated rituals and modes of realisation are manifested in Roman Catholic religious culture in particular ways. The centrality of the Mass as a dramatic realisation of the sacred in the mundane world is that which is most distinctive of the Catholic Christian tradition. Durkheim, who viewed Catholic Christianity from his own location within Judaic culture, observed that Catholicism was:

> inconceivable without the ever-present idea of Christ and his ever-practised cult; for it is by the ever-living Christ, sacrificed each day, that the community of believers continues to communicate with the supreme source of the spiritual life.
>
> (p. 33)

The institutional Roman Catholic Church has for centuries been the repository of 'the sacred mysteries' of Christianity, of its ritual modes and of its regulatory structures, of relations with other faiths and with non-faith and of its whole relationship with the profane world. While the history of Roman Catholicism provides many examples of the sharp separation between the sacred and the profane noted by Durkheim (the enclosed religious life of monasteries and convents being just one illustration), Catholic Christianity has always been characterised by two contrasting forms of relation to the external world. On the one hand there has been the notion that 'retreat from the world' may be necessary if the fullness of spiritual integrity and wisdom is to be obtained. On the other hand, there has been the imperative, from Christ Himself, to 'go out and convert all nations'. The history of Catholic practice thus illustrates forms of cultural retreatism (for the perfection and protection of the sacred) existing at one and the same time with forms of cultural imperialism (for disseminating the knowledge of the sacred to a wider world). In the formal discourse of the Church what sociologists might style 'cultural imperialism' is perceived and expressed in a discourse of 'mission'. From a Catholic perspective, the Church has a sacred mission to take the message of Christ to the ends of the earth. The dialectic of 'retreat' and 'mission' in Catholic religious culture generates some internal tensions and contradictions which have to be worked out in different historical periods, social and cultural settings and within the social institutions of the Church. The Catholic school, as one of the most significant social institutions of the Church, has been caught up in tensions between 'retreat' and 'mission' both in its historical circumstances and in its present role in modern society.

The Catholic school: retreat and mission

The dialectic of retreat and mission has shaped and patterned Catholic schooling in England and the USA in particular ways, although the discourse and the concepts have themselves developed across different historical periods. It is a commonplace of Catholic educational history that Catholic schools in England, the USA and Australia were, in their origins, constructed and constituted as citadels and fortresses for the preservation of the faith in a hostile external environment characterised by a dominant Protestant order, continuing anti-Catholic prejudice and the growing influence of secularisation. Whereas various schemes were proposed for the integration of Catholic children and youth into state and publicly provided educational systems, the Catholic bishops and the Catholic religious orders were clear that the preservation of Catholic religious culture required separate provision. As a policy imperative this can be seen in the declaration of the first synod of the province of Westminster, following the restoration of the Catholic hierarchy in 1850:

> The first necessity . . . is a sufficient provision of education adequate to the wants of our poor. It must become universal . . . to . . . prefer the establishment of good schools to every other work . . . We should prefer the erection of a school, so arranged as to serve temporarily for a chapel, to that of a church without one.[11]

The Catholic school in England from its origins was clearly intended to be a cultural and faith bastion against the potentially polluting effects of hegemonic Protestantism and secular rationalism. The Catholic school was constituted as another form of church and its duty was to transmit and renew the sacred truths of the Catholic faith and an understanding of its discourse, symbols and ritual practices among its largely poor and working-class adherents. In addition, Catholic schooling faced the particular challenge at this time of providing a socio-cultural and religious provision for a large influx of Irish immigrants whose distinctive Catholic faith had to be 'saved' from potential corruption in Protestant England. Thus it was that Catholic schools were constructed at first in a mode of cultural retreatism, defence and separation from a profane world that was seen to threaten their integrity. The concept of the integrity of the Catholic school, which is a main theme of this present study, surfaced early in the discussions between the Catholic hierarchy and government representatives. Cardinal Manning made it very clear to the British Prime Minister in 1870 that:

> the integrity of our schools as to (i) Doctrine (ii) religious management and the responsibility of the Bishops in these respects, cannot be touched without opening a multitude of contentions and vexations.[12]

Given these concerns to preserve the integrity of Catholic religious and educational culture it is not surprising that the dominant model of the Catholic school became that of 'retreat from the world'. As McLaughlin *et al.* (1996) remark:

> The bishops were single-minded in their attempt to maintain a religious subculture against perceived threats of an increasingly secular society and what they saw as an emerging secular state school system. As a result the Church carried out its educational role in relative isolation from the wider state maintained education system.
>
> (pp. 4–5)

A similar imperative shaped the formation of Catholic schools in the USA as McLaughlin *et al.* (1996) point out:

> Bishop Bernard McQuaid of Rochester typifies the attitude that won out. He saw schools as protective walls. In order 'to protect children from the "wolves of the world" who were destroying countless numbers of the unguarded ones' he committed the Church to building those walls and he added, 'if the walls are not high enough, they must be raised; if they are not strong enough, they must be strengthened'.
>
> (p. 9)

Bishop McQuaid's statement provides a dramatic exemplification of the policy imperatives for the first stages of Catholic schooling in England and in the USA. To escape the depredations of the 'wolves of the world', Catholic children and youth needed to be safe in the cultural retreat of the Catholic school, with strong cultural insulations from the external, profane world. While therefore the dominant characteristic of early Catholic schooling was a form of cultural retreatism and defence, this did co-exist with a conception of educational mission. However, the mission of this period (i.e. the nineteenth and early twentieth centuries) may be described as one of *internal mission*.

The internal mission of Catholic schooling in England was primarily to the industrial working class in the major conurbations of London, Liverpool, Lancashire, Birmingham, Manchester, Newcastle and the North-East, a considerable proportion of whom were of Irish origin.[13] It is symbolic of this distinctive educational mission to the poor that one of the key agencies of the Catholic Church in matters of educational policy and provision in the period 1847 to 1906 was the Catholic Poor School Committee, the forerunner of the contemporary Catholic Education Service. Before the deliberations of the Second Vatican Council (1962–5) gave particular emphasis to the notion of 'a preferential option for the poor' as a defining characteristic of Catholic social and educational activity, a very clear option for the poor already existed in Catholic schooling provision in England. This was a necessary option for the poor (rather than a preferential one) and arose from the demographic fact that the Catholic community in England was largely poor, working class and immigrant Irish. The crucial internal mission of Catholic schooling in England in the nineteenth and early twentieth centuries was to provide religious, personal and educational formation for the children of the Catholic poor in elementary schools of reasonable quality. Cardinal Manning[14] was a noted champion of working-class causes in the latter part of the nineteenth century. As Roberts (1996) notes:

> The Catholics, under the leadership of Cardinal Manning, provided a vast range of social institutions to help the poor, destitute and handicapped in human society.
>
> (p. 128)

A key social institution was the Catholic elementary school and the mission for the Cardinal and the bishops was to attempt to provide a place in a Catholic school for every Catholic child. This *mission of universal access* was regarded by the Catholic hierarchy as not only a sacred duty but also a prudential one. Failure to make such provision could lead to Catholic parents sending their children to locally provided Board schools which gave a technically secular education but were viewed by the bishops as Protestant in ethos. The mission of Catholic elementary schooling was, among other things, to save the Catholic poor from the potential corruptions of secularism and of Protestantism.

While the overwhelming and dominant educational mission of the Catholic Church in England was the provision of universal and adequate elementary education for its working-class adherents, some thought had to be given to the education of other Catholic social classes. Beales (1950, p. 367) has pointed out that whereas the 'mission of universal access' was the preoccupation of the Catholic bishops, what may be called the 'mission of leadership' was largely the work of the religious orders.[15] Catholic independent schools and Catholic grammar schools were established in the nineteenth and early twentieth centuries to provide an education for leadership for the sons and daughters of the relatively small Catholic upper and middle classes. Catholic grammar schools which offered free secondary education after 1944 to Catholic boys and girls who demonstrated 'scholarship' merit and talent were to become an important channel for upward social mobility in the Catholic community. This educational mission of leadership formation resulted in the creation of a more substantial Catholic middle class which was to have a significant influence in public and professional life, in the life of the Church and in the future development of the Catholic educational mission.[16]

The Catholic school and secularisation

In Durkheim's (1971) analysis, profane culture has the potential to pollute and devalue sacred culture but its potential to do this is always constrained. It is constrained by the fact that in Durkheim's study, sacred culture is in an acknowledged position of hierarchical superiority to that of profane culture. That which is profane is subservient to and contained within the jurisdiction of the rules and the principles of the sacred. The integrity of the sacred is also preserved by the existence of strong cultural insulations from the world of the profane. While these conditions remain, sacred culture is not fundamentally threatened by the existence of profane culture.

However, the development of secularisation in the modern world from the Enlightenment to the present day presents the agencies of sacred culture with a more powerful and sharper challenge. Secularisation represents the denial of the validity of the sacred and of its associated culture and its replacement by logical, rational, empirical and scientific intellectual cultures in which the notion of the transcendent has no place. Secularisation involves a significant change in the cultural power relations of any society. Berger, in his influential study *The Social Reality of Religion* (1973), expresses it in this way:

> By secularization we mean the process by which sectors of society and culture are removed from the domination of religious institutions and symbols . . . Secularization manifests itself in the evacuation by the Christian churches of areas previously under their control and influence.
>
> (p. 113)

While secularisation changes intellectual culture and power relations, it also operates to affect the world view of many individuals so that religious concepts, religious discourse and religious sensitivities are simply irrelevant to the everyday business of life. This is what Berger (1973) refers to as 'a secularisation of consciousness':

> Put simply this means that the modern West has produced an increasing number of individuals who look upon the world and their own lives without the benefit of religious interpretations.
>
> (p. 113)

Protestantism, in Berger's perspective, has left itself open to the depredations of secularisation because it has historically involved itself in a process of reducing the scope and the symbolism of the sacred in its religious practice. Catholicism, on the other hand, is for Berger a stronger adversary of secularisation because of the internal richness of its sacred culture:

> The Catholic lives in a world in which the sacred is mediated to him through a variety of channels . . . the sacraments of the church, the intercession of the saints, the recurring eruption of the 'supernatural' in miracles . . . a vast continuity of being between the seen and the unseen.
>
> (p. 117)

Berger is actually making a large assumption here that most Catholics are in fact 'living' in the richly symbolic world of the sacred which he describes. While at a theological and historical level the notion of 'a vast continuity of being between the seen and the unseen' is distinctive of Catholic religious culture, the extent to which most Catholics are immersed in that culture, whether in the Church or in the school, is more problematic in contemporary settings.

There is debate about the wider cultural and intellectual significance of the process of secularisation in modern society. For some, it represents the liberation of humanity from the myths and obscurantism of religious domination; in short, a true form of human enlightenment in which reason comes to occupy the place formerly assigned to God. For others, secularisation represents a crucial loss of the sense of transcendence in human existence and with it the sense of ultimate meaning and purpose for humanity. The domination of 'reason' from this perspective represents the arrival of a potentially calculative, bloodless and inhumane cultural form.

White (1995) in *Education and Personal Well-Being in a Secular Universe* celebrates the arrival of secularisation and of the growth in intellectual and personal maturity which, from his perspective, it represents. For White:

> The replacement of a Christian by a secular utilitarian ethic by the end of the eighteenth century meant abandoning all notions of other-worldly felicity.
>
> (pp. 4–5)

In this major cultural and intellectual transformation, the realisation of personal autonomy as independence from the idea of God, from tradition and social custom and from significant others became a new form of personal maturity, allowing new forms of self-determination:

> Collectively, we are not given ethical direction by forces outside ourselves, whether these are natural or transcendental; we have worked this out over millennia from our own resources.
>
> (pp. 8–9)

Recognising the need for new sources of personal well-being (in the absence of other-worldly felicity) and for an awareness of a secular cosmic framework (in the absence of a divine framework), White argues that schools could find in aesthetic education,[17] understood in its widest sense, a powerful alternative to religious education and that philosophy of education could have a key role 'in illuminating the place of a non-religious . . . Cosmic framework in the education of our children' (pp. 18–19).

If secular humanist philosophers such as White are concerned to provide a viable and meaningful framework for secular education, others, such as Hirst (1974, 1976, 1994), have argued that the whole idea of a Christian education (or of any faith-based education) is not defensible in the modern world. Hirst's argument is that with an Enlightenment emphasis upon the primacy of rationality, logic, empirical evidence and manifest truth criteria, the search for knowledge and understanding, which is education, cannot be based upon the unverifiable propositions of the Christian faith or of any faith. The autonomy of education, as with the autonomy of the person, cannot be constrained by the prior formulations, dogma and catechism of religious belief. The educational enterprise must be entirely free of the limiting effect of ideological commitment whether that commitment is religious or political in nature. Hirst's prime target is, however, religious ideology[18] in education:

> Just as intelligent Christians have come to recognise that justifiable scientific claims are autonomous and do not, and logically cannot, rest on religious beliefs, so also, it seems to me, justifiable educational principles are autonomous. That is to say, that any attempt to justify educational principles by an appeal to religious claims is invalid.
>
> (1976, pp. 155–7)

What this argument fails to recognise is that there has not been, and in human society, cannot be, a school or an educational experience which is entirely autonomous, objective, neutral and ideologically free. Schools in Europe were first formed in the ideology (or faith) of Catholic Christianity, whereas the vast majority of them are now located in the ideology (or faith) of secular humanism. Schools are not scientific laboratories. They are, crucially, person-forming, citizen-forming and society-forming social institutions, and as such they always have been, and they are likely always to be, influenced by external ideologies of various types – religious, secular, humanist, political, atheist. If therefore the historically and politically formed enterprise of schooling (as opposed to the abstract and theoretical notion of education) will always be located within a given ideological and cultural framework, then other means have to be found to protect the integrity and relative autonomy of intellectual and educational processes.[19] Secular schools as opposed to religious schools are not ideologically free zones. Secularism has its own ideological assumptions about the human person, the ideal society, the ideal system of schooling and the meaning of human existence. While these assumptions may not be formally codified into a curriculum subject designated 'secular education' as an alternative to 'religious education', they characteristically permeate the ethos and culture of state-provided secular schools and form a crucial part of the 'hidden curriculum'.[20]

Writers and researchers such as McLaughlin (1990, 1992, 1996) and Bryk *et al.* (1993) have argued that contemporary Roman Catholic schooling (as opposed to pre-Vatican II forms of schooling) provides a viable and defensible mode of liberal education in a secular age, although one marked by tensions and dilemmas. Bryk *et al.* (1993) conclude their detailed empirical study of Catholic schooling in the USA with these observations:

> Catholic educators must struggle to discern the valuable contributions of this larger, secular culture, while maintaining fidelity to the religious ideals that have vitalized Catholic schools since Vatican II. Such *openness with roots* [my emphasis] inevitably creates organisational tensions and dilemmas.
>
> (pp. 334–5)

Bryk *et al.* recognise that this new Vatican II principle of 'openness with roots' in Catholic schooling faces an internal reaction and backlash from those Catholics who fear the effects of openness and who wish to return to the certainty and security of pre-Vatican II theological, liturgical and educational roots. However, the authors of *Catholic Schools and the Common Good* (1993) believe that Catholic schooling as a form of defensible liberal education in a secular culture must continue to develop the Vatican II emphasis upon openness:

> An alternative conception – one that we have stressed here – envisions Catholic schools as a realization of the prophetic Church that critically engages contemporary culture. Anything that even remotely smacks of 'indoctrination in the mind of the Church' can seriously undermine this more public function . . . From this perspective, Catholic education represents an invitation to students both to reflect on a systematic body of thought and to immerse themselves in a communal life that seeks to live out its basic principles.
>
> (p. 335)

The notion that a secular form of liberal education is the only defensible educational experience which can be offered in modern society has been criticised from a philosophical perspective by McLaughlin. For him, it is clearly a right of parents in a democratic and pluralist society to shape the early education of their children according to the beliefs, values, principles and ideologies which they regard as important. It is also clearly a democratic right of parents to commit their children to faith-based schooling of a religious nature. However, McLaughlin is also aware of the rights of children and young people as they mature, to come to their own reasoned position on religious and ideological issues, morality and principles for living, i.e. to aspire to relative autonomy. In his view, a modern form of Catholic schooling characterised by 'openness with roots' can be a synthesis of these two legitimate positions:

> Such schooling can be seen to be compatible with liberal, democratic principles, not least by providing a particular substantial starting point for the child's eventual development into autonomous agency and democratic citizenship.

> (1996, p. 147)

The positions of both Bryk *et al.* (1993) and McLaughlin (1996) on the possibilities for a Catholic schooling in a secular age which synthesises both 'roots' and 'critical openness' may seem to external observers to be unduly optimistic about changes in educational culture brought about by the new spirit of Vatican II. Pervasive historical myths and images of Catholic schooling, such as the well-known statement attributed to the Jesuits, 'Give me the child until he is seven, and I will give you the man', make many external observers believe that Catholic schooling is, in practice, a strong and effective form of indoctrination.[21] At the level of the institutional Roman Catholic Church, the stance of Pope John Paul II does not seem to be one of encouraging critical openness in the religious and social institutions of the Church. It is a commonplace of Catholic communities in the UK and in the USA to observe that the new spirit of openness inaugurated by Vatican II in the 1960s is no longer in the ascendant in the institutional Church.[22] What are the implications of this for the educational cultures and practices of contemporary Catholic schools? Given the paucity of detailed school-based educational research on Catholic schooling, it is difficult to answer this question.[23] We do not know, in any comprehensive sense, what the effects of post-Vatican II religious and cultural change have been on the internal cultures of Catholic schools. Neither do we know what the consequences for Catholic schools have been as a result of the very different external conditions – religious, socio-economic and ideological – in which they now operate. Part of the intention of this study is to probe some of these important issues.

If the relative underdevelopment of empirical educational research into the nature and effectiveness of Catholic schooling in a secular age is surprising, the relative underdevelopment of a Catholic philosophy of education in a secular age is even more surprising. It might have been expected that, with attacks upon the legitimacy and defensibility of Catholic schooling produced by secular humanist philosophers, a countervailing defence would have been constructed by Catholic philosophers. In fact, this has not happened in any comprehensive sense. One of the reasons for this would seem to be that many Catholic educators in the past (largely priests and members of religious orders) were confident that they had an authoritative exposition and defence of Catholic education in the writings of St Thomas Aquinas.

Writing in 1964, Archbishop Beck commented upon 'the vitality of thought' of the 'Angelic Doctor' and of the continuing relevance of his 'Christianized Aristotelianism' to contemporary Catholic education. In particular, he argued that St Thomas's greatest work, the *Summa Theologica*, could be regarded as 'an educational document of the highest importance' because it involved an exposition of a complete philosophy of the person derived from the fundamental proposition 'God is the first principle of things' (p. 114).

It seems likely that the religious and intellectual pre-eminence of St Thomas Aquinas[24] overshadowed and partly inhibited subsequent attempts to rearticulate and recontextualise a Catholic philosophy of education to face the challenges of secularism.

Reviewing the field in 1995, Carr *et al.*, while acknowledging that 'Important resources for the rational articulation and defence of a distinctively Catholic conception of education are indeed to be found in the philosophy of St Thomas' (p. 176), called for new efforts to produce a contemporary Catholic philosophy of education. Such an attempt would involve drawing upon the wisdom of St Thomas but also integrating this with the work of neo-Thomists such as Maritain (1961, 1964) and the work of contemporary Catholic philosophers such as MacIntyre[25] (1981, 1988, 1990) and Taylor[26] (1989). In the absence of a fully articulated Catholic philosophy of education for modern culture, Catholic educators have in practice used as a resource the formal publications and declarations on Catholic education of the institutional Church. These publications, mediated by the Sacred Congregation for Catholic Education, later renamed the Vatican Congregation, have provided the main source of theological, philosophical and educational guidance for lay Catholic educators. In so far as contemporary Catholic schooling, in England at any rate, can lay claim to an articulated theoretical framework, it has been derived from these 'documents for guidance' rather than from the developed insights of formal scholarship.

Notes

1 See Morris (1994, 1998a, 1998b) and Catholic Education Service (1995a).
2 Arthur (1995, p. 119) notes that: 'As recently as March 1989 the Association of Metropolitan Authorities passed a resolution which found voluntary aided schools "damaging" to the interests of education in some localities'. Some radical Labour councils in London and Liverpool were hostile to the existence of Catholic schools on ideological grounds, despite the fact that many Catholics were Labour voters.

3 The title of Hornsby-Smith's early study. *Catholic Education; The Unobtrusive Partner* (1978), conveys a sense of the marginality of the Catholic sector in the 1960s and 1970s in educational policy terms.

4 See Grace (1998b).

5 Quoted in Durkheim (1971, pp. 24–5). This was first published in 1912.

6 Ibid, p. 422.

7 Ibid, p. 415.

8 Ibid, p. 419.

9 See Thatcher (1993, p. 626). In this infamous assertion Margaret Thatcher demonstrated a form of aggressive individualism totally at odds with the principles of Catholic religious and social teaching.

10 It should be made clear that Durkheim was commenting upon the role of religion in the societies which he studied. His own personal stance was secular and he looked forward to the time when the idea of society would replace that of religion and the church as a unifying social and moral force.

11 Quoted in Arthur (1995, p. 15).

12 Ibid, p. 34.

13 For the uneasy relation between English Catholicism and the Irish, see Hickman (1995).

14 See McClelland (1962) and Selby (1974).

15 The mission of leadership for upper- and middle-class Catholic youth was particularly evident in the educational work of the Benedictines, the Dominicans, the Jesuits, the Society of the Sacred Heart, The Institute of the Blessed Virgin Mary and the Ladies of Mary, among others.

16 In the provision of Catholic grammar schools many religious orders were involved, including (for boys) the Christian Brothers, the De La Salle Brothers, the Franciscans, the Jesuits, the Oratorians, the Marists, the Salesians and the Xaverians, and (for girls) the Faithful Companions of Jesus, the Dominican Sisters, the Sisters of Notre Dame, the Sisters of St Paul, the Sisters of La Retraite and the Ursulines, among others. Many of the headteachers interviewed later in this study had received their secondary education and spiritual formation in schools run by these orders.

17 For a similar argument see Abbs (1995).

18 From a secular perspective, religious ideas cannot be accepted as a revelation of truth from a divine source but rather as an ideology in the service of religious interest groups. It should be noted however that Hirst does not utilise the concept of ideology in his writings.

19 In the last instance, the protection of notions of intellectual integrity and of the relative autonomy of the learner is a major responsibility of education professionals in all categories of school and college. Whether external conditions allow them to exercise that responsibility is another matter.

20 'Hidden curriculum' refers to the ways in which school ethos, organisation and practice educate pupils in addition to the outcomes of the formal taught and visible curriculum.

21 For an important discussion of concepts of indoctrination, see Snook (1972) and Astley (1994). Astley points out that until this century, indoctrination had the neutral meaning of teaching or instruction. It acquired pejorative associations later. In a pejorative sense, it has frequently been applied to Catholic education, implying that it has been a process for the imprinting of the mind with dogma and catechism. Given the large number of lapsed Catholics in contemporary society this suggests that the idea of Catholic indoctrination is not true, or if true, has not been very effective.

22 See, for instance, Winter (1985).

23 For a review of available studies, see Chapter 4.
24 See Mayer (1929) and Donlon (1952). For a valuable recent collection of the writings of Thomas Aquinas, see McInerny (1998), and for new reflections upon his continuing relevance for education see Arthur *et al.* (1999).
25 Writing of 'some consequences of the failure of the Enlightenment Project', MacIntyre (1981) argues that

> the problems of modern moral theory emerge clearly as the product of the failure of the Enlightenment project. On the one hand the individual moral agent, freed from hierarchy and teleology, conceives of himself and is conceived of by moral philosophers as sovereign in his moral authority. On the other hand the inherited, if partially transformed rules of morality have to be found a new status, deprived as they have been of their older teleological character and their even more ancient categorical character as expressions of an ultimately divine law. If such rules cannot be found a new status which will make appeal to them rational, appeal to them will indeed appear as a mere instrument of individual desire and will.
>
> (p. 62)

The implication of MacIntyre's argument is that secular rules of morality have failed to find a new status (comparable with the 'will of God') and that therefore a state of moral anomie in modern society has resulted.
26 Taylor's major text, *Sources of the Self,* argues for the necessity of an ontological basis for ethics and morality: 'one or another ontology is in fact the only adequate basis for our moral responses, whether we recognise this or not. A thesis of this kind was invoked by Dostoyevsky and discussed by Leszek Kolakowski in a recent work: "If God does not exist, then everything is permitted"' (p. 10).

Bibliography

Abbs, P. (1995) 'The Spiritual in Art and Culture', *Salisbury Review,* June, pp. 27–31.

Arthur, J. (1995) *The Ebbing Tide: Policy and Principles of Catholic Education,* Leominster: Gracewing Publications.

Arthur, J., Walters, J. and Gaine, S. (1999) *Earthen Vessels: The Thomistic tradition in education,* Leominster: Gracewing Publications.

Astley, J. (1994) *The Philosophy of Christian Religious Education,* Alabama: Religious Education Press.

Beales, A. C. F. (1950) 'The Struggle for the Schools', in G. A. Beck (ed.) *The English Catholics, 1850–1950,* London: Burns Oates.

Beck, G. A. (1964) 'Aims in Education: Neo-Thomism', in T. H. B. Hollins (ed.) *Aims in Education,* Manchester: Manchester University Press.

Berger, P. (1973) *The Social Reality of Religion,* London: Penguin.

Bryk, A., Lee, V. and Holland, P. (1993) *Catholic Schools and the Common Good,* Cambridge, MA: Harvard University Press.

Carr, D., Haldane, J., McLaughlin, T. and Pring, R. (1995) 'Return to the Crossroads: Maritain Fifty Years On', *British Journal of Educational Studies,* Vol. 43, No. 2, pp. 162–78.

Catholic Education Service (1995a) *Quality of Education in Catholic Secondary Schools,* London: CES.

Donlon, T. C. (1952) *Theology and Education,* Dubuque, Iowa: W M Brown.

Durkheim, E. (1971) *The Elementary Forms of the Religious Life: A Study in Religious Sociology*, London: Allen and Unwin.

Grace, G. (1998b) 'Critical Policy Scholarship: Reflections on the Integrity of Knowledge and Research', in G. Shacklock and J. Smyth (eds) *Being Reflexive in Critical Educational and Social Research*, London: Falmer Press.

Hickman, M. (1995) *Religion, Class and Identity: The State, the Catholic Church and the Education of the Irish in Britain*, Aldershot: Avebury.

Hirst, P. (1974) *Moral Education in a Secular Society*, London: University of London Press.

Hirst, P. (1976) 'Religious Beliefs and Educational Principles', *Learning for Living*, Vol. 15, pp. 155–7.

Hirst, P. (1994) 'Christian Education: A Contradiction in Terms?', in J. Astley and L. Francis (eds) *Critical Perspectives on Christian Education*, Leominster: Gracewing Publications.

Hornsby-Smith, M. (1978) *Catholic Education: The Unobtrusive Partner*, London: Sheed and Ward.

Hume, B. (1997) 'The Church's Mission in Education', in *Partners in Mission: A Collection of Talks by Bishops on Issues Affecting Catholic Education*, London: Catholic Education Service.

MacIntyre, A. (1981) *After Virtue: A Study in Moral Theory*, London: Duckworth.

MacIntyre, A. (1988) *Whose Justice? Which Rationality?*, London: Duckworth.

MacIntyre, A. (1990) *Three Rival Versions of Moral Enquiry*, London: Duckworth.

Maritain, J. (1961) *Education at the Crossroads*, New Haven, CT: Yale University Press.

Maritain, J. (1964) *The Aims of Education*, New Haven, CT: Yale University Press.

Mayer, M. (1929) *The Philosophy of Teaching of St Thomas Aquinas*, New York: Bruce.

McInerny, R. (1998) *Thomas Aquinas: Selected Writings*, London: Penguin.

McLaughlin, T. (1990) 'Parental Rights in Religious Upbringing and Religious Education Within a Liberal Perspective', Ph.D. thesis, University of London.

McLaughlin, T. (1992) 'The Ethics of Separate Schools', in M. Leicester and M. Taylor (eds) *Ethics, Ethnicity and Education*, London: Kogan Page.

McLaughlin, T. (1996) 'The Distinctiveness of Catholic Education', in *The Contemporary Catholic School*, London: Falmer Press.

McLaughlin, T., O'Keefe, J. and O'Keeffe, B. (eds) (1996) *The Contemporary Catholic School: Context, Identity and Diversity*, London: Falmer Press.

McClelland, V. (1962) *Cardinal Manning*, Oxford: Oxford University Press.

Morris, A. B. (1994) 'The Academic Performance of Catholic Schools', *School Organisation*, Vol. 14, No. 1, pp. 81–9.

Morris, A. B. (1998a) 'Catholic and Other Secondary Schools: An Analysis of OFSTED Inspection Reports 1993–1995', *Educational Research*, Vol. 40, No. 2, pp. 181–90.

Morris, A. B. (1998b) 'So Far, So Good: Levels of Academic Achievement in Catholic Schools', *Educational Studies*, Vol. 24, No. 1, pp. 83–94.

Roberts, I. D. (1996) *A Harvest of Hope: Jesuit Collegiate Education in England 1794–1914*, St Louis: The Institute of Jesuit Sources.

Sacred Congregation for Catholic Education (1977) *The Catholic School*, Homebush, NSW: St Paul Publications.

Selby, D. E. (1974) 'The Work of Cardinal Manning in the Field of Education', Ph.D. thesis, University of Birmingham.

Snook, I. A. (ed.) (1972) *Concepts of Indoctrination,* London: Routledge & Kegan Paul.

Taylor, C. (1989) *Sources of the Self: The Making of the Modern Identity,* Cambridge: Cambridge University Press.

Thatcher, M. (1993) *The Downing Street Years,* London: HarperCollins.

White, J. (1995) *Education and Personal Well-Being in a Secular Universe,* London: London Institute of Education.

Winter, M. (1985) *Whatever Happened to Vatican II?,* London: Sheed and Ward.

Chapter 2

Catholic schools

The renewal of spiritual capital and the critique of the secular world

Catholic Schools: Mission, Markets and Morality, 2002, (Ed). G. Grace, 236–240, RoutledgeFalmer.

Bourdieu (1986) has referred to three forms of capital which need to be considered in analysing any educational system, i.e. economic capital, whose effects are mediated by social class inequalities in the lives of students; social capital constituted in different access to supportive social networks; and cultural capital viewed as language, knowledge and 'style' differentially available to students in their homes. To this may be added, for the analysis of faith-based schooling systems, the concept of *spiritual capital*. Spiritual capital is defined here as *resources of faith and values derived from commitment to a religious tradition.*[1] Bourdieu argues that cultural capital is a power resource which can have an existence independently of economic capital[2] and this argument can be extended to include spiritual capital. Spiritual capital can be a source of empowerment because it provides a transcendent impulse which can guide judgement and action in the mundane world. Those within education whose own formation has involved the acquisition of spiritual capital do not act simply as professionals but as professionals and witnesses.

The Catholic schooling system internationally has benefited from the presence of significant spiritual capital among its school leaders. This leadership cadre has been recruited from priests, teaching Brothers and Sisters of various religious orders and from lay men and women who have acquired a sense of educational vocation through their own Catholic schooling and college experiences. In terms of the maintenance and enhancement of the Catholic educational mission, this cadre of leaders (despite the individual failings of some of its members) has been overall a powerful asset for the system – the animating spiritual capital of Catholic schooling.

This study has analysed the dilemmas arising for some Catholic secondary school leaders in urban areas in England as they face the contemporary challenges of mission, market and morality in rapidly changing conditions. Among the major challenges that have been highlighted are nurturing spirituality in the young against external pressure for secularism, hedonism and materialism; renewing and revivifying Catholicity to meet the needs of contemporary adolescents; mediating between the moral teachings of the institutional Church and the mores of youth culture; teaching the importance of personal and social justice and the dignity of the person; strengthening Catholic values of community, solidarity and the common good in the face of the imperialism of market values and competitive individualism in education; and holding to traditional Catholic concepts that academic success and empowerment are intended to be used in the service of others.

While variations in the responses to these challenges of the sixty schools have been demonstrated, what emerges overall is a recognition that the majority of these Catholic school leaders have drawn upon their resources of spiritual capital in discerning the way forward and in giving leadership on the educational policies and practices of their schools. Using their understanding of the fundamental principles of the Catholic faith and of its associated moral and value positions, the Catholic headteachers of this study have, in the main, attempted to maintain the mission integrity of Catholic schooling in the face of many external pressures which could compromise that integrity. The sources of their own spiritual capital have included the significant effects of their own secondary schooling and college experiences (the influence of religious orders being prominent), a family background of prayer and regular attendance at Mass, their own current prayer life and religious practice, and professional opportunities for development and reflection upon the spiritual context of Catholic schooling.

As this study has shown, future generations of school leaders and teachers in Catholic education are unlikely to benefit from this matrix of sources for spiritual capital. The reduced influence of the religious orders in schooling and in teacher formation and radical changes in the religious life of families have resulted in a weakening of this matrix. There is evidence[3] that many candidates for the headship of Catholic schools in England can now talk confidently about achievements in test scores and examinations, business planning and budgets, marketing and public relations, but are relatively inarticulate about the spiritual purposes of Catholic schooling. This is a major contradiction in a system of schooling which exists to give the nurture of spirituality a top priority and it demonstrates that the traditional spiritual capital of Catholic school leadership is a declining asset. This would not matter so much if extensive action for the renewal of such capital was being undertaken in courses and programmes offered by Catholic professional development agencies in England. However, there is little evidence yet that such provision is being made on the scale required by contemporary conditions.[4]

This study argues that the spiritual capital of the Catholic schooling system in England (and by implication elsewhere) is what has provided the dynamic drive of its mission in the past and helped it to preserve, in the main, its mission integrity in the challenges of the present. The renewal of its spiritual capital thus becomes the crucial question for the continuance of its *distinctive* mission in the future. This is a major conclusion of the research project.

'Transmission of the charism' is one way of speaking about and implementing the processes which are needed in Catholic education. A number of religious orders, e.g. the Jesuits, the Salesians, the De La Salle and the Christian Brothers, the Marists, the Sisters of Notre Dame, the Faithful Companions of Jesus and the Sisters of Mercy, have organised programmes for the spiritual formation of their lay successors as headteachers and teachers. However, there is also considerable scope for what may be called the *transmission of a lay charism* to a new generation of educators. Programmes using experienced or recently retired Catholic headteachers as mentors for new Catholic educators have much potential. With a specific focus upon the ways in which spirituality can relate to educational policy and practice, such programmes can be a valuable counter-cultural agenda to that provided by secular courses of headteacher 'training'. Such charism transmission now seems essential for the future of Catholic education.

It could be argued that a limitation of this research and of its conclusions regarding spiritual capital arises from its concentration upon school leadership roles, in particular those of headteachers. While headteachers in English Catholic schools are significant influences upon mission, ethos and effectiveness, they are only part of the larger enterprise of the Catholic school. The writer accepts that limitations of research resources have resulted in limitations of the analytical scope of this study. It is fully recognised that the resources of spiritual capital in Catholic schooling extend well beyond that possessed by individual headteachers. Spiritual capital is also constituted in school governing bodies, in classroom teachers, in priests and school chaplains, in parents and not least in the students themselves. A comprehensive analysis of the resources of spiritual capital in contemporary Catholic schooling would require examination of all these constituencies and of their future roles in spiritual regeneration. There have been indications during this research of the crucial importance of these other constituencies in the renewal of Catholic schooling. Among developments reported by headteachers as significant in the spiritual lives of the schools were the impact of Christian teachers of other denominations,[5] the importance of lay school chaplains and the contributions of senior students ready to take the leading role in the enhancement of the religious and spiritual programmes of the school. In other words, while the spiritual capital of Catholic schooling from traditional sources may be in decline there is some evidence that it is being renewed from other sources, when these sources are used creatively.

Wilson (1999), in his analysis of the decline of religious certainty in Europe, nevertheless concludes his influential book *God's Funeral* with the observation that 'the immense strength of the Catholic idea played a demonstrable role in the collapse of the Soviet Communist system' (p. 354). If the great challenge to Catholicism in the past, i.e. that of communist atheism with imperialist intentions, has declined, a new challenge and a new imperialism has emerged, i.e. that of global capitalist values. Soros (1999) has charted the nature of this new cultural and economic imperialism and has concluded 'that market values have assumed an importance at the present moment in history that is way beyond what is appropriate and sustainable' (p. 46).

Usher and Edwards (1994, p. 175), in their study of the effects of globalisation upon education, have argued that national objectives in education will soon be limited to 'fulfilling the requirements of the economy under conditions of global competition'. However, what is remarkable about the growing literature on globalisation and education, including the work of Usher and Edwards (1994), Green (1997) and others, is that the role of religion is generally ignored. The fact that world-based religions such as Catholic Christianity and Islam are international power sources which have missions other than those of economic globalisation appears to be marginalised in the globalisation analyses and debates. This is yet another example of the effects of secular marginalisation upon contemporary intellectual culture which this book hopes to challenge. There can be no comprehensive understanding of the economic, social and cultural effects of globalisation which does not take fully into account the countervailing influences of major religious cultures and organisations.

One of the countervailing institutions against the hegemony of market materialism, individual competitiveness and commodity worship is the Catholic Church and its various agencies internationally. Among these, Catholic schools are crucial in the contemporary struggle for the formation of young people and for the shaping of their consciousness.[6] Such schools strive to renew a culture of spirituality, virtue and service to the common good in an increasingly materialist and individualistic global market.

In *Religion and the Secular City* Cox (1984, pp. 170–1) made the prescient observation that:

> If freedom once required a secular critique of religion, it can also require a religious critique of the secular.[7]

The very existence of Catholic schools and indeed of all faith-based schools constitutes part of the religious critique of the secular, without which both culture and freedom would be diminished.

Notes

1 Spiritual capital, in this definition, is a resource of faith and values possessed by all faith-based schools and not only by Catholic ones.
2 However, much of Bourdieu's work is directed to show that in practice these two forms of capital are highly interrelated.
3 During the course of the fieldwork, the researcher received such evidence from a range of individuals involved in the selection and appointment of new headteachers in Catholic schools.

4 This comment relates to the situation in the UK. There is more evidence of this provision in higher education institutions in the USA and Australia.
5 There has been a traditional Catholic preoccupation with the percentage of Catholic teachers in each secondary school. This research has shown that this is a simplistic approach to the question of school ethos. Teachers of other Christian denominations were widely reported by the headteachers as being significant spiritual assets for the schools when compared with lukewarm or nominal Catholic teachers.
6 Catholic schools may be viewed as agencies for the renewal of spiritual capital among the young, i.e. working against the materialistic spirit of global capitalism.
7 Quoted by Purpel (1989). I am grateful to David Purpel for the location of this quotation.

Bibliography

Bourdieu, P. (1986) 'The Forms of Capital', in J. McPherson (ed.) *Handbook of Theory and Research for the Sociology of Education*, New York: Greenwood Press.

Cox, H. (1984) *Religion and the Secular City*, New York: Simon and Schuster.

Green, A. (1997) *Education, Globalization and the Nation State*, London: Macmillan.

Purpel, D. (1989) *The Moral and Spiritual Crisis in Education*, New York: Bergin and Garvey.

Soros, G. (1999) *The Crisis of Global Capitalism*, London: Little, Brown.

Usher, R. and Edwards, R. (1994) *Postmodernism and Education: Different Voices, Different Worlds*, London: Routledge.

Wilson, A. N. (1999) *God's Funeral*, London: John Murray.

Chapter 3

Renewing spiritual capital

An urgent priority for the future of Catholic education internationally

International Studies in Catholic Education, 2010, 2(2), 117–128.

When researching the responses of 60 Catholic school leaders to their demanding work in English inner-city secondary schools, I encountered evidence of a deep vocational commitment. These headteachers were clearly drawing upon a spiritual and religious resource that empowered them and which gave them a sustained sense of mission, purpose and hope in their educational work. In the research report which followed, I referred to this sustaining and inspirational factor as 'spiritual capital'. What I did not do, as some critics have pointed out, was to provide an adequate historical and theoretical elaboration to this concept that might be used in future research and academic writing. This is an attempt to remedy that omission and to provide a more detailed understanding of what spiritual capital is, and of its crucial relevance for the future effectiveness and integrity of the Catholic education mission worldwide.

On the emergence of the concept of spiritual capital

During my fieldwork research for the book *Catholic schools: Mission, markets and morality* (Grace 2002a) I had the opportunity to interview 60 Catholic secondary-school leaders working in schools largely serving inner-city and other deprived urban communities in London, Liverpool and Birmingham in the UK. These school leaders were not simply theorists of 'the preferential option for the poor' in Catholic education, they were front-line practitioners and agents of its realisation in the everyday activities of the schools. In their professional lives they encountered crises, conflict and challenges from many sources as they attempted to develop educational cultures characterised by faith, hope, love, moral and social formation and the fulfilment of talents according to Catholic principles.[1]

On the one hand, the communities that they served were frequently marked by the dysfunctional effects of poverty, unemployment, broken families, drug and alcohol abuse and criminality in general. In other words, the structural dysfunctions and contradictions of the wider society were present in a concentrated form in the localities in which they tried to realise the Catholic educational mission. They had to deal with the consequences of this as mediated by the behaviour and attitudes of the young people who entered their schools from these disadvantaged communities. To be a Catholic school leader in such contexts was to encounter day-to-day challenges to one's own faith, hope, love and charity.

On the other hand, the English state in the 1980s and 1990s intensified its expectations for academic performance and 'output' of measurable examination results, regardless of the social and economic challenges which individual schools faced. Schools which failed to show year-on-year improvement in their academic results, would be subject to a process of 'naming and shaming', as local and national media reported these 'results' to a wider public.

To be a Catholic school leader in these contexts at this time was to experience the long historical tension between 'rendering to Caesar' and 'rendering to God' now in an intensified form. The English state ('Caesar') was making academic demands upon the schools of the inner-city, which made no allowance for the many difficulties (at the level of staffing, students and community support) that the school leaders encountered. For all their efforts, public humiliation might be the result.

In these circumstances it would not have been surprising if my interviews with these 60 school leaders had revealed a group of men and women who were low in morale, exhausted, embittered and in the process of losing hope about the Catholic school mission in the urban front line. However, this was not the case. While there were variations in the responses which they gave to particular issues, I became aware that I was encountering a constant factor across most of the sample, a factor of vocational commitment. The majority of these headteachers, in their demanding work in challenging urban schools, were clearly drawing upon a spiritual and religious resource that empowered them and gave them a sustained sense of mission, purpose and hope in their work.

In the last chapter of *Catholic schools* I tried to reflect upon this unexpected outcome by referring to this 'constant factor' as 'spiritual capital' possessed by these school leaders. What I did not do, as some critics have pointed out, was to provide an adequate historical and theoretical elaboration of this concept which might be used in subsequent research and academic writing. What follows is an attempt to remedy this defect and to provide a more detailed elaboration of spiritual capital and of its relevance for the future of Catholic education.

Pierre Bourdieu: education and forms of capital

My use of the concept of 'spiritual capital' in Catholic education was strongly influenced by my reading of the work of the French social theorist Pierre

Bourdieu and, in particular, by his paper 'The forms of capital' (Bourdieu 1986) and his article 'Genesis and structure of the religious field' (Bourdieu 1991).

Bourdieu (1986) referred to three forms of capital which need to be considered in analysing any educational system: economic capital, whose effects are mediated by social class inequalities in the lives of students; social capital, constituted in different access to supportive social networks; and cultural capital, viewed as resources of knowledge, language and appropriate social relations differentially available to students in their homes. As he argued: 'It is in fact impossible to account for the structure and functioning of the social world unless one reintroduces capital in all its forms and not only in the one form recognised by economic theory' (Bourdieu 1986, 242).

In his 1991 article Bourdieu introduced a further category, i.e. 'religious capital'. In his analysis of the 'religious field', he suggested that religious capital was: 'the monopolization of the administration of the goods of salvation by a body of religious specialists . . . of a deliberately organised corpus of secret (and therefore rare) knowledge' (Bourdieu 1991, 9).[2] This maintained a strict boundary between the priesthood (possessed of religious capital) and the laity (excluded from such capital).

As David Swartz (1997) observed in his valuable overview of Bourdieu's work, all these various forms of capital are also forms of power, whether they are material, social, cultural or religious, and for Swartz this constitutes a 'political economy of symbolic power' (Swartz 1997, 65).

However, what I was trying to describe, arising out of my research analysis was not a political economy of symbolic power instantiated in social and cultural structures, but rather a symbolic power instantiated in individual school leaders.

They were not, in general, possessed of religious capital[3] (in the manner described by Bourdieu) but they were possessed of individual spiritual capital which was, on the basis of my analysis, a source of personal power. This was not 'power over', but it was 'power to maintain' an educational mission and to animate and inspire others in that mission. In this way I extended Bourdieu's analysis of socially structured forms of power-capital, to include a form of power-capital that was located in people.

My preliminary and inadequate attempts to elaborate this concept were expressed in 2002 as: 'resources of faith and values derived from commitment to a religious tradition'; and also in the form:

> Spiritual capital can be a source of empowerment because it provides a transcendent impulse which can guide judgement and action in the mundane world. Those within education whose own formation has involved the acquisition of spiritual capital do not act simply as professionals but as professionals and witnesses.
>
> (Grace 2002a, 236)[4]

This left many questions unanswered, for instance, how did these school leaders come to be possessed of spiritual capital and what other forms of spiritual capital might exist in other participants in the schools? Another crucial question was that, if the acquisition of spiritual capital by these school leaders had been an historical process, how was spiritual capital being renewed or not, in their successors as leaders and also among Catholic school teachers and school governors in general? What does 'spiritual' mean in these contexts?[5] These questions and others will now be considered in more detail.

Spiritual capital, theological literacy and charism

It is necessary, in elaborating the meaning of spiritual capital as a feature of Catholic education, to distinguish it from two related terms that can be found in the literature. These terms are 'theological literacy' and 'charism'.

In 2007, Nick Weeks, formerly Diocesan Director of Schools for the diocese of Lancaster, made an original contribution to the field in his text *Theological literacy and Catholic schools*. Weeks argued that faced with many contemporary challenges, what was required from Catholic school leaders, governors and teachers was a higher level of theological literacy which he defined as: 'Theological literacy is the ability to communicate knowledgeably how the faith of the Church relates to contemporary everyday experience . . . ' (Weeks and Grace 2007, 8).

While Catholic schools were involved in the development of new forms of literacy such as information technology and computer literacy, the development of theological literacy among both teachers and students, was, Weeks argued, relatively neglected and this threatened the long term vitality, authenticity and distinctiveness of the Catholic education mission. Such literacy was essential.

There are clearly important relationships between the concept of 'theological literacy' and of 'spiritual capital', but there are also qualitative differences which will be discussed later.

The concept of 'charism' now makes frequent appearances in the literature of Catholic education and, once again, there are obvious relationships between charism and spiritual capital but, at the same time, some differences.

In a ground-breaking article, 'Transmission of the charism: A major challenge for Catholic education', John Lydon (2009) provided a detailed and scholarly examination of the various meanings of charism and of their relevance for the future of Catholic education. In essence, charism refers to a special gift of the Holy Spirit given by the grace of God to those individuals who are called to various forms of leadership with the capacity to inspire others in the mission of salvation.[6] Lydon shows how the charism of inspired leadership was given to individuals such as St Paul, St Francis of Assisi and the founders of major religious congregations such as St Ignatius and St John Bosco.

In the case of the many religious congregations with missions in education established from the Counter-Reformation to the present day, Catholic educational history records an impressive number of charismatic leaders including John Baptist de la Salle, Angela Merici, Mary Ward, Madeleine Sophie Barat and others who had the capacity to inspire disciples in the educational missions of the Church in the modern period.[7]

In what senses, therefore, can spiritual capital be distinguished from theological literacy, on the one hand, and charism on the other? Theological literacy, as defined by Weeks and Grace (2007), involves a command of theological knowledge, an ability to communicate it effectively and to relate it to the challenges of everyday life. Charism is a particular gift of the Holy Spirit to certain individuals empowering them to become charismatic leaders of new movements in the Church. Spiritual capital, it can be argued, draws upon theological literacy but adds to it the dimension of a personal witness to faith in practice, action and relationships. Spiritual capital compared with charism is also a form of personal empowerment but not of such a high order – it is not the dramatic charism and charisma of exceptional leadership but rather the sustaining resource for everyday leadership in Christian living and working.[8]

It is the argument of this paper that it is spiritual capital understood at this level that has historically provided the animating force and dynamic motive power of Catholic schooling internationally. The crucial question for the future is: are the reserves of spiritual capital in the Catholic school system being renewed or is the system in contemporary conditions living on a declining asset?

The Church, lay Catholics and witnesses to faith

In 1982 the Congregation for Catholic Education issued an important document, *Lay Catholics in schools: Witnesses to faith*. Recognising the continual decline in the number of priests and members of religious orders working in Catholic schools, the document sought to provide a serious theorisation of the vocation of the lay Catholic educator and of the concept of an education profession as a form of vocation. This was stated in 'ideal type' constructs:

> the Catholic educator must be a source of spiritual inspiration . . . The lay Catholic educator is a person who exercises a specific mission within the Church by living the faith . . . with an apostolic intention . . . for the integral formation of the human person.
>
> (Congregation for Catholic Education 1982, 14)

The whole document can be read as an attempt by the Church to reconstitute lay Catholic teachers in schools as a mediated form of a religious congregation albeit secular and not bound by formal vows. They were, however, expected to be a source of spiritual inspiration and to have an apostolic intention in their work. Lay Catholic teachers were called upon to become witnesses to faith in the school context:

> The more completely an educator can give concrete witness to the model of the ideal person that is being presented to the students, the more this ideal will be believed and imitated . . . It is in this context that the faith witness of the lay teacher becomes especially important. Students should see in their teachers the Christian attitude and behaviour that is often absent from the secular atmosphere in which they live.
>
> (Congregation for Catholic Education 1982, 19)

It can be argued that what the Church was attempting to do at this historical juncture was to reconstitute its declining resources of spiritual capital in education (as the religious congregations weakened) by generating new resources of spiritual capital in the lay school leaders and teachers who had become the contemporary agents of the education mission in many countries. The *Lay Catholics in schools* document identified a need for processes of permanent formation (Congregation for Catholic Education 1982, 36) to be available for the religious and spiritual nurture of the lay missionaries of education in school and called upon bishops, priests and religious congregations to provide such formation.

Much of the formal teaching of the Catholic Church is provided in the mode of 'apostolic exhortations'. The 1982 analysis and suggestions from the Congregation for Catholic Education in Rome followed this historical pattern. It was a document of exhortation to the international Catholic community to recognise the seriousness of declining spiritual capital in Catholic schooling and to take action to reconstitute it in new forms.

This provokes the necessary question – in such circumstances is exhortation alone sufficient to meet the scale of the major transformations required in the spiritual formation of the next generation of Catholic educators?

On the formation of spiritual capital

In 2006 Archbishop Michael Miller, CSB, then Secretary of the Congregation for Catholic Education in Rome, reflected upon the changes from religious to lay leadership in the Catholic schools of the USA.

Archbishop Miller noted that in 1965 there were 180,000 religious sisters in the USA compared with fewer than 75,000 in 2006 and that religious women now constituted less than 4% of the professional staff of Catholic schools, while 95% of the teachers were lay persons. He concluded that: 'The shift to lay leadership in Catholic schools which has followed from the dearth of religious, presents its own set of challenges' (Miller 2006, 4–5).

Reflecting upon these challenges the Archbishop implied that consecrated religious in Catholic education had been possessed of special characteristics (which I would call spiritual capital) arising from their lengthy formation:

> Because of their special consecration, their particular experience of the gifts of the Spirit, their constant listening to the word of God, their practice of discernment, their rich heritage of pedagogical traditions . . . and their profound grasp of spiritual truth, consecrated persons are able to be especially effective in educational activities.
>
> (Miller 2006, 4)[9]

This is, I believe, a particularly clear statement about the ways in which spiritual capital was instantiated in the members of religious congregations across the world who were responsible for the development and leadership of the Catholic education systems internationally. Thus John Baptist de la Salle insisted that the members of his teaching congregation must be thoroughly formed in three core values: 'The spirit of faith', 'zeal in the ministry of teaching' and 'trust in God's Providence and Holy Will' (Koch et al. 2004, 21).

As laypersons have increasingly come to replace religious as both school leaders and teachers, Archbishop Miller points out that: 'To be effective bearers of the Church's educational tradition, laypersons who teach in Catholic schools need a religious formation that is equal to their . . . professional formation' (Miller 2006, 5). This opens up the question, are Catholic laypersons, now school leaders and teachers, receiving such extended and in-depth religious and spiritual formation as did their predecessors?

The formation experiences of 60 Catholic headteachers in England

In interviews conducted with 60 school leaders involved in my research project (1997–2000) questions were asked about their own formation experiences.[10] This revealed that many of them had come from family backgrounds of prayer and regular attendance at Mass, which had been reinforced by attendance at Catholic primary schools. Particularly influential, according to their accounts, was their subsequent attendance at secondary schools under the jurisdiction of religious congregations and their further attendance at teacher education colleges also operated by religious congregations. As a result of these latter influences, 15 of these school leaders had encountered their own vocational call to the religious life and had become members of congregations such as the Society of Jesus, the Sisters of Mercy, the Sisters of Notre Dame, the Faithful Companions of Jesus, the Congregation of La Sainte Union, the Sisters of Charity of St Paul, the Society of the Sacred Heart, the De La Salle Brothers and the Irish Christian Brothers.

The majority of the research participants who had not encountered a call to the religious life, witnessed to the experience of having acquired a strong sense of lay vocation for teaching as a result of the role models they had observed among their religious teachers and college lecturers. As one of them expressed it:

> I saw teaching as a vocation. It was on a par, believe it or not, with going into the priesthood. I have always taught in Catholic schools. I think it's an enormous challenge to actually spread the Faith in a community like this.
>
> (Headteacher of St Dominic's in a deprived community in Liverpool, Grace 2002a, 135–136)

Questioned about their personal constructs of the Catholic educational mission (as distinct from formal statements of the Church and the formal commitments of school mission documents)[11] over half of the sample made strong and explicit references to faith leadership and conveyed a committed sense of personal spiritual vocation as central to their conceptions of the role of a Catholic school leader. This sense of personal mission was expressed in various ways:

> The question is what have you personally got to bring and the answer is, one's own relationship with Christ . . . to be a role model where it is quite clear that one's own beliefs and practices are firmly rooted in the teachings of Christ and built on a prayer life not neglected because of 'busyness'.
>
> (Female lay headteacher)

> The importance of regular attendance at spiritual retreats. I think that has allowed me to focus. It is not well behaved boys, it is not school uniform, it is not academic results. At the end of the day the mission is achieved through spirituality.
>
> (Male lay headteacher)

> I always give priority to some spiritual aspect of the life of the school. I try to do that to remind myself and the community at large that the purpose of the mission of this place is to further the Christian ethos.
>
> (Female religious headteacher)[12]

It can be argued from the research evidence[13] that this particular sample and generation of Catholic school leaders had been significantly influenced by formative experiences arising from their home backgrounds, their Catholic school education and their teaching formation in colleges operated by religious congregations. There was evidence that transmission of spiritual capital had taken place from religious congregations to these mainly lay headteachers in forming a distinct sense of teaching as a vocation.

Some of them explicitly acknowledged this during the course of the interviews. They were possessed of resources of spiritual capital derived from these formative experiences which sustained them during the day-to-day trials of inner-city headship.

This is a leadership phenomenon which must be apparent across the whole international network of Catholic schools. What is happening to Catholic school education internationally now is that with the decline in the numbers of consecrated persons as leaders and teachers in the schools, the spiritual capital of these religious has been passed on to a first generation of lay leaders and teachers who have experienced the formative influence of their charisms. This first generation are the inheritors of the animating spiritual capital in education formerly possessed by members of the religious congregations. The reconstitution of spiritual capital in Catholic education has, therefore, in many locations completed (for better or worse) its first stage transmission process. The urgent question now to be considered is: what is happening to this spiritual capital in subsequent transmission processes?[14]

The renewal of spiritual capital in contemporary Catholic education

In commenting on these transmission processes, in the context of Catholic schools in the USA, Archbishop Miller argued that: 'It is up to the ecclesial community to see to it that such formation is required of and made available to all Catholic school educators . . . In this regard, Catholic universities have a special responsibility to assist Catholic schools' (Miller 2006, 5). Have Catholic universities and colleges responded to this need?

Reviewing the situation in the USA, Sister Patricia Helene Earl, IHM (2007) has noted that, while programmes to assist the formation of Catholic school principals have been established in a number of universities, the focus of the programmes has been largely upon relevant educational and theological knowledge. She argues that in addition to such knowledge content, 'teachers also need guidance to develop their spirituality' (Earl 2007, 55). In her chapter in the *International handbook of Catholic education*, Earl outlines an innovative programme of 'Spirituality and virtues' seminars provided by the Arlington Diocese, Virginia in conjunction with Marymount University. However, given that this is described as an 'original' approach to this issue, it suggests that programmes for the formation of spiritual capital among Catholic school leaders and teachers are not yet a significant feature of Catholic higher education in the USA.

The findings of the *International handbook of Catholic education* (Grace and O'Keefe 2007) seem to confirm this situation as applying also to the programmes offered by Catholic universities and colleges across the world.

Each contributor to the *Handbook* was invited to identify the challenges for Catholic schools in over 30 different societies and to report upon the responses being made to these challenges. A close reading of the 45 chapters in the *Handbook* reveals very little evidence that Catholic universities and colleges across the world are assisting diocesan administrations in programmes designed to strengthen spiritual capital among school leaders and teachers. However, the natural historical constituency to organise programmes for the transmission of spiritual capital is clearly the religious congregations with missions in education. Lydon (2009) reports the initiatives being taken by the Salesians and there is evidence of the provision of programmes of spiritual formation by the Jesuits, the De La Salle and Christian Brothers, the Marists, the Sisters of Notre Dame and the Sisters of Mercy among others. What we lack is any sense of a coordinated policy in this crucial area (as suggested by Archbishop Miller 2006) or any extensive research and evaluation studies to draw together the outcomes of such programmes.

In the opinion of Thomas Groome: 'If the foundation charisms of religious institutions cannot be broken open among teaching colleagues, there will be no alternative but to call it [the Catholic education project] off' (Groome 2001; quoted in Lydon 2009, 51). This is probably overstating the case, because charisms or spiritual capital exist in other forms,[15] but given the central significance of spiritual capital in the formation of Catholic school leaders and teachers, present responses to the challenge do appear to be disturbingly *laissez faire*. In other words, there does not seem to be enough practical response to the need to regenerate spiritual capital among lay Catholic educators, exhortation alone has not produced enough practical programmes to meet the scale of the contemporary challenge.

The conferences of Catholic bishops internationally, who have responsibility for the mission integrity of Catholic schools in each country, should place the renewal of spiritual capital in Catholic education high on their priority agendas and should give leadership in encouraging (and even requiring) formation programmes to be created by various agencies.

Failure to do this will result in the inevitable depletion of the historical deposit of spiritual capital in our schools and the gradual incorporation of Catholic schools into a secularised and marketised contemporary educational culture.[16]

Seeing spiritual capital as an urgent priority

It is now possible to make a more developed historical and theoretical elaboration of the concept of spiritual capital, as understood in the Catholic tradition in education, than that first attempted in 2002. In summary form, spiritual capital may be said to be:

- resources of faith and values derived from a vocational commitment to a religious tradition (in this case the Catholic tradition);

- a source of vocational empowerment because it provides a transcendent awareness that can guide judgement and action in the mundane world so that those whose own formation has involved the acquisition of spiritual capital do not act in education simply as professionals but as professionals and witnesses;
- a form of spirituality in which the whole of human life is viewed in terms of a conscious relationship with God, in Jesus Christ and the saints, through the indwelling of the Spirit;
- a form of spirituality which has been the animating, inspirational and dynamic spirit which has empowered the mission of Catholic education internationally largely (although not exclusively) through the work of religious congregations with missions in education in the past;
- a form of spirituality now in urgent need of renewal in the contemporary world of Catholic education faced with growing secularisation, ideologies of secularism,[17] global marketisation and materialism and the decline of religious congregations in the field of education; and
- a form of spirituality which needs to be reconstituted in lay school leaders and teachers by formation programmes which help them to be Catholic witnesses for Christ and not simply professional deliverers of knowledge and skills as required by the secular state and the secular market.

It is hoped that this article will encourage all relevant agencies in Catholic faith and culture to provide the formation programmes which are necessary for this great transformation.

Acknowledgements

I thank the two anonymous referees of this paper whose comments on the first draft have been of great assistance to me.

Notes

1 In relation to the fulfilment of talents (academic results), the Catholic 'formula' has always been: Fulfilment of talents + commitment to the common good = the good Catholic citizen. This was clearly expressed by the Congregation for Catholic Education in its 1977 text *The Catholic school*: 'This is the basis of a Catholic school's educational work. Education is not given for the purposes of gaining power ... Knowledge is not to be considered for material prosperity and success but as a call to serve and to be responsible for others' (Congregation for Catholic Education 1977, 43). See Grace (2002b) for a discussion of 'the challenge of academic success' in Catholic schools.

2 One anonymous referee of this paper has described this as 'a very tendentious definition' which should be challenged. In his view the Church's 'goods of salvation' have not been 'a deliberately organised corpus of secret knowledge', but a treasure to be shared openly with everyone. While Bourdieu (1991) emphasises the power relations of doctrine and liturgy, this referee emphasises their openness to all.

3 Of the 60 school leaders, 45 were laypersons and 15 were extant or former members of religious congregations. In Bourdieu's terms it could be said that some of these latter were possessed of religious capital in addition to spiritual capital.

4 In arriving at this definition I was greatly influenced by the profound statement of Pope Paul VI in his *Apostolic Exhortation: Evangelii Nuntiandi*: 'Modern man listens more willingly to witnesses than to teachers, and if he does listen to teachers it is because they are also witnesses' (Pope Paul VI 1975, 23). See also *Lay Catholics in schools: Witnesses to faith* (Congregation for Catholic Education 1982).

5 There are many definitions of spirituality. The one used in this paper may be expressed as: 'In Catholic Christian terms, spirituality is the whole of human life viewed in terms of a conscious relationship with God, in Jesus Christ and the saints, through the indwelling of the Spirit and lived within the Church as the community of believers'. I am grateful to an anonymous referee for help in formulating this definition.

6 Lydon shows that many religious congregations with missions in education are currently involved in programmes called 'transmission of the charism' for the benefit of their lay successors as school leaders and teachers. However, it could be argued that if charism is an exceptional gift of the Holy Spirit to certain individuals, it cannot easily be transmitted in a formation programme. There is a case for saying that what these programmes are attempting to do is to renew the resources for spiritual capital, as defined in this paper, for the empowering of a new lay leadership in the schools.

7 In his classic study, *The evolution of educational thought* (English translation), Emile Durkheim (1977) devoted three chapters to an analysis of the educational impact in France of the Jesuit order founded and inspired by Ignatius Loyola. Durkheim recognised that the Jesuits were able to be educationally effective for many reasons but a crucial one was their sense of personal spiritual mission. This sustained them in the many struggles which they encountered in developing their educational work in France. Durkheim believed that secular education in France needed to acquire a similar 'sustaining resource' and this would be a secular form of morality, what we might call secular moral capital. As Peter Collins observes in the translator's Introduction:

> Ultimately Durkheim hoped that these lectures would result not merely in the acquisition of knowledge by future teachers but in the generation of a new educational faith – a secular faith certainly, but nevertheless one which would issue in passionate commitment to the vocation of teaching.
>
> (Durkheim 1977, xx)

The Jesuits had spiritual capital. Durkheim wanted the teachers of France to have moral capital in a new secular context.

8 I want to argue that this 'sustaining resource' is for most people, what I have called 'spiritual capital'. However, it can be noted that Archbishop Michael Miller, CSB, describes this in other terms: 'I believe that men and women, precisely as members of the lay faithful have their own charism of teaching, independent of the charism of a particular religious congregation' (Miller 2006, 6).

9 Archbishop Miller is quoting from the *Apostolic Exhortation, Vita Consecrata* of Pope John Paul II (1996, 96). See also, *Consecrated persons and their mission in schools: Reflections and guidelines* (Congregation for Catholic Education 2003).

10 See Grace (2002a, 245) for the interview schedule and pages 236–240 for first reflections on spiritual capital.

11 In schools founded by religious congregations it was interesting to note that references to the founding charisms had been incorporated into contemporary

mission statements, e.g.: 'Jesuit education is inspired by the vision of St Ignatius Loyola in which God reveals his love for us in all things. The aim of Jesuit education is the formation of people of competence, conscience and compassion who are men and women for others' (Pope Paul III School, London); 'In the spirit of St John Bosco we turn our efforts to those who stand in special need because of the lack of material or emotional security' (St Robert Bellarmine School, Liverpool). For other examples see Grace (2002a, 129–130).

12 See Grace (2002a, 135) for these and other statements.

13 This research evidence can also include the findings of the large-scale (and now classic) study by Anthony Bryk, Valerie Lee and Peter Holland, *Catholic schools and the common good* (Bryk et al. 1993). In noting the importance of social capital in explaining the effectiveness of the schools, they also identified another crucial factor which they called 'inspirational ideology'. This included:

> The power of the symbolic . . . it is here that Catholic religious tradition is most directly manifest . . . the words and life of the 'man called Christ' stimulates reflections about how students should live as persons-in-community. The notion of the 'Kingdom of God' offers a vision toward which human effort should be pointed. Finally, the image of the 'resurrection destiny' nurtures hopefulness . . . Here is the sustaining force for the day-in and day-out struggle against tyranny, poverty and injustice. Such images evoke our humanness. They add depth to a schooling process that is otherwise dominated by a rhetoric of test scores, performance standards and professional accountability.
>
> (Bryk et al. 1993, 303)

Could this be 'spiritual capital' by another name?

14 Wallace (2000, 191), viewing the issue from a US perspective, expresses the question in dramatic terms: 'There is a major identity crisis occurring in Catholic schools. The dramatic shift from religious to lay personnel raises the question of whether or not some Catholic schools are becoming private schools with a religious memory but a secular presence'.

15 I recognised this in earlier writing:

> It is fully recognised that the resources of spiritual capital in Catholic schooling extend well beyond that possessed by individual headteachers. Spiritual capital is also constituted in school governing bodies, in classroom teachers, in priests and school chaplains, in parents and not least in the students themselves.
>
> (Grace 2002a, 238)

We clearly need to research the various sources and forms of spiritual capital which exist within the whole community which constitutes the Catholic school.

16 Such an outcome was predicted by James Arthur in his study of Catholic secondary schools in England (Arthur 1995). While not endorsing all of Arthur's suggestion about a weakening culture of Catholicity in the schools, my own research pointed to problems at the level of school leadership:

> There is evidence that many candidates for the headship of Catholic schools in England can now talk confidently about achievements in test scores and examination results, business planning and budgets, marketing and public relations but are relatively inarticulate about the spiritual purposes of Catholic schooling. This is a major contradiction in a system of schooling which exists to give the nurture of spirituality a top priority.
>
> (Grace 2002a, 237)

17 For important distinctions between secularisation and secularism see Arthur (2009).

References

Arthur, J. 1995. *The ebbing tide: Policy and principles of Catholic education.* Leominster, UK: Gracewing Publications.

Arthur, J. 2009. Secularisation, secularism and Catholic education. *International Studies in Catholic Education* 1, no. 2: 228–39.

Bourdieu, P. 1986. The forms of capital. In *Handbook of theory and research for the sociology of education,* ed. J. G. Richardson, 241–58. New York: Greenwood Press.

Bourdieu, P. 1991. Genesis and structure of the religious field. *Comparative Social Research* 13: 1–44.

Bryk, A., V. Lee, and P. Holland. 1993. *Catholic schools and the common good.* Cambridge, MA: Harvard University Press.

Congregation for Catholic Education. 1977. *The Catholic school.* Vatican City, Italy: Libreria Editrice Vaticana.

Congregation for Catholic Education. 1982. *Lay Catholic in schools: Witnesses to faith.* Vatican City, Italy: Libreria Editrice Vaticana.

Congregation for Catholic Education. 2003. *Consecrated persons and their mission in schools.* Vatican City: Libreria Editrice Vaticana.

Durkheim, E. 1977. *The evolution of educational thought: Lectures on the formation and development of secondary education in France.* London: Routledge & Kegan Paul.

Earl, P. 2007. Challenges to faith formation in contemporary Catholic schooling in the USA: Problem and response. In *International handbook of Catholic education,* ed. G. Grace and J. O'Keefe, 37–60. Dordrecht, The Netherlands: Springer.

Grace, G. 2002a. *Catholic schools: Mission, markets and morality.* London: RoutledgeFalmer.

Grace, G. 2002b. Mission integrity: Contemporary challenges for Catholic school leaders. In *Second international handbook of educational leadership and administration,* ed. K. Leithwood and P. Hallinger, 427–49. Dordrecht, The Netherlands: Kluwer Academic Press.

Grace, G., and J. O'Keefe, eds. 2007. *International handbook of Catholic education.* 2 Vols. Dordrecht, The Netherlands: Springer.

Koch, C., J. Calligan, and J. Gros, eds. 2004. *John Baptist de la Salle: The spirituality of Christian education.* New York: Paulist Press.

Lydon, J. 2009. Transmission of the charism: A major challenge for Catholic education. *International Studies in Catholic Education* 1, no. 1: 42–58.

Miller, M. 2006. *The Holy See's teaching on Catholic schools.* Manchester, NH: Sophia Institute Press.

Pope John Paul, II. 1996. *Apostolic exhortation: Vita Consecrata.* Vatican City, Italy: Libreria Editrice Vaticana.

Pope Paul, VI. 1975. *Apostolic exhortation: Evangelii Nuntiandi.* Vatican City, Italy: Libreria Editrice Vaticana.

Swartz, D. 1997. *Culture and power: The sociology of Pierre Bourdieu.* Chicago, IL: University of Chicago Press.

Wallace, T. 2000. We are called: The principal as faith leader in the Catholic school. In *Catholic school leadership,* ed. T. Hunt, T. Oldenski and T. Wallace, 191–203. London: Falmer Press.

Weeks, N., and G. Grace. 2007. *Theological literacy and Catholic schools.* London: Institute of Education, CRDCE.

Part 2

The preferential option for the poor

Chapter 4

Catholic schools and the common good

What this means in educational practice

Professional Focus Series, 2000, No. 2, 2–10.

In 1977 the Sacred Congregation for Catholic Education issued from Rome a foundational document, *The Catholic School*, which expressed the new spirit arising from Vatican II of openness in Catholic education and of service to the common good of persons and of society. This was outlined at the level of both general principles for action and also of specific groups for which there should be a preferential option for action.

At the level of general principle, the mission for Catholic schools was expressed in these terms:

- 'For the Catholic school mutual respect means service to the Person of Christ. Cooperation is between brothers and sisters in Christ. A policy of working for the common good is undertaken seriously as working for the building up of the kingdom of God.'

  (p46)

- 'The Catholic school community therefore is an irreplaceable source of service, not only to the pupils and its other members but also to society. Today especially one sees a world which clamours for solidarity and yet experiences the rise of new forms of individualism. Society can take note from the Catholic school that it is possible to create true communities out of a common effort for the common good.'

  (p47)

In terms of specific groups seen to be particularly in need of the services of Catholic education, *The Catholic School* is clear about what the priorities should be:

- 'First and foremost the Church offers its educational service to the poor or those who are deprived of family help and affection or those who are far from the faith. Since education is an important means of improving the social and economic condition of the individual and of peoples, if the Catholic schools were to turn its attention exclusively or predominantly to those from the wealthier social classes it could be contributing towards maintaining their privileged position and could thereby continue to favour a society which is unjust.'

(pp44–45)

The intention of the Sacred Congregation was to try to breathe a new spirit into the structures and processes of Catholic schooling so that notions of openness, working for the common good and a particular mission to the poor (in economic terms, family support terms and faith terms) should have greater salience. The extent to which this intention actually had an impact upon Catholic educational practice can only be assessed on a country by country basis in the light of subsequent developments.

When the 1977 document referred to 'the rise of new forms of individualism' in various parts of the world it was making a perceptive observation about the growing influence of certain sociopolitical and economic ideologies which were rising to power at this time. New Right ideologies of competitive individualism, free market economies, a reduced social and economic role for the state and the extension of market values and practices into all forms of institutional life were beginning to affect government policies in many countries. A number of these policies appeared to be at odds with Catholic social teaching and in particular with Catholic conceptions of the common good. In the United Kingdom, under the governments of Margaret Thatcher and John Major in the 1980s and early 1990s, a radical series of school reforms extended the influence of 'new forms of individualism' within the educational system. This was an attempted transformation of the very nature of education and of schooling which I have described (Grace, 1995 p21) in these terms: 'While "mission statements" are being constructed for English schools it is being increasingly understood that the "mission" which counts is success in a competitive market situation for schooling. . . . education is regarded as a commodity; the school as a value-adding production unit; the headteacher as chief executive or managing director; the parents as consumers and the ultimate aim of the whole enterprise is to achieve a maximum value-added product which keeps a school as near to the top of the league table of success as is possible.'

As a counter-cultural response to these developments, the Catholic Bishops of England and Wales issued in 1997 a foundational document with the title, *The Common Good in Education*. This expressed the principles of Catholic social teaching in education in these terms:

- 'Education is not a commodity to be offered for sale. The distribution of funding solely according to the dictates of market forces is contrary to the Catholic doctrine of the common good. Teachers and pupils are not economic units whose value is seen merely as a cost element on the school's balance sheet. To consider them in this way threatens human dignity. Education is a service provided for society for the benefit of all its young people, in particular for the benefit of the most vulnerable and the most disadvantaged – those whom we have a sacred duty to serve. Education is about the service of others rather than the service of self.'

(p13)

A distinctive Catholic position of education as a service for the common good of society is here strongly reaffirmed. This emphasis upon service was also integrated with observations on human dignity,

- 'Every member of a school or college community possesses a basic dignity that comes from God and is therefore worthy of respect. This includes students, teaching and support staff, governors, parents and, in particular, the disadvantaged and those with special needs. In Catholic education we are challenged by Christ to see his presence in our neighbour . . . That is why the poor and the disadvantaged in financial, social, academic or spiritual terms must be our primary concern . . . The church's social vision should likewise be evident in the organisation and management of the classroom and in the relationships between and among staff and students. As members of the school community governors, staff . . . and students together with their parents should be enabled to participate, as appropriate, in policy making and encouraged to share in the responsibility for the common good of all within and beyond the school itself.'

(p7)

- 'We believe each person possesses a basic dignity that comes from God, not from any human quality or accomplishment, not from race or gender, age or economic status. The test therefore of every institution or policy is whether it enhances or threatens human dignity and indeed human life itself.'

(p6)

It is apparent from these assertions that the Catholic bishops were concerned that the application of market values in education and that the emphasis upon 'new forms of individualism' would have the effect, in practice, of undermining the human dignity and worth of those students in education who did not, or could not, contribute strongly to the school's 'company results'. In a market conception of schooling, disadvantaged students might not be seen as a good investment for Education plc.

The fact that Catholic schools are in the service of the common good not only of Catholic communities but also of the wider society has been stressed in the Vatican's most recent declaration, *The Catholic School on the Threshold of the Third Millennium* (Congregation for Catholic Education 1998).

- 'The Catholic school's public role is clearly perceived. It has not come into being as a private initiative but as an expression of a public character. It fulfils a service of public usefulness and, although clearly and decidedly configured in the perspective of the Catholic faith, is not reserved to Catholics only, but is open to all those who appreciate and share its educational project. This dimension of openness becomes particularly evident in countries in which Christians are not in the majority or developing countries where Catholic schools have always promoted civil progress and human development without discrimination of any kind.'

(p44)

As will be seen in section three of this paper, Catholic schools can make a strong claim to having served the educational, social and political good of a number of societies – a service for the benefit of all citizens and not simply of Catholic citizens.

The Catholic Church has always understood that the realisation of the common good mission in Catholic education depends ultimately on a sense of special vocation among its school principals, headteachers and teachers. The Catholic position is that just as the school is not a factory or a business, the status of teacher is not a job but a vocation. This was clearly expressed in the Vatican publication, *Lay Catholics in Schools: Witnesses to Faith* (1982) and has recently been emphasised by Pope John Paul II in an address to the National Assembly of Italian Catholic Schools (October 1999):

- 'The educational capacity of every scholastic institution largely depends on the quality of the people who are part of it and, in particular, on the competence and dedication of its teachers . . . I therefore turn with affection, gratitude and trust to you, teachers of Catholic schools, both religious and lay people who often work under difficult conditions and are forced to accept an inadequate salary. I ask you always to put your heart into your work sustained by the certainty that you are thus participating in a special way in the mission Christ entrusted to his disciples.'[1]

Without a strong conception of vocation among teachers in Catholic schools the mission of common good service in education is likely to become vulnerable to the influences of contemporary commercial and market ideologies in education and to secular emphases upon academic and skills productivity alone.

What the Church's teaching could mean in educational policy and practice

It is clear from the previous section that Catholic education involves a principled commitment to the advancement of the common good. But what are the implications of this for educational policy and practice? It is useful to think of these implications from three perspectives: *a)* whole society implications; *b)* local community implications; and *c)* individual school implications.

a) Whole society implications

Catholic schools have a commitment to contributing towards the common good of the societies of which they are a part. In terms of educational practice this could mean the realisation of the mission in the following ways:

Christian citizenship education

Catholic schools could be, and should be, at the forefront of educating in theory and in practice for democratic citizenship formulated to mean an active political involvement in national projects to advance the common good. The very concept of citizen implies commitments and concerns beyond self, family and local community. At the most developed level, i.e. 'citizen of the world' it implies a solidarity with peoples beyond the national boundaries. Children and young people have an understanding of political relations in society (as the past history of South Africa demonstrates). What they need from Catholic schools is a Christian view of how to be concerned, active and responsible citizens in the building of a new South Africa, and the building of a better world.

Development of 'common good' talents and skills

The Catholic educational position has always been that it is not sufficient simply to develop the intelligence, talents and skills of young people on an individual or 'self-fulfilment' basis. This could lead to the creation of talented and clever but also self-centred and materially acquisitive individuals with no regard for any conception of a common good. The Catholic position is that intelligence, talents and skills are to be developed in Catholic education to the highest possible degree, along with a religious and moral understanding that such personal empowerment is to be used for the benefit of others.

The Catholic formula is: developed talents and skills + common good moral commitments = the good Catholic citizen.

Strengthening the spiritual and moral culture of society

In every society different cultures representing different values, world views and ways of being in the world co-exist and in many cases conflict in particular historical periods. In contemporary conditions, two developments provide a challenge to the integrity and influence of spiritual and moral culture, including that represented by the Catholic schooling system. These developments are the globalisation of the influence of international capitalist agencies in economic relations and the growing influence of secularisation in intellectual and cultural relations. While the spread of international capitalism to many countries has brought clear material benefits, the danger of its pervasive influence especially through advertising, has also brought, as the Pope has warned, the challenge of *materialism*. The possibility exists that human life may become the pursuit of consumer goods rather than the pursuit of common goods.

At another level, that of secularisation in the modern world, the very idea of God is marginalised or entirely removed from consideration and the discourse of the sacred becomes weaker as the discourse of utilitarian concerns (economic planning, bureaucratic requirements, technological innovations, consumer choice) becomes stronger.

In this context an important mission for Catholic schools everywhere is to try to act as a counter-cultural force to strengthen spiritual and moral culture in society, to keep alive notions of the common good and of social justice and to inspire and prepare young people to defend Gospel values in an age in which they are under threat.

The implications of this for educational policy and practice are considerable. School principals and teachers will need to have forms of continuing professional development and practical courses of study which will empower them to be knowledgeable and persuasive in the articulation of the Catholic faith and of its spiritual, social and moral teachings. Catholic bishops and Catholic Institutes of Education everywhere have a clear responsibility to provide such courses for their Catholic educators.[2]

b) Local community implications

An obvious implication of Catholic school commitment, especially to the service of the poor and powerless, is that Catholic schools should be predominantly located in those communities in any society which are poor and powerless. In this way, the Catholic school can act as a beacon of hope (where hope is in short supply), a community resource (where resources are in short supply) and a witness to Christ (where this witness is most needed).

In terms of educational practice, the realisation of the local community mission of Catholic schools could involve the following:

Forming local community leaders

One consequence of a successful academic Catholic education is that talented young people tend to leave their local rural and small town communities in pursuit of career opportunities and of social mobility in the organisations of the big city. This is an understandable progression and it may lead to opportunities to work for the common good at national and even international levels. However, this tendency results in the loss of talent and of potential leadership in the rural and small town communities from which these students originated. The common good, at the local level, may not be helped by this process which has been described as 'up – and out for the individual'.

Catholic schools can play a part in modifying these tendencies in two ways. Firstly, the schools can focus their educational programmes to show young people the possibilities for being socially mobile and in pursuit of the common good or of being local and in pursuit of the common good (what Gramsci has called 'organic intellectuals'). Secondly, the school could provide a resource base for adult and continuing education where local 'mature students' could be educated for leadership roles in the local community. Serious attention to the provision of adult and continuing education is a necessary part of the strategy of strengthening the common good outcomes of education at the local community level.

Forming a community network of schools

The realisation of notions of the common good in educational practice seems to imply that a group of Catholic schools in a given locality will want to act as a supportive community network of schools and not simply as a number of individual and competitive units. School partnerships, consortia, cluster groups and community networks should therefore be a defining and distinctive feature of Catholic school organisation. In such Catholic collectivities, schools would be able to help and support each other by the sharing of resources, partnership planning for teachers' continuing professional development, teacher exchange, joint planning for staff recruitment, helping any school in particular difficulties, joint purchase of resources through consortia arrangements, joint responses to government education initiatives and partnership arrangements to deal with difficult and challenging pupils.

Such community networks of schools will not only strengthen the schools which are members of them but they will also strengthen the larger communities of which they are a part. The whole exercise can also be viewed as a practical example of Christian democracy in action and a significant contribution to the advancement of the common good.

c) Individual school implications

Most Catholic schools in their mission statements say that they are loving and happy communities, permeated by the spirit of Christ and characterised by a culture and ethos which shows respect for the dignity and worth of all persons in the school and which operates upon principles of high expectations for teachers and pupils, a supportive and encouraging environment, and a Catholic school climate which while ordered and effective is at the same time understanding and forgiving. But do Catholic schools in their practice live up to the principles of their mission statements? It is easier to write the principles of a school's mission statement than to live the principles in the everyday pressures and preoccupations of school life. And yet, if there is to be a distinctive conception of Catholic school culture and ethos[3] and if there is to be a distinctive conception of Catholic school effectiveness (Grace 1998), then Catholic schools always have to strive to live out the commitments of their mission statements. The great danger in all forms of school life is that despite a formal commitment to the dignity and respect of all the pupils, *in practice certain pupils receive more dignity and respect than others*. These privileged pupils may be, in different school situations, those who are regarded as quick and clever, polite and diligent, clean and attractive, religious and moral, or they may be pupils from particular home backgrounds and culture (social class, racial/ethnic, regional, religious). The understandable tendency in everyday school life is to give more positive attention, time, praise, recognition and status to those pupils who meet the school's expectations of the model or ideal pupil and who bring credit to their teachers and to the school's reputation.

However, if Catholic schools are seriously trying to live out their common good commitments to *all* of their pupils, then, it could be argued, they have to try to resist these tendencies to 'love only those who love you'. Catholic schools have to try to show as much concern for, and respect of, the pupils who do not fulfil the ideal pupil role, i.e. those who are disruptive and challenging, those who are slow to learn, those who are disorganised and irresponsible, etc.

These considerations may cause Catholic schools to examine their educational practice in these respects:

Celebrating the talents and achievements of all

to give forms of public recognition which extend beyond academic and sporting prowess alone to include other contributions to school and community life, to the religious life of the school, to creative achievements of all kinds and to ideas of 'progress made'.

Organising to encourage the development of the talents of all

to consider whether various forms of grouping for teaching and learning (streaming, tracking, setting, ability grouping, ability tables) may work against common good achievement.

Policies for discipline and punishment

to consider whether certain forms of discipline and punishment are appropriate for Christian schools which say that they are permeated by the spirit of Christ[4] and that they believe in respect for all persons.

Policies against bullying, racism and sexism

to consider whether the school has formulated such policies, with the collaboration of parents and pupils, and whether the school is monitoring the effectiveness of such policies in practice.

Policies on pupil exclusions and expulsions

to consider what can be done for those pupils whose sustained disruptive behaviour makes it necessary for them to be removed from their own school community.

Respecting and supporting the teachers

to consider whether the school as an organisation and the Diocese as the administrative authority are pursuing policies which contribute to the common good of the teachers in Catholic schools in terms of their working conditions and salaries and general support services.

Notes

1 As reported in *L'Osservatore Romano* 1 December 1999, p8.
2 The Catholic Institute of Education in South Africa is responding to these needs in its provision of courses and conferences for Catholic educators and in its publications eg Potterton, 1999.
3 For a view that Catholic school religious distinctiveness may be weakening at secondary level in England, see Arthur, 1995. However, for a view that Catholic schools are particularly well placed to develop a communitarian agenda in education, see Arthur and Bailey, 2000.
4 As McLaughlin (1997, p25) puts it: 'If Catholic schools have Christ as the raison d'etre for their existence, then leadership in Catholic schools must reflect the leadership of Jesus Christ, adapted to the contemporary context'.

References

Arthur, J. (1995), *The Ebbing Tide: Policy and Principles of Catholic Education*. Leominster: Gracewing Publications.

Arthur, J. and Bailey, R. (2000), *Schools and Community*. London: Falmer Press.

Bryk, A., Lee, V. and Holland, P. (1993), *Catholic Schools and the Common Good*. Cambridge MA: Harvard University Press.

Catholic Bishops of England and Wales (1997), *The Common Good in Education*. London: Catholic Education Service.

——— (1997), *A Struggle for Excellence: Catholic Secondary Schools in Urban Poverty Areas*. London: Catholic Education Service.

——— (1999) *Foundations for Excellence: Catholic Primary Schools in Urban Poverty Areas*. London: Catholic Education Service.

Christie, P. (1990), *Open Schools: Racially Mixed Catholic Schools in South Africa 1976–1986*. Johannesburg: Ravan Press.

Congregation for Catholic Education (1998), *The Catholic School on the Threshold of the Third Millennium.* Vatican City: Libreria Editrice, Vaticana.

Conroy, J. (ed.) (1999), *Catholic Education: Inside-out and Outside-in.* Dublin: Lindisfarne Books.

Grace, G. (1995), *School Leadership: Beyond Education Management.* London: Falmer Press.

—— (1998), 'Realising the Mission: Catholic Approaches to School Effectiveness' in R. Slee, G. Weiner, and S. Tomlinson (eds) *School Effectiveness for Whom? Challenges to the School Effectiveness and School Improvement Movements.* London: Falmer Press.

—— (2001, forthcoming), 'St Michael's Roman Catholic Comprehensive School, Billingham' in M. Maden (ed.) *Success Against the Odds: Five Years On.* London: Routledge Falmer.

—— (2002, forthcoming), *Catholic Schools: Mission, Markets and Morality.* London: Routledge Falmer.

Mbeki, T. (1999), *A Nation at Work for a Better Life.* Pretoria: GCIS.

McLaughlin, D. (1997), 'Leadership in Catholic Schools: A Touchstone for Authenticity' in J. McMahon, H. Neidhart and J. Chapman (eds) *Leading the Catholic School.* Richmond: Victoria, Spectrum Publications.

Pope John Paul II (1999), Address to the National Assembly of Italian Catholic Schools, Rome *L'Osservatore Romano N.48.*

Potterton, M. (1999), *Quality for All: Improving the Quality of Catholic Schools.* Johannesburg: Catholic Institute of Education.

Sacred Congregation for Catholic Education (1977), *The Catholic School.* Vatican City, Libreira Editrice, Vatican.

—— (1982) *Lay Catholics in Schools: Witnesses to Faith.* London: Catholic Truth Society.

South African Catholic Bishops (1980), *The Bishops Speak.* Pretoria: SACBC.

—— (1989) *Community Serving Humanity.* Pretoria: SACBC.

Vatican Congregation for Education (1988), *The Religious Dimension of Education in a Catholic School.* Dublin: Veritas.

Chapter 5

'First and foremost the Church offers its educational service to the poor'

Class, inequality and Catholic schooling in contemporary contexts

International Studies in Sociology of Education, 2003, 13(1), 35–55.

This article is based upon the assumption that a comprehensive construct of sociological enquiry in education must include engagement with specific faith-based educational systems in various settings. The analysis presented here attempts to advance that process of engagement by examining, both theoretically and empirically, the role of contemporary Catholic schooling and its relations with class, inequality and social reproduction from an international perspective. The article outlines some critical perspectives on traditional Catholic culture and education using concepts drawn from the work of Gramsci and of Bourdieu. The transformative potential of the Second Vatican Council (1962–1965) is then discussed, followed by a consideration of contemporary empirical studies of Catholic schooling. Throughout the analysis, Gramsci's concept of an ideological 'war of position' is applied to the internal relations of the Catholic Church and of Catholic education internationally. The need for further research into the power relations of the Catholic Church is indicated.

Critical perspectives on traditional Catholic culture and education

Antonio Gramsci (1891–1937) recognised the power and influence of the Catholic Church as an educational agency. However, for Gramsci the Church's work in education had become incorporated to serve the interests of the dominant classes, bureaucratised as an agency for the social reproduction of the Church itself and overly preoccupied with the dissemination of a mystical and other-worldly ideology.

In his classic essay 'The Intellectuals', Gramsci argued that 'all men (*sic*) are intellectuals . . . but not all men have in society the function of intellectuals' and made the important observation that 'school is the instrument through which intellectuals of various levels are elaborated' (Gramsci, 1978, pp. 9–10). Developing his famous distinction between 'traditional intellectuals' and 'organic intellectuals', Gramsci represented the Catholic Church as an educational agency which absorbed many of the potential organic intellectuals of the working class and recontextualised them to become traditional intellectuals in the service of a conservative status quo. Working from Marx's original observation that religion conserves the social order by contributing to the legitimation of the power of the dominant and to the domestication of the dominated, Gramsci argued that:

> the ecclesiastics (traditional intellectuals) for a long time . . . held a monopoly of important services – religious ideology, schools education, morality, justice, charity, good works, etc. The category of ecclesiastics can be considered the category of intellectuals organically bound to the landed aristocracy.
>
> (p. 7)

From this perspective, those who became priests or nuns ceased to be organically linked to their class of origin and became part of an ideological superstructure of domination.

In more recent times, Bourdieu (1991) in his observations on 'the religious field' has developed a similar argument:

> The relationship of homology obtaining between the position of the church in the structure of the religious field and the position of the dominant fractions of the dominant classes in the field of power and in the structure of class relations . . . makes the church contribute to the conservation of political order.
>
> (p. 33)

Both of these critical writers, while emphasising the relations of correspondence between the Church and dominant orders viewed historically, have also noted the existence of ideological struggles and power conflicts associated with this relationship. Gramsci observed that the dominant intellectual position of the ecclesiastics was challenged by the emerging position of other professional and secular intellectuals. Bourdieu (1991, p. 33) has noted that the relation of homology which he describes 'does not exclude tensions and conflicts between political and religious power'. However, the emphasis here is upon what might be called the field of external conflict, i.e. that between church intellectuals and secular intellectuals, or church versus state. Much less attention is given to what can be called the field of internal conflict, in this case the Catholic Church and its internal theological, power, social and ideological struggles. This relative lack of attention to internal conflicts within Catholicism is probably the result of perceptions of the institutional Church as monolithic, authoritarian and subject to strong internal surveillance (e.g. Vatican Curia, Holy Office/Inquisition, the Papacy). Nevertheless this social construct of the Church oversimplifies both the historical internal relations of the Church and its contemporary internal relations. As I have written elsewhere (Grace, 2001, p. 490):

> Church–State relations in educational policy and practice are not the meeting of two monoliths either in conflict or in alliance on specific questions. They are rather a more complex manoeuvring of interest groups located within both the structures of the state and the structures of the Church.

In other words, more analytical attention needs to be given to the socio-cultural and political role of the contemporary Catholic Church in its internal conflicts and the attempted transformations of its theology, culture and social teaching.

The Second Vatican Council (1962–1965): the potential for transformation

Given the extensive literature on this subject,[1] it is only possible here to outline some of the major themes emerging from this radical event in the development of the Catholic Church. Hastings (1991, p. 525) has argued that:

> There can be no question that the Vatican Council was the most important ecclesiastical event of this century. . . . It so greatly changed the character of by far the largest communion of Christendom.

The Council was radical in theological, social and political terms, and in the pontificates of John XXIII (1958–1963) and Paul VI (1963–1978) a process of cultural and institutional transformation was launched. This process involved attempts to develop a new conception of the Church as not simply clerical but constituted as 'the people of God'; a greater emphasis upon collegial authority; a new principle of openness and dialogue with the world, other Christian denominations, other faiths and those with no faith; a renewed corpus of Catholic social teaching centred on 'a preferential option for the poor'; a new conception of sin as not simply individual but also social and structural, and a changed socio-political stance in international relations. This last involved a move from the traditional denunciations of Marxism and of communist regimes as atheistic and oppressive to a more extensive criticism of structures of oppression and exploitation ('structures of sin') constituted in capitalism, in race relations (apartheid in South Africa) and in socio-political and economic relations in various parts of the world, such as Latin America.

From the 1960s to the present a considerable ideological and power struggle has characterised the internal relations of the Catholic Church, as the advocates of the Vatican II transformations seek to develop a new 'theology of praxis'[2] and the traditionalists and conservatives attempt to resist it. This has amounted to an internal 'war of position', an analytical concept which Gramsci originated but which he would not have expected to occur within the structures of the Church itself.

The war of position can be traced across all the reforming themes of the Vatican Council but attention here will be confined to three of them.

From social charity to social justice

Charity as a concept and practice was a feature of traditional Catholic culture as it sought to alleviate the worst excesses of oppressive structures in the past, whether of feudalism or of capitalism. Social justice as a concept only entered the formal discourse of the Catholic Church when it was first used by Pius XI in his encyclical *Quadragesimo Anno* (1931). In this document Pius made crucial distinctions between social charity and social justice:[3]

> A charity which defrauds the worker of his just wage is no true charity but a hollow name and a pretence . . . Doles given out of pity will not exempt a man from his obligations of justice . . . True charity, on the contrary, is the virtue which makes men try to improve the distribution of goods as justice requires.

This emphasis was taken up and developed much further in the spirit of Vatican II thinking by Pope Paul VI in the encyclical *Populorum Progressio* (1967) and in the document *Justice in the World* (1971) produced by the Synod of Bishops in Rome. Paul Vallely and other contributors to the text *The New Politics: Catholic social teaching for the twenty-first century* (Vallely, 1998) have pointed to the great significance of these statements, especially as a critique of international capitalism and international trade relations. *Justice in the World* was explicit about the structural injustice involved in post-imperialism which had resulted in a 'new form of colonialism in which the developing nations will be the victims of the interplay of international economic forces.'[4]

Populorum Progressio criticised the ideology of liberal capitalism:[5]

> Certain concepts have arisen . . . that present profit as the chief spur to economic progress, free competition as the guiding norm of economics and private ownership of the means of production as an absolute right, having no limits or concomitant social obligations. This unbridled liberalism paves the way for a particular type of tyranny.

With such statements, produced at the highest levels, the Catholic Church was attempting to show that it was *not* in correspondence with the ideologies of dominant orders, but rather in a counter-cultural stance of social critique. This changed position was not simply manifest in formal statements, but was also being realised in a theology of praxis. An emphasis upon the praxis of liberation became evident at this time. The Council of Latin American Bishops meeting in Medellín, Colombia in 1968 took up ideas of a theology of liberation, ideas of conscientisation and of a transfer of power to the poor through literacy and education. The effect of this new thinking emanating from Latin America was apparent in the discourse of the document *Justice in the World*:[6]

> God reveals himself to us as the liberator of the oppressed and the defender of the poor.

The appearance of a liberation theology in Latin America and later in other Catholic contexts challenged long-standing concepts of religion and the Church as 'the opium of the people' and substituted the possibility that they might become agencies for conscientisation and liberation.

From conservative theology to liberation theology?

Thomas Oldenski (1997, p. 79), in *Liberation Theology and Critical Pedagogy in Today's Catholic Schools,* gives a valuable account of the new theological and educational understandings as articulated by a number of writers in Latin America:

> Liberation theology rejects the dominating theological discourses of a pervasively Eurocentric cultural experience of religion, spirituality and even church, in attempting to reconstruct these theological concepts and religious practices. Liberation theology criticizes how the Eurocentric churches historically used and currently use power.

Liberation theology presents a new understanding of what it means to be Christian in a transformative way. It suggests that the act of believing in Jesus includes a belief in social justice as a prime virtue and in the reality of evil as the social injustice that dominates and marginalises oppressed people:[7]

> One exercises Christian faith by participating in the transformation of society toward a more just and democratic practice and establishing a solidarity with . . . the poor and the victims of gender, class and race oppression.

The Vatican II impulse to reform traditional Catholic practice and theology had resulted in Latin America in the possibility that the Catholic Church might not be, in Gramsci's terms, 'organically bound to the landed aristocracy' but rather, that some of its clerical members (priests, Jesuits and nuns) might become organically bound to oppressed social groups.

In his study of the discourses and practices of liberation theology and of critical pedagogy, Oldenski demonstrates how these two cultural innovations interacted and developed in a symbiotic way. Paulo Freire produced his classic work, *Pedagogy of the Oppressed* (1968), in the same year that the Council of Latin American Bishops at Medellín was expressing 'a preferential option for the poor'. There is evidence of Freire's early involvement with the Catholic Church in Brazil and in the development of the praxis of liberation theology. In the latter part of his career, as a professor in the Faculty of Education at the Catholic University of São Paulo, he was involved in a large project of popular education sponsored by the Archdiocese of São Paulo.[8]

Although liberation theology and its advocates have received many setbacks during the conservative pontificate of John Paul II (1978–), a discourse and practice of liberation, solidarity, option for the poor, conscientisation and education for critical literacy continues to be active in Latin America and in other settings which have been influenced by these radical transformations. In particular, Basic Christian Communities (Swope, 1992) represent a new form of adult education in deprived locations with radical potential. While some bishops and priests remain in the role of traditional intellectuals serving the institutional church and dominant political elites, others are attempting to become organic intellectuals in the service of 'the people of God' and of the oppressed classes. These organic intellectuals of what Freire (1984) has called the 'Prophetic Church' face not only censure from the traditional Church authorities, but also the direct violence of dominant power elites (as the assassination of Archbishop Oscar Romero and of many priests and nuns demonstrates).

It cannot be said that liberation theology and the critical pedagogy of conscientisation that goes with it has transformed the Catholic Church, Catholic culture or even Catholic education. What can be said, however, is that these radical influences are present in the internal war of position which characterises the contemporary Catholic Church. While under present hierarchical relations their influence may be muted and constrained, changes in hierarchy could result in more extensive transformations in all of these sectors.

New directions for Catholic education?

In 1977 the Sacred Congregation for Catholic Education (SCCE) issued from Rome a foundational document, *The Catholic School*, which expressed Vatican II's new spirit of openness and service to the common good.[9] This was outlined at the level both of general principles for action and also of specific groups for which there should be a preferential option for action. What might be called the foundation charter for contemporary international

Catholic education set out three regulative principles for the future development of Catholic schooling: commitment to the common good, commitment
to solidarity and community, and commitment to the service of the poor.
The first of these was expressed as a theology of praxis:

> For the Catholic school, mutual respect means service to the Person of
> Christ. Cooperation is between brothers and sisters in Christ. A policy
> of working for the common good is undertaken seriously as working for
> the building up of the kingdom of God.
>
> (SCCE, 1977, p. 46)

The second represented a counter-cultural and oppositional stance to the
emergence of New Right forms of aggressive individualism in public policy
in a number of contexts:

> Today one sees a world which clamours for solidarity and yet experi-
> ences *the rise of new forms of individualism* [my emphasis]. Society can
> take note from the Catholic school that it is possible to create true com-
> munities out of a common effort for the common good.
>
> (p. 47)

The third involved a radical commitment to the poor (comprehensively
defined):

> First and foremost the Church offers its educational service to the poor,
> or those who are deprived of family help and affection, or those who
> are far from the faith. Since education is an important means of improv-
> ing the social and economic condition of the individual and of peoples,
> if the Catholic school was to turn attention exclusively or predomi-
> nantly to those from the wealthier social classes it could be contributing
> towards maintaining their privileged position and could thereby con-
> tinue to favour a society which is unjust.
>
> (pp. 44–45)

In the internal war of position within the Catholic Church after Vatican II,
this radical manifesto for Catholic schooling appeared to signal an advance
for the advocates of reform as a significant attempt to recontextualise the
Church's educational mission.

However, the document itself was addressed for the consideration of
'episcopal conferences', that is, the Conferences of Catholic Bishops around
the world responsible for the administration and policy formation of their
educational systems. The reforming principles of *The Catholic School* thus
might be taken up with enthusiasm in some contexts, with caution in others
and, in conservative settings, virtually ignored.

It is an interesting comment on the enduring power of conservative interests within the Catholic Church, even after Vatican II, that whereas the encyclical *Humanae Vitae* (1968) on birth control was declared to be binding upon all Catholics, the important document on social teaching *The Catholic School* was offered for their 'consideration'.

The extent to which the intentions of *The Catholic School* have been implemented can only be assessed on a country-by-country basis. The history and sociology of this attempt to recontextualise Catholic schooling has yet to be written from an international perspective. Such a large comparative exercise will require an examination of the role of Conferences of Catholic Bishops in various parts of the world as mediators and (in Bernstein's terms) 'relays' for educational reform.

In England and Wales, the Conference of Catholic Bishops did reaffirm the principles of the 1977 document. As the United Kingdom experienced New Right ideologies of competitive individualism, free market economics, a reduced social and economic role for the state and the extension of market values and practices into public policy under the governments of Margaret Thatcher and John Major in the 1980s and early 1990s, the Catholic Bishops made their response. This consisted of major counter-cultural statements, *The Common Good and the Catholic Church's Social Teaching* (Catholic Bishops Conference of England and Wales, 1996) and, on educational policy, *The Common Good in Education* (Catholic Education Service, 1997). These powerful statements demonstrated opposition to the 'new forms of individualism' which were being implemented in economic and social policy and in the radical series of school reforms enacted in the 1980s in the UK.

The Common Good in Education was particularly explicit in opposing the marketisation of education, which it saw as deleterious to poor and disadvantaged communities:

> Education is not a commodity to be offered for sale. The distribution of funding solely according to the dictates of market forces is contrary to the Catholic doctrine of the common good. Teachers and pupils are not economic units whose value is seen merely as a cost element on the school's balance sheet. To consider them in this way threatens human dignity. Education is a service provided by society for the benefit of all its young people, in particular for the benefit of the most vulnerable and the most disadvantaged – those whom we have a sacred duty to serve. Education is about the service of others rather than the service of self.
>
> (p. 13)

Both of these important documents of Vatican II social teaching provided an alternative agenda for Catholic schools in England and Wales. While government policy encouraged them to think of ways of being individually 'successful' in a market economy for schooling, the Catholic bishops exhorted them to hold fast to solidarity, community, and a preferential option for the poor. Catholic schools, in other words, were caught up in an ideological struggle in education which had profound consequences for class, inequality and social reproduction. How each school located itself in this struggle was the outcome of a complex matrix of influences including the power of the interventionist state, the social teaching of Vatican II (as mediated within each diocese), the location and market position of a school, the religious and ideological commitment of Catholic head teachers and governors, and the involvement of a more active parental group. This, which Brown (1990) has called 'the ideology of parentocracy', became significant in England in the 1980s and early 1990s.

The war of position within Catholic schooling in England and Wales was not simply a struggle between Church and State. It was a more complex engagement in which a confident and enlarged sector of the Catholic middle class (largely parents) could be decisive in determining the direction of educational policy for local areas and schools.[10]

Catholic schooling in contemporary contexts: some studies

The empirical study of Catholic education internationally is remarkably under-developed (Grace, 2002). With almost 200,000 schools (primary and secondary) serving almost 50 million students in a great variety of socio-cultural, political and economic settings, the international world of Catholic schooling remains largely unknown, not only by sociologists of education but also by many educational researchers and scholars. This lack of knowledge about contemporary Catholic schooling systems does not, however, prevent academics and educators from expressing strong (generally negative) opinions about the consequences of Catholic schooling for personal and intellectual autonomy, class relations and inequality, social harmony, race relations, gender relations and the social reproduction of bigotry and divisiveness.[11]

The small selection of empirical studies of Catholic schooling presented in this article cannot deal comprehensively with all of these negative attacks. They *can* demonstrate that evidence-based argument is required in this field rather than the recycling of prejudice and ideological assertions, and that when such evidence is considered the relationship of Catholic schooling to class and inequality issues is more nuanced than its critics have allowed.

In Latin America[12] (in particular, Chile) the research of Swope (1992) has demonstrated the radical potential of Basic Christian Communities (BCCs) in deprived urban locations as informal agencies for adult education. Some of these agencies, influenced by the principles of liberation theology and by Freirian approaches to conscientisation, have created new contexts for

Catholic adult education. As Swope has shown, the formal insulation of Catholic schooling from external social, political and economic relations has been broken down in the BCCs, where 'church discourse', 'domestic discourse', 'economic discourse' and 'political discourse' are brought together to create new forms of a Catholic educational text and a Catholic Christian pedagogy. Swope also demonstrates that some theologians, priests and members of religious orders (especially Jesuits) associated with the work of the BCCs have taken up the role of organic intellectuals for working-class and peasant communities in that continent.

The BCCs in Chile, Brazil and elsewhere in Latin America represent new Vatican II ways of 'being Church' and 'being school'. More research is needed to trace the extent of BCC organisation, the responses of the institutional Church to these developments and the current vitality of these agencies in changing economic and political conditions. While such research is supported by the Jesuit-sponsored Centro de Investigation y Desarrollo de la Educacion (CIDE) in Santiago and by institutions such as the Catholic University of São Paulo, the research resources in Latin America are not extensive. In contrast, the USA has been the main location for empirical research into contemporary Catholic education and its relations with class, inequality and social reproduction.

Catholic schooling in the USA has historically been associated with educational services for the poor and disadvantaged, especially immigrant communities of Irish, Italian, Polish, German and Hispanic cultural origin. Research on such provision and on its relative effectiveness has been undertaken in a series of studies, including Vitullo-Martin (1979), Cibulka et al (1982), Greeley (1982), Raudenbush & Bryk (1986), Coleman & Hoffer (1987), Convey (1992), Bryk et al (1993), O'Keefe (1996) and Oldenski (1997). Many of these studies show that such educational provision has had good outcomes for poor and disadvantaged students in terms of academic achievement, progress to higher education and subsequent social mobility. Cibulka et al (1982), for instance, in a study of fifty Catholic elementary schools with ethnic minority enrolments of at least 70% (in Chicago, Detroit, Los Angeles, Milwaukee, Newark, New Orleans, New York and Washington), found that such schools were serving families which were larger and poorer that the average American family. Many were single-parent families, and more than half of the families were not Catholic. Generally, students in these schools achieved better results than students in neighbouring public schools. Cibulka and his co-researchers noted the existence of high levels of commitment and dedication (vocation) among the teachers in these schools, about 30% of whom were members of religious orders.

Although the question of relative achievement must be approached with great caution,[13] what this and other research demonstrates is that Catholic schooling can be a powerful and community-enhancing resource in inner-city and deprived urban locations. Such educational services meet the needs not only of the Catholic poor but also of other disadvantaged groups, including significant numbers of black students who are not Catholic.

The major American research study on class, inequality and social reproduction, from a Catholic perspective, is the text by Anthony Bryk, Valerie Lee and Peter Holland, *Catholic Schools and the Common Good* (1993). Using large-scale statistical data from the *High School and Beyond* federal project and related information, and extending this by detailed fieldwork in seven Catholic high schools (in Los Angeles, Boston, Baltimore, Cleveland, Louisville and San Antonio), the research team focused upon the search for answers to the question:

> How do Catholic high schools manage simultaneously to achieve relatively high levels of student learning, distribute this learning more equitably with regard to race and class than in the public sector and sustain high levels of teacher commitment and student engagement?
>
> (p. 297)

Analysis, especially of the fieldwork data, suggested the importance of four factors in the 'Catholic school effect': academic structure and learning culture (bookishness), internal and external community networks (social capital), devolved governance (autonomy) and 'inspirational ideology' (a sense of mission and purpose). Bryk et al also found strong commitments to social justice in these post-Vatican II American high schools, expressed in two educational 'missions': one to the socio-educational advance of those disadvantaged in class and race terms, and the other to the formation of socio-political and social justice awareness among elite students:[14]

> Although we have emphasised the education of disadvantaged students, we note that Catholic schools also advance an important agenda in the education of their more advantaged counterparts. In schools with large proportions of low-income students, the social justice mission of Vatican II is tangibly manifested . . . The concern for social justice however is also manifest in the schooling of the advantaged. Catholic schools deliberately strive to inculcate an understanding for and a commitment to social justice in all their students. Many of these students are likely to move into powerful positions in society as adults . . . The Catholic school emphasizes to its students the value of leadership for social justice and hopes that this message will become internalised in adulthood.
>
> (pp. 340–341)

For post-Vatican II schooling in the USA, as the research of Bryk et al and others have demonstrated, a new form of theological, social and educational praxis is in the process of formation. In this Catholic praxis, the spiritual, the moral and the social are necessarily interconnected as categories. There can be no authentic love of God (a manifestation of the spiritual) which is not at the same time linked to living a good life (a manifestation of the moral) and to loving and helping one's neighbour (a manifestation of social concern and social justice). It does however seem unlikely that the Catholic system is the only faith-based educational provision which has such spiritual, moral and social justice commitments. Systems established by Jewish, Islamic and Hindu communities and by other Christian communities would claim to have such characteristics arising from their faith commitments.

In the field of race relations, studies such as Irvine & Foster's *Growing Up African American in Catholic Schools* (1996) suggest that some Catholic schools are aware that social justice involves the creation of anti-racist educational environments. However, the most significant examples of Catholic schools and the praxis of anti-racism are to be found, as might be expected, in South Africa. In 1989, the Pontifical Commission for Justice and Peace at the Vatican issued a guidance document for all Catholics on matters concerning race relations (Pontifical Commission for Justice and Peace, 1989). This document, *The Church and Racism: towards a more fraternal society* included, among other things, a commitment to the eradication of racism within its own institutions.

As Pam Christie (1990) has shown, the Catholic Church in South Africa had anticipated this declaration by over a decade. In a post-Vatican II spirit of reform the South African Catholic Bishops Conference (SACBC) took a stand in opposition to the apartheid state policy of racial separation in schooling by passing a resolution in favour of 'the integration of Catholic schools'. Nevertheless, there were internal differences in the church about the wisdom of such a strategy:

> This initiative did not occur as a single, uncontested thrust within the Catholic church. There were differences of opinion not so much on the principle of opening as on strategy . . . with regard to dealings with the government and on the interpretation of 'open' as opposed to 'integrated'.
>
> (p. 19)

Christie's research demonstrates that in the struggle to establish racially mixed Catholic schools in South Africa between 1976 and 1986, women in religious teaching orders were crucial in overcoming such institutional caution:

> There is evidence of the autonomy of individual schools in decision-making and also evidence of the leadership of women religious in the open schools movement . . . The strategy of the sisters in pre-empting state approval and pushing against the law, in effect overtook the legalistic and cautious strategy of the brothers. There is no doubt that women

religious were the leaders of school integration and gave the movement much of its shape.

(p. 22)

While Jesuits gave leadership to a Christian praxis of liberation in Latin America, women religious gave leadership to a similar movement in South Africa. In both class and race relations a post-Vatican II theology and social teaching was developing more radical forms of Catholic educational practice than had ever been seen in the past.

By comparison, the transformations of Catholic schooling in the UK, Ireland and Australia have been much less dramatic in their nature and more muted in their outcomes. Nevertheless, in each of these contexts studies show some transformations relating to a Vatican II renewal of Catholic education. My study of 60 Catholic secondary schools in London, Liverpool and Birmingham (Grace, 2002) found that such schools were providing valuable educational services to inner-city and deprived working-class communities and were fulfilling the Vatican II commitment that 'first and foremost the Church offers its educational services to the poor'. At the same time such schools were active in social justice and citizenship formation as well as more traditional forms of social charity. Many of these schools were open to Christians of other denominations and to members of other faiths. A significant number of the school leaders (the head teachers) indicated that the Vatican II principles of Catholicism relating to openness and dialogue, social justice commitments and 'new ways of being Church' had influenced the educational environments which, with others, they were trying to develop in the schools. In some areas (particularly Birmingham), Catholic secondary schools had developed partnership and community educational networks[15] in opposition to government-sponsored concepts of individual entrepreneurial schools competing in the educational marketplace. These English Catholic secondary schools had a stance towards issues of class, inequality and social reproduction in education that was qualitatively different to that of their predecessors. Their mission statements proclaimed both religious and social justice ideals in education and many of them attempted to realise these ideals in practice. While they were clearly focused upon academic success and social mobility goals for their largely working-class students, these instrumental purposes were nearly always related to an ethic of 'academic success for service and not simply for self'.[16] The discourse of school mission statements cannot be taken as evidence for educational outcomes but it does provide an important indicator of a school's publicly declared purposes and an agenda against which its 'mission integrity' can be evaluated.

Research on Catholic schooling in Scotland has been stimulated by the work of Paterson (1991, 2000a, 2000b). In a major quantitative study of

345 secondary schools, 61 of which were Catholic, Paterson (1991, p. 95) concluded that:

> We can propose that the large change in the ranking of the Catholic sector indicates some especially effective school practices, good enough to overcome the disadvantage of whole communities.

While emphasising the role of Catholic schools as agencies for social mobility, Paterson later (2000a) argued that their strong community networks (social capital) and ethos of service could be 'a source of ideas for how civic culture and democracy could be renewed.' (p. 46) This is a provocative and radical thesis, given the long association of Catholic culture with hierarchy and authoritarianism rather than with democratic practice. However, it usefully highlights another aspect of the internal contradictions of contemporary Catholicism and of the war of position within it on matters to do with power, authority and governance. A Vatican II conception of collegiality and of the importance of 'the People of God' finds itself set against a centuries-old tradition of hierarchy and of what Collins (1997) calls 'a papal monarchism, absolute and infallible'.[17] The resolution of these contradictions within the institutional Church and its various agencies will not be accomplished quickly. Catholic conservatism formed over centuries will not be easily transformed by a few decades of Vatican II radicalism.

The relative conservatism of Catholic education in Ireland and in Australia seems to bear out this observation. The Catholic Church in Ireland exercises a degree of control and influence on educational policy and practice which is probably unparalleled in contemporary Europe.[18] Writing from a standpoint of critical sociology, Drudy & Lynch (1993) make some sharp comments upon the contradictions in Catholic schooling in Ireland, especially those relating to 'the preferential option for the poor':

> The churches themselves are key institutions in the upholding of fee-paying secondary schools, which fits uneasily with their claim that their primary concern is for the poor and underprivileged.
>
> (p. 86)

Nevertheless, even in this conservative cultural setting evidence of some transformation can be discerned.[19] The Conference of Major Religious Superiors (CMRS), in which religious sisters are prominent, commissioned a series of research surveys such as *Inequality in Schooling in Ireland* (CMRS, 1988), *Education and Poverty* (CMRS, 1992) and *Women for Leadership in Education* (Conference of Religious in Ireland, 1994). As in South Africa, it appears that some religious sisters in Ireland are providing a leadership for the recontextualisation of Catholic schooling.[20]

In an overview of research on Australian Catholic schools, O'Keefe (1999) has suggested that while research on religious, moral and spiritual formation, i.e. on the reproduction of Catholicity, is quite extensive, research on class and inequality issues is undeveloped. Early ethnographic work such as that of Angus (1988) had suggested that the academic goals of Australian Catholic schools may have caused some marginalisation of their religious, moral and social formation goals. The founding of the Australian Catholic University in 1991 seems likely to widen the scope of research with more emphasis upon the role of Catholic schools in the sector of class, inequality and race relations in Australian education. A potential research agenda has been outlined by Duignan & d'Arbon (1998), but this awaits extensive empirical investigation. There is informal evidence that the Catholic school system in Sydney, for instance, operates a policy of 'common good' redistribution of resources which works to support Catholic schools in deprived and relatively poor communities, but no systematic research has yet evaluated this policy.[21]

This limited review of research studies in international Catholic education has demonstrated the existence in some sectors of Vatican II educational transformations, which can be represented as:

- radical: e.g. Brazil, Chile, South Africa
- moderate: e.g. England, Scotland, USA
- conservative: e.g. Australia, Ireland

The 'position' of Catholic schooling in relation to class, inequality and social reproduction is not a simple and unitary matter. On the contrary, it is characterised by a high degree of internal differentiation across the world, related to local power structures (secular and ecclesiastical), class, economic and race relations, and historical social and cultural conditions existing in various societies. As the war of position within Catholicism in its various cultural settings continues in the 21st century, the key question is whether Catholic schooling will strengthen its alliance with and service to the poor and oppressed, or instead become increasingly incorporated to serve the interests of a globalised and materially 'successful' elite and an expanded Catholic middle class for whom academic success is the main purpose of schooling.

Acknowledgement

As I have argued elsewhere (Grace, 1998, p. 214), 'a research network acting in the role of "critical friend" can assist the individual researcher in maintaining the integrity of comprehensive analysis of relevant power and social relations in education'. The value of such critical friends has been well exemplified in the comments I have received from two anonymous referees of this journal. I recognise their importance in the reshaping of this paper and refer to them in the notes. I thank them sincerely for their perceptive and thoughtful observations, which have sharpened this writer's awareness of the power mission of the Catholic Church as well as of its spiritual and moral mission and of the contradictions which this creates.

Notes

1 See Flannery (1998), Vallely (1998) and Winter (2002).
2 The theology of praxis developed in the writings of Gutierrez (1988, 1990) and Boff (1987) may be compared, in the religious realm, with Gramsci's concept of 'a philosophy of praxis'.
3 Quoted in Calvez & Perrin (1961, p. 164).
4 Quoted in Vallely (1998, p. 73).
5 See Vallely (1998, p. 14).
6 See Vallely (1998, p. 76).
7 While evidence of greater class and race solidarity can be discerned in the post-Vatican II Church, it must be noted that its stance on gender relations and matters of sexual orientation has not changed significantly. As the anonymous referee of this paper has commented: 'The Roman Catholic Church's position in relation to the education of women has been profoundly conservative, especially in relation to reproductive rights in all countries. The Church is blind to issues of gender injustice . . . It was, and is, deeply antipathetic to people who are gay, lesbian or bisexual. It has been highly selective and partial in its definition of the "poor"'.
8 Oldenski (1997, pp. 70–71).
9 A Vatican II principle of openness in Catholic education was expressed in the document *The Catholic School* (Sacred Congregation for Catholic Education, 1977) in these terms: 'In the certainty that the Spirit is at work in every person, the Catholic school offers itself to all, non-Christians included' (p. 66). This principle has been reiterated in the Vatican's most recent statement on education, *The Catholic School on the Threshold of the Third Millennium* (Congregation for Catholic Education, 1998, p. 44): 'The Catholic school . . . is not reserved to Catholics only but is open to all those who appreciate and share its qualified educational project.'
10 See the work of Arthur (1994, 1995) for an analysis of the influence of parental power within the English Catholic educational community.
11 See Grace (2003).
12 See Cariola (1971).
13 For a more detailed discussion see Grace (2002, chapters 4 and 7).
14 Catholic justification for educational work with elite students in private and high-status schooling has always been based upon assumptions that this is a possible way to help the poor by the religious and socio-political 'conversion' of the rich. A historical and sociological evaluation of these assumptions has yet to be undertaken.
15 See Foley & Grace (2001).
16 For examples, see Grace (2002, pp. 127–128).
17 Daniel Goldhagen (2002), in his searing analysis of the role of the Catholic Church in the Holocaust, observes that 'almost since its inception, the Church has been a political institution, vying for this-worldly power at least as much as it tended to other-worldly affairs' (p. 90), and concludes that 'the Church's many predicaments are enmeshed in its being a political institution' (p. 257). It is recognised that the Catholic Church's own power relations are crucial to

understanding both its historical and its contemporary role in international affairs. It is hoped to develop this perspective in future writing.

18 I am grateful to the anonymous referee for drawing my attention to the need for greater structural location of the Catholic Church in various societies, and in particular for the following observation: 'While the Roman Catholic Church had a standing and position in South Africa and in Brazil in the post-Vatican II era, it was not itself a part of the elite in the way that it was in a country like Ireland. The Roman Catholic Church was the dominant cultural institution in Ireland from the middle of the 19th century . . . and as such was deeply implicated in the business of the State. It was an integral part of the power elite and this may well explain its conservatism.'

19 See O'Sullivan (1996).

20 For similar evidence from the USA, see Casey (1993).

21 'Informal evidence' refers here to statements made by Brother Kelvin Canavan, Director of Schools for the Archdiocese of Sydney, to the writer.

References

Angus, L. (1988) *Continuity and Change in Catholic Schooling: an ethnography of a Christian Brothers' college in Australian society.* London: Falmer.

Arthur, J. (1994) Parental Participation in Catholic Schooling: a case of increasing conflict, *British Journal of Educational Studies,* 42(2), pp. 174–190.

Arthur, J. (1995) *The Ebbing Tide: policy and principles of Catholic education.* Leominster: Gracewing.

Boff, C. (1987) *Theology and Praxis.* Maryknoll: Orbis.

Bourdieu, P. (1991) Genesis and Structure of the Religious Field, *Comparative Social Research,* 13, pp. 1–44.

Brown, P. (1990) The 'Third Wave': education and the ideology of parentocracy, *British Journal of Sociology of Education,* 11, pp. 65–85.

Bryk, A., Lee, V. & Holland, P. (1993) *Catholic Schools and the Common Good.* Cambridge, MA: Harvard University Press.

Calvez, J.-Y. & Perrin, J. (1961) *The Church and Social Justice.* London: Burns & Oates.

Cariola, P. (1971) The Thought of the Church and the Future of Catholic Education in Latin America, *Religious Education,* 66, pp. 419–424.

Casey, K. (1993) *I Answer with My Life: histories of women teachers working for social change.* New York: Routledge.

Catholic Bishops Conference of England and Wales (1996) *The Common Good and the Catholic Church's Social Teaching.* London: Catholic Bishops Conference.

Catholic Education Service (1997) *The Common Good in Education.* London: Catholic Education Service.

Christie, P. (1990) *Open Schools: racially mixed Catholic schools in South Africa 1976–1986.* Johannesburg: Raven Press.

Cibulka, J., O'Biren, T. & Zewe, D. (1982) *Inner-city Private Elementary Schools.* Milwaukee: Marquette University Press.

Coleman, J. & Hoffer, T. (1987) *Public and Private High Schools: the impact of communities.* New York: Basic Books.

Collins, P. (1997) *Papal Power.* Blackburn, Victoria: HarperCollins.

Conference of Major Religious Superiors (CMRS) (1988) *Inequality in Schooling in Ireland*. Dublin: CMRS.

Conference of Major Religious Superiors (CMRS) (1992) *Education and Poverty*. Dublin: CMRS.

Conference of Religious of Ireland (CORI) (1994) *Women for Leadership in Education*. Dublin: CORI.

Congregation for Catholic Education (1998) *The Catholic School on the Threshold of the Third Millennium*. Vatican City: Libreria Editrice Vatican.

Convey, J. (1992) *Catholic Schools Make a Difference: twenty-five years of research*. Washington, DC: National Catholic Educational Association.

Drudy, S. & Lynch, K. (1993) *Schools and Society in Ireland*. Dublin: Gill & MacMillan.

Duignan, P. & d'Arbon, T. (Eds)(1998) *Leadership in Catholic Education*. Strathfield, New South Wales: Australian Catholic University.

Flannery, A. (Ed.)(1998) *Vatican Council II: the conciliar and post-conciliar documents. Vol. 1*. New revised edition. New York: Costello, and Dublin: Dominican.

Foley, J. & Grace, G. (2001) *The Birmingham Catholic School Partnership: holding to common good values in a market competitive age*. London: Institute of Education/Centre for Research and Development in Catholic Education.

Freire, P. (1968) *Pedagogy of the Oppressed*. Harmondsworth: Penguin.

Freire, P. (1984) Education, Liberation and the Church, *Religious Education*, 79(4), pp. 524–545.

Goldhagen, D. (2002) *A Moral Reckoning: the role of the Catholic Church in the Holocaust*. London: Little, Brown.

Grace, G. (1998) Critical Policy Scholarship: reflections on the integrity of knowledge and research, in G. Shacklock & J. Smyth (Eds) *Being Reflexive in Critical Educational and Social Research*. London: Falmer.

Grace, G. (2001) The State and Catholic Schooling in England and Wales: politics, ideology and mission integrity, *Oxford Review of Education*, 27(4), pp. 489–500.

Grace, G. (2002) *Catholic Schools: mission, markets and morality*. London: Routledge Falmer.

Grace, G. (2003) Educational Studies and Faith-Based Schooling: Moving from Prejudice to Evidence-Based Argument', *British Journal of Educational Studies*, 51, pp. 149–167.

Gramsci, A. (1978) *Selections from the Prison Notebooks of Antonio Gramsci*. Edited by Q. Hoare & G Nowell Smith. London: Lawrence & Wishart.

Greeley, A. (1982) *Catholic High Schools and Minority Students*. New Brunswick, NJ: Transaction Books.

Gutierrez, G. (1988) *A Theology of Liberation*. Maryknoll: Orbis.

Gutierrez, G. (1990) *The Power of the Poor in History*. Maryknoll: Orbis.

Hastings, A. (1991) *A History of English Christianity 1920–1990*. London: SCM Press.

Irvine, J. & Foster, M. (Eds)(1996) *Growing Up African American in Catholic Schools*. New York: Teachers College Press.

O'Keefe, J. (1996) No Margin, No Mission, in T. McLaughlin, J. O'Keefe & B. O'Keeffe (Eds) *The Contemporary Catholic School: context, identity and diversity*. London: Falmer.

O'Keefe, J. (1999) Research on Catholic Education: a view from Australia, *Catholic Education*, 2(3).

Oldenski, T. (1997) *Liberation Theology and Critical Pedagogy in Today's Catholic Schools*. New York: Garland.

O'Sullivan, D. (1996) Cultural Exclusion and Educational Change: education, church and religion in the Irish Republic, *Compare*, 26(1), pp. 35–49.

Paterson, L. (1991) Trends in Attainment in Scottish Secondary Schools, in S. Raudenbush & J. Willms (Eds) *Schools, Classrooms and Pupils: international studies of schooling from a multilevel perspective*. San Diego: Academic Press.

Paterson, L. (2000a) Catholic Education and Scottish Democracy, *Journal of Education and Christian Belief*, 4(1) pp. 337–349.

Paterson, L. (2000b) Salvation through Education? The changing social status of Scottish Catholics, in T. Devine (Ed.) *Scotland's Shame? Bigotry and sectarianism in modern Scotland*. Edinburgh: Mainstream.

Pontifical Commission for Justice and Peace (1989) *The Church and Racism*. London: Catholic Truth Society.

Raudenbush, S. & Bryk, A. (1986) A Hierarchical Model for Studying School Effects, *Sociology of Education*, 59, pp. 1–17.

Roman Synod (1971) Justice in the World, in M. Walsh & B. Davies (Eds) (1991) *Proclaiming Justice and Peace: papal documents from Rerum Novarum to Centesimus Annus*. Alabama: Twenty-Third Publications.

Sacred Congregation for Catholic Education (1977) *The Catholic School*. Homebush, New South Wales: St Paul Publications.

Swope, J. (1992) The Production, Recontextualising and Popular Transmission of Religious Discourse in Eight Basic Christian Communities in Santiago, Chile. PhD Thesis, University of London.

Vallely, P. (Ed.)(1998) *The New Politics: Catholic social teaching for the twenty-first century*. London: SCM Press.

Vitullo-Martin, T. (1979) *Catholic Inner-City Schools: the future*. Washington, DC: US Catholic Conference.

Winter, M. (2002) *Misguided Morality: Catholic moral teaching in the contemporary church*. Aldershot: Ashgate Publishing.

Part 3

Faith-based schools, religion and academe

Chapter 6

Educational studies and faith-based schooling

Moving from prejudice to evidence-based argument

British Journal of Educational Studies, 2003, *51*(2), 149–167.

Much of the political and public debate about faith-based schooling is conducted at the level of generalised assertion and counter-assertion, with little reference to educational scholarship or research. There is a tendency in these debates to draw upon historical images of faith schooling (idealised and critical); to use ideological advocacy (both for and against); and to deploy strong claims about the effects of faith-based schooling upon personal and intellectual autonomy and the wider consequences of such schooling for social harmony, race relations and the common good of society.

This paper will attempt to review some of these controversies in the light of recent educational and research studies. Particular attention will be given to research investigations of Catholic schooling systems in various cultural and political contexts, studies which are largely unknown outside the Catholic community.

In addition to reviewing educational studies of faith-based schooling, the paper will offer critical appraisal of the main arguments in the debate and it will also outline a possible research agenda for future inquiry in this sector of educational studies.

1. Secular marginalisation and research on faith-based schooling

Michael Gallagher (1997, p. 23) has argued that 'secular marginalisation' has become a dominant feature of Western contemporary intellectual culture with the result that 'in the academic and media worlds . . . religion is subtly ignored as unimportant'. The effects of such marginalisation can be seen in educational studies and research by the general neglect of the faith-based dimension of any major issue under investigation. A detailed scrutiny of the literature on globalisation and education, policy studies, school effectiveness and school leadership or of the conference programmes of organisations such as the American Educational Research Association or the British Educational Research Association will demonstrate this lacuna.

The assumption appears to be that research into faith-based schooling is a somewhat exotic minor activity primarily of interest and relevance to those in the various faith communities but hardly (post-Enlightenment) a major concern for mainstream educational research and discourse.[1] Thus it may be argued that while faith-based schools may have come 'out of the ghetto' in terms of their relations with external agencies, this process does not seem to have happened to the same extent in educational scholarship and research.

The outcome of this is that significant studies of globalisation and educational policy struggles in education, school effectiveness investigations and school leadership analysis take place as if the existence of faith-based schooling systems was peripheral to the central questions being raised. However, it is very clear in the cases cited that the values, worldview, principles and commitments of various faith communities *are* implicated in any understanding of such major educational issues. A comprehensive construct of educational inquiry must include engagement with specific faith cultures in given educational situations.

If mainstream educational study and research has largely ignored the relevance of faith-based cultures (until recently) it must also be noted that the various faith communities themselves have not given much priority to researching the cultures and outcomes of their particular schooling systems. Just as there has always been an uneasy relation between faith and reason, there has also been an uneasy relation between faith and research. Research can produce results which are disturbing to the faithful and for this reason some religious authorities have not encouraged systematic and critical investigations of their own schooling systems.[2]

The results of mainstream marginalisation on the one hand and of faith-based closure on the other has meant that research into faith-based schooling systems is remarkably underdeveloped given the extent and scale of faith-based educational provision internationally. The general absence of large-scale and sophisticated investigations of faith-based schooling has had a number of unfortunate consequences. One of these is that much of the current political and public debate about faith-based schooling has been conducted at the level of prejudiced and generalised assertion and counter-assertion with little reference to research. There is a tendency in these debates to draw upon dated historical images of faith schooling, to use ideological advocacy (both for and against) and to deploy strong claims about the effects of faith-based schooling upon personal and intellectual autonomy, social harmony, race relations and the common good of society.

A typical example of this may be found in the pages of the *Times Educational Supplement* of 23 February 2001 where special features on faith-based schooling were given headlines such as 'God help us' and 'No faith in the absurd'. An article on this topic by Professor Richard Dawkins, Professor of Public Understanding of Science at Oxford University, was headlined as saying: 'Sectarian religious schools serve only to promote prejudice, confusion and division' and 'religious violence as seen in Northern Ireland is stoked by segregated schools'. Dawkins's own assertion in the article was that religious schools 'can be deeply damaging, even lethally divisive' (p. 17).

The implication of these statements (for which no research evidence is cited) is that wherever community conflict exists (especially in Northern Ireland) a major causal factor is the existence of faith-based schooling systems. It will be argued later that such claims represent an ahistorical, decontextualised and oversimplified view of the causes of such conflict. What complicates political and public debate on faith-based schooling is that the great majority of participants (including Professors of Public Understanding . . .) actually know very little about the contemporary educational culture and practice of schools. Despite this lack of knowledge, many are prepared to make strong claims about how these schools operate and about their effects upon personal development and social harmony. This amounts to a form of intellectual prejudice (perhaps in some cases of ethnic and racial prejudice) where arguments are based upon distorted or partial knowledge or, as in the case of Northern Ireland, an assumption of guilt by association. Given the importance of these issues not only for national harmony and understanding but also for international understanding, the need for systematic, scholarly and impartial research on faith-based schooling is very clear.

2. The Catholic schooling system: partial images and contemporary research

The Catholic schooling system is probably the largest faith-based educational provision internationally, involving about 120,000 Catholic schools serving almost 50 million students in a wide range of socio-economic, political and cultural settings worldwide.[3] In many countries there is also a significant Catholic presence in higher education. This international system of education has been subject, to a greater or lesser extent in different parts of the world, to the renewal of Catholic theological and social teaching emanating from the Second Vatican Council (Flannery, 1998).

In a recent review of empirical research studies of Catholic schooling in the USA, England, Scotland, Ireland and Australia (Grace, 2002), I found that the USA has provided not only the largest data source for other researchers but also theoretical concepts and research paradigms which have been used by researchers in other cultural settings. This is hardly surprising given the Catholic population of that country (60 million), the number of Catholic universities and colleges and the strong empirical traditions of American social enquiry and intellectual life. While the findings of this research corpus cannot simply be extrapolated to other socio-historical and cultural locations, they do provide some empirical indicators, which need to be examined in those locations.

3. Research on Catholic schools in the USA

a. On religious, moral and social formation and attitudes

Two of the leading researchers of these issues in the USA are Andrew Greeley and Anthony Bryk, both University of Chicago professors of social and educational inquiry. Greeley, with others, studied the effects of Catholic schooling post-Vatican II (i.e. after 1965) upon the religious and social values and attitudes of adolescents. The studies were reported in 1976, 1982 and 1989. Greeley *et al.* found that Catholic secondary schooling in this period had experienced a significant cultural and educational transformation. The impact of the reforms of the Second Vatican Council (1962–1965) was apparent in an educational culture which was much more open to debate and dialogue and to relations with the wider society than had been the case with the defensive Catholic 'citadel schools' of an earlier period. This new culture of relative openness had produced a more mature understanding of Catholicism among many adults but it had also resulted in changed attitudes to other faith communities. Summing up his research and that of others, Greeley (1998, pp. 182–183) posed the question:

> Are Catholic schools (in the USA) divisive? Do they produce men and women who are more likely to be prejudiced than those who go to public schools?

On the basis of the available research Greeley responded:

> Quite the contrary, those who attend Catholic schools are less prejudiced than Catholics who attend public schools and less prejudiced than all public school graduates. Moreover, they are also more likely to be pro-feminist. All of these statements are true even when social class and educational achievement are held constant.

> (*ibid.*, p. 183)

A similar research conclusion has been provided by Anthony Bryk, Valerie Lee and Peter Holland in *Catholic Schools and the Common Good* (1993). Following a comprehensive review of existing research and in-depth analysis of secondary schools in Boston, Baltimore, Cleveland, Louisville, San Antonio and Los Angeles, Bryk *et al.* concluded:

> Traditional argument against public support for Catholic schools – the fear of religious establishment, social divisiveness and elitism seem ungrounded. We discern nothing fundamentally undemocratic about Catholic schools' educational philosophy of person-in-community and their ethical stance of shaping the human conscience toward personal

responsibility and social engagement. To the contrary, these religious understandings order daily life and its outcomes in very appealing ways. It is not narrow, divisive or sectarian education but rather an education for democratic life . . .

(p. 341)

The implications of these research findings are that the world of post-Vatican II Catholic education is a very different cultural, religious and educational environment to that of the pre-conciliar period. Modern forms of Catholic education are, at their best, providing religious, moral and social formation which is respectful of the spiritual and intellectual autonomy of students, open to debate, dialogue and scepticism and sensitive to the responsibilities of good citizenship and to the traditions of other faiths.[4]

While the research of Greeley *et al.* and of Bryk does not provide definitive empirical answers to these contested issues, they do at least constitute an evidence-based argument that representations of Catholic schooling as authoritarian, indoctrinatory and socially divisive are based upon dated historical images of, or assumptions about, the nature of Catholic education. If these misrepresentations of Catholic schooling can exist in political and public debate, it suggests that misrepresentation of the contemporary schooling systems of other faith communities can also exist. One of the obvious ways to deal with these misrepresentations is that more large-scale, systematic and in-depth research should be undertaken into the cultures and practices of contemporary faith-based schools.

b. On educational service to the poor and disadvantaged

Catholic schooling in the USA has historically been associated with educational provision for the poor and disadvantaged and especially for immigrant communities of Irish, Italian, Polish and other European origins. Research on such provision and on its relative effectiveness has been undertaken in a series of studies, including Vitullo-Martin (1979), Cibulka *et al.* (1982), Greeley (1982), Raudenbush and Bryk (1986), Coleman and Hoffer (1987), Convey (1992), Bryk *et al.* (1993) and O'Keefe (1996). Many of these studies show that such educational provision appears to have good outcomes for poor and disadvantages students. Cibulka *et al.* (1982), for instance, in a study of 50 Catholic elementary schools with ethnic minority enrolments of at least 70 per cent located in Chicago, Detroit, Los Angeles, Milwaukee, Newark, New Orleans, New York and Washington, found that such schools were serving families which were larger and poorer than the average American family. Many were single parent families and *more than half of the families were not Catholic.* Generally students in these schools performed at higher achievement levels than students in neighbouring public schools (however, relative achievement levels are controversial – see below). Cibulka and his co-researchers noted the existence of high levels of motivation and dedication (vocation) among the teachers in these schools, about 30 per cent of whom were members of religious orders.

Although the question of relative achievement levels has to be scrutinised more carefully, what such research does demonstrate is that faith-based schooling, in this case Catholic schooling, can be a powerful and community-enhancing resource in inner-city and other deprived urban locations. What also emerges from these studies is that Catholic schooling in such locations does not simply meet the educational needs of the Catholic poor but also the needs of the non-Catholic poor including significant numbers of disadvantaged black students in inner-city America.

A faith-based schooling system which has a positive mission to the educational and social service of the poor would appear to be a major cultural asset in any society. It seems difficult to sustain the charge or image of 'elitism' in the face of such evidence.

c. On contribution to the common good of society

The major American research study on this subject, Bryk *et al.* (1993), concludes in these terms:

> Although we have emphasised the education of disadvantaged students, we note that Catholic schools also advance an important agenda in the education of their more advantaged counterparts. In schools with large proportions of low-income students, the social justice mission of Vatican II is tangibly manifested . . . The concern for social justice however is also manifest in the schooling of the advantaged. Catholic schools deliberately strive to inculcate an understanding for and a commitment to social justice in all their students. Many of these students are likely to move into powerful positions in society as adults . . . The Catholic school emphasises to its students the value of leadership for social justice and hopes that this message will become internalised in adulthood.
>
> (pp. 340–341)

The notion of Catholic schooling as having a narrow sectarian remit is based upon an out-moded pre-Vatican II image of Catholic education. What those outside the Catholic educational community do not understand is how significant a social justice and common good mission has become in modern Catholic educational practice.[5] For post-Vatican II schooling, as the research of Bryk *et al.* (1993) and others demonstrated, the spiritual, the moral and the social are necessarily interconnected as categories. There can be no authentic love of God (a manifestation of the spiritual) which is not at the same time linked to living a good life (a manifestation of the moral) and to loving and helping one's neighbour (a manifestation of social concern and social justice). It seems unlikely that the Catholic system is the only faith-based education mission which has such spiritual, moral and social justice purposes.

d. On school effectiveness and academic outcomes

The question of the relative academic effectiveness of the Catholic school system is a very controversial one in the USA and elsewhere. While there are studies which appear to show (after controlling for the relevant variables) that Catholic schools achieve better academic outcomes than comparable public schools, there are also studies which question such conclusions or the research methodologies involved. Researchers such as Coleman and Hoffer (1982) and Bryk *et al.* (1993) point to the positive effects of certain features of Catholic educational culture such as 'social capital', 'strong internal sense of community', 'structured environments', 'sense of mission' and 'vocational commitment of teachers'. Critics such as Lauder and Hughes (1999) and Goldstein (2001)[6] suggest that the prior achievement and the cultural background of students entering Catholic secondary schools largely accounts for their successful academic outcomes.

For the USA, Convey (1982, p. 6) makes a judicious summing up:

> Self-selection prevents a conclusive answer to whether or not Catholic schools are more effective than public schools. Studies that compare Catholic schools with public schools can never eliminate the possibility that some unmeasured or otherwise uncontrolled attribute of students that is associated with self-selection is responsible for a significant amount of the differences between the Catholic and public schools . . . The possibility that the observed differences between Catholic schools and public schools are more a function of the type of students who enrol in each, rather than anything to do with the school, can never be completely eliminated.

In terms of the public debate about faith-based schooling, some potentially negative developments can result in the school effectiveness sector. The apparent academic success (as opposed to the value-added success) of faith-based schools may be appropriated by political and ideological interest groups which want to criticise the effectiveness of public schooling. In other words, faith-based schooling can be incorporated into a larger ideological struggle about the provision of education in terms which are derogatory to public schooling – and terms which are not endorsed by the faith community itself. These negative developments have emerged in the USA and are becoming apparent in other societies.

Part of the hostility to Catholic schools in the USA may be accounted for by this political strategy of using the relative academic success of such schools as a weapon to undermine the reputations and status of public schools in the eyes of parents. It is important to note that Catholic educators and researchers have sought to distance themselves from such a strategy. As Convey's 1992 statement shows, there is both a professional and a research recognition that qualitative differences exist between faith-based schooling and public schooling in the USA which prevent simplistic comparisons of academic outcomes. Research in the USA on the Catholic faith-based schooling system suggests that critical assertions about social divisiveness, indoctrination, authoritarianism, elitism and narrow sectarian focus cannot be sustained by empirical studies of post-Vatican II schooling. On the contrary, Catholic schools can be seen to have a spiritual, educational and social mission which contributes to the common good of American society.

4. Research on Catholic schools in other contexts

Empirical research on post-Vatican II Catholic schooling in the UK, Ireland and Australia is beginning to show similar findings to that conducted in the USA, although particular dilemmas and contradictions have become apparent in each socio-cultural setting. Changed approaches to religious, moral and social formation and a much stronger emphasis upon commitment to social justice and the common good is a feature of Catholic schooling in these contexts. This is apparent in research findings in the UK from the work of Hornsby-Smith (1978, 1999, 2000), Arthur (1995), O'Keeffe (1997, 1999), Paterson (2000), Grace (2001, 2002); in Ireland in the work of O'Sullivan (1996) and Feheney (1998, 1999) and in Australia in the work of Flynn and Mok (2002).

My own recent study of Catholic schools in London, Liverpool and Birmingham drew its evidence base from fieldwork visits to schools and communities (largely in inner-city and deprived urban locations), from a study of school documentation, Ofsted reports and Section 23 (Diocesan Inspector's) reports, from interviews with 60 Catholic headteachers and from focus-group discussions with 50 senior students (Year 10) in five London schools.

This research gives empirical support to the proposition that post-Vatican II Catholic schooling in England has undergone considerable transformation. While the faith of Catholic Christian belief remains fundamental, a significant transformation has taken place in the realisation of its spiritual message, the mode of its educational process, its relation to the personal autonomy of the young and its relation to other faiths and to the wider world. Although it is a faith-based system I would argue, from the evidence available, that it is entirely compatible with the principles of a liberal education and with the principles of a democratic and socially caring society.

On a larger international scale, it is evident that the Catholic schooling system and other faith-based systems have a crucial role to play in globalisation struggles. With the collapse of the Soviet Communist system, George Soros (1999) has pointed out that a new cultural imperialism has emerged, i.e. that of global capitalist values. Soros has charted the nature of this new global imperialism, and has concluded 'that market values have assumed an importance at the present moment in history that is way beyond what is appropriate and sustainable' (p. 46).

It can be argued that faith-based schools are one of the countervailing institutions against the global hegemony of market materialism, individual competitiveness and commodity worship. Their role could be crucial not only in the preservation of various forms of spiritual and moral values but also in struggles of solidarity and social justice internationally.

5. Northern Ireland: faith schooling and community conflict

In recent political and public debate about faith-based schooling, Northern Ireland, either directly or by implication, has been used as the paradigm case of the negative consequences of such a system. Thus, in the direct mode, the Humanist Philosophers' Group in their publication *Religious Schools: the case against* (2001, p. 35) assert:

> We have clear evidence . . . from Northern Ireland where the separa-tion of Catholic and Protestant schools has played a significant part in perpetuating the sectarian divide.

However, it may be noted that no sources of evidence are cited to substanti-ate this assertion. In another mode, Richard Dawkins (2001, p. 17) argues:

> Why do people in Northern Ireland kill each other? It is fashionable to say that the sectarian feuds are not about religion, the deep divides in that province are not religious, they are cultural, historical, economic. Well, no doubt they are . . . [but] . . . if Protestant and Catholic children ceased to be segregated throughout their school days, the troubles in Northern Ireland would largely disappear. . . .

It is important to note the use of ideological as opposed to scholarly lan-guage in this extract. Potentially significant structural causes of the troubles in Northern Ireland which refer to cultural, historical and economic rela-tions are described as 'fashionable' explanations, while the thrust of the article is to suggest that faith-based schooling is the fundamental cause of the problem. This is an example of what has already been called the 'guilt by association' mode of analysis. It may reasonably be asked whether Pro-fessor Richard Dawkins would accept such an analysis in his own field of evolutionary biology.

In fact, assertions such as these represent an ahistorical, decontextualised and oversimplified view of the Northern Ireland situation, as any serious scrutiny of relevant literature demonstrates. In the 1970s, systematic investigation of this issue in relation to the British government's (1973) White Paper, *Northern Ireland Constitutional Proposals*, resulted in the following conclusion:

> To make the educational system itself the scapegoat for all the ills of Northern Ireland would obscure problems whose origins are of a much more complex character.
>
> (HMSO, 1973, p. 7)

and the research of O'Donnell (1977, p. 155) reported that:

> religion, *per se*, plays an insignificant role in the stereotypes of Northern Ireland. Power is the crucial factor.

A review of the impact of faith-based schooling in Northern Ireland by A.M. Gallagher of the Centre for the Study of Conflict, University of Ulster, noted that:

> despite years of discussion there is no consensus in the research literature on the impact of segregated schools on attitudes and behaviour.
>
> (1992, p. 354)

John Greer, a leading researcher in this field, reporting his own investigations into 'openness', defined as 'the willingness of pupils to value members of the other tradition as neighbours, relatives, workers . . .' concluded from a large-scale survey of over 2,000 pupils in secondary schools (9 Catholic, 10 Protestant) that:

> Throughout the age range for both sexes and both denominational groups there was a positive relationship between attitude towards religion and openness. The young people most favourably disposed towards religion were also most open to members of the other religious groups. This is an important finding, contradicting the notion that in Northern Ireland religiosity increases closedness to 'the other side'.
>
> (1993, p. 458)

Of course, all of these considered statements and research findings are open to challenge on conceptual, methodological and analytical grounds but what does become clear from a survey of the literature is that assertions which suggest that faith-based schooling in Northern Ireland is 'deeply damaging, even lethally divisive' can only have a base in prejudice or ideology and not in scholarship and research.

6. The future: a research agenda for faith-based schooling

With the growing importance of faith-based schooling systems internationally there is an obvious need for more systematic research and inquiry into their spiritual, moral and intellectual cultures and into their educational and social outcomes. Such research will need to be impartial, comprehensive and sensitive to the pluralist range of faith traditions and faith communities. In addition to studies of the various forms of Christian educational provision (Catholic, Anglican, Methodist, Baptist, Evangelical etc.) such research will need to focus upon Islamic, Jewish, Sikh, Buddhist and other schools founded by major faith communities. To combat ignorance and prejudice about how different forms of faith-based schooling actually operate in the contemporary world, systematic inquiry is necessary. This means that research trusts, foundations and also government agencies must recognise that such research has become mainstream and is no longer a marginal activity. It also means that the authorities of the various faith communities must be prepared to open their schools to such impartial inquiry. There are some encouraging signs that this is beginning to happen. My own research into Catholic schools in London, Liverpool and Birmingham was funded by the Leverhulme Trust and supported by twelve religious orders with missions in education.[7] In Jewish education, an important research report by Oliver Valins, Barry Kosmin and Jacqueline Goldberg has recently been published with the title *The Future of Jewish Schooling in the United Kingdom* (2001).[8] In the Anglican community the amount of research activity is increasing with the scholarly work of Leslie Francis, Jeff Astley, William Kay and Priscilla Chadwick.[9] The foundation of the Islamic Academy at Cambridge in the 1980s has prepared the ground for such systematic inquiry in that community.

However, as Harry Judge of Oxford University has recently argued, it is also important that researchers from *outside* the various faith communities should scrutinise the operations of faith-based schooling systems.[10] This would contribute helpfully to the process known as triangulation where a specific cultural phenomenon is viewed and analysed from a number of different perspectives. Some examples of this do exist in the work of Walford (2000, 2001) on Christian Evangelical schools and of Halstead (1995) and Hewer (2001) on Muslim schools, but much more needs to be done.

A possible research agenda for the future, it is suggested, could include some of the following main areas for investigation.

a. Faith schools and community relations

The impact of faith schools upon community relations appears to be a priority area for research inquiry given that large claims are made on this subject with little reference to empirical evidence. A comprehensive examination of the subject would require an investigation of community perceptions, attitudes and evaluations of such schools at both adult and youth levels. For instance, does the existence of such schools contribute to perceptions of the 'strangeness' or 'otherness' of particular faith and ethnic communities in ways which seem negative for community and race relations? In other words, investigations of what might be called the external social consequences of faith schools are required. At the same time (because they are interrelated) research is needed in specific community contexts on the internal cultures and educational programmes of both state schools and faith schools. In particular, the extent and effectiveness of programmes of multicultural and anti-racist education in such schools should be evaluated and also the content and pedagogic methods used in all programmes of religious and moral education. For faith schools their own mission integrity should be a focus of self-evaluation as well as of external inquiry. Given that all the major faiths proclaim missions of love, peace, harmony, forgiveness and reconciliation (often formally expressed in school mission statements), a leading question for them all is, do the educational cultures, programmes and relationships in their schools contribute to the enhancement of these characteristics in their students and in wider community relations? Does the faith, in educational terms, lead young people to an open and caring relationship with others beyond their immediate community, or does it lead to closure and prejudice?

b. Faith schools and contribution to the common good

This is a related but wider area of investigation. To the extent that public funds are used in support of faith schools, can it be shown that such schools contribute to the common good of society and not simply to the particular good of the faith community?[11] Existing research evidence suggests that the common good effects of faith-based schooling can be demonstrated in various ways. The classic text on this subject, by Bryk *et al.* (1993), has shown empirically the substantial contribution made by Catholic schools to community resourcing and educational progress in American inner cities. It has also shown that such provision has been at the service of students who are not Catholic, especially from black disadvantaged groups. Further research is needed to see how general this common good effect is in faith schools in other contexts. There is also the fascinating and very under-researched question of what effect does a faith-based schooling have on adult men and women in their personal, social and public lives? My own research, using personal oral history accounts of the long-term effects of a Catholic schooling, showed some interesting indications. While there were adults who had found it an oppressive experience, there appeared to be more who had found it a positive experience which they related closely to the principles and practice of their public lives in politics, social and educational service, community work and contemporary feminist writing.[12] If the long-term outcome of faith-based schooling is the sort of adult citizen it helps to form, then we need to know more about this by systematic inquiry among adults from different faith communities. Here is a major field for oral history research in the future.

c. Faith schools, markets and mission integrity

Mission integrity may be defined as *fidelity in educational practice, and not just in public rhetoric, to the distinctive and authentic principles of a faith-based schooling.* As already mentioned, the leaders of faith schools have a particular responsibility to monitor and evaluate the contemporary practice of their schools to try to ensure that this is an authentic realisation of the faith and of its educational and social principles. In the contemporary competitive market-place of education which schooling has become in the UK, faith-based schools run the risk of becoming incorporated into the market materialist culture. The pursuit of improved academic results year upon year (as published in league-table results) may lead faith schools to adopt market strategies which are at odds with the values and principles of their own mission statements. I have tried to set out the challenges to Catholic schools (and by implication to other faith schools) in these terms:

> If a market culture in education encourages the pursuit of material interests, what becomes of a Catholic school's prime commitment to religious, spiritual and moral interests? If calculation of personal advantage is necessary for survival in the market, how can Catholic schools remain faithful to values of solidarity and community? If schools in a market economy in education must show good 'company' results in academic success and growing social status, what becomes of the Catholic principle of 'preferential option for the poor'? [. . .] The temptation in a market economy for schooling is to try, by manipulation of admission policies and exclusion policies, to maximise the number of potentially 'profitable' students and to reduce the number of challenging and uncooperative pupils.
>
> (2002, pp. 180–181)

What is needed for all faith-based schools is research which examines how they are responding to these challenges and achieving market survival and even 'success' without seriously compromising their mission integrity. In this research sector the relations between faith schools and state schools in specific communities is clearly an important topic.

d. Faith schools, liberal education and democratic culture

Critics of faith-based schools often imply that the pedagogical climate of such organisations is inimical to the realisation of a liberal education or of the formation of democratic citizenship. This view is premised on the assumption that the particular faith in question is absolutist, closed to liberal intellectual discourse and, in its own internal power relations, incompatible with modern democratic culture and citizenship. As suggested earlier in this paper, such assumptions may be based upon out-dated and distorted understandings of a particular faith community. To try to establish a more reliable evidence base in this sector, in-depth studies of particular faith school cultures are needed with a focus on liberal education practice and on citizenship formation.[13] Philosophers of education, such as Terence McLaughlin (1996), have argued that certain forms of religious schooling are compatible with a liberal and democratic education, especially if they are characterised by what McLaughlin and others have described as 'openness with roots', i.e.

> providing a particular substantial starting point for the child's eventual development into autonomous agency and democratic citizenship.
>
> (p. 147)

We need extensive empirical research to investigate to what extent the phenomenon of 'openness with roots' exists in the cultures and practices of various forms of faith-based schooling.

e. Faith schools: the views and experiences of students

Ruddock and Flutter (2000, p. 86) argue that both educational research and school improvement projects have been impoverished by lack of serious attention to the perspectives of pupils:

> This traditional exclusion of young people from the consultation process, this bracketing out of their voice, is founded upon an outdated view of childhood which fails to acknowledge children's capacity to reflect on issues affecting their lives.

If mission integrity should be a central concept for the evaluation of faith-based schooling (as is argued in this paper) then it follows that students in faith schools are crucial participants and evaluators of that concept in practice. Faith-based schooling and all forms of schooling must be open to the critical evaluation of the students in the system. Sensitive and facilitating research into students' views and experiences is integral to a research agenda for the future.

As the Humanist Philosophers' Group (2001, p. 12) point out:

> Autonomous commitment to beliefs is something which religious believers ought to value.

If faith-based schools wish to reject the charge that they are engaged in the religious indoctrination of the young rather than presenting an experience of, and dialogue with, a faith, then they must be prepared to listen to the voice of their own students. The students will be an important source of evidence about whether or not 'openness with roots' actually describes their educational experiences.

The overall argument of this paper is therefore that it is time to move on from prejudiced or ideological assertions about faith-based schooling to evidence-based argument. Faith-based schooling systems internationally have been a marginalised field for educational inquiry. A research agenda of major issues awaits scholarly and impartial investigation which can helpfully inform both policy-making and public debate about faith-based schooling in contemporary society.

Notes

1 There are some exceptions to this general neglect. See, for instance, Halpin (2001) and O'Keeffe (1997, 1999).
2 This would appear to be the case in Ireland, for instance. McDonagh (1991, p. 72) noted, 'Relatively little has been done in Ireland to evaluate our schools from the perspective of Catholic education . . . The overwhelming reality is that the Irish Church has not to date responded to the invitation to evaluate schools under its authority.'
3 See Pittau (2000).
4 For evidence in support of these assertions, see Grace (2003) forthcoming.
5 See Catholic Bishops' Conference of England and Wales (1996) and Catholic Education Service (1997).
6 Personal paper to the author. See Grace (2002) chapter 7.
7 Religious orders in the UK and Ireland which supported the CRDCE research project included the Society of Jesus, De La Salle Brothers, Christian Brothers, Faithful Companions of Jesus, Sisters of Charity of St Paul (Selly Park), Salesians of Don Bosco, Benedictines of Ampleforth, Sisters of Notre Dame, Society of the Holy Child Jesus, Sisters of Mercy, Institute of the Blessed Virgin Mary and Loreto Sisters, La Retraite Sisters, Servite Sisters, Congregation of Our Lady of the Missions and the Missionaries of the Sacred Heart (Dublin).
8 See also Miller (2001).
9 Given this corpus of research on Anglican schools it is remarkable that none of this is cited in the Dearing Report (2001) *The Way Ahead: Church of England Schools in the New Millennium.*
10 Personal letter to the writer (18 April 2002).
11 As John Sullivan (2001, p. 176) comments, 'Unless Catholics can show that their desire for a distinctive form of education is not vulnerable to accusations of being inward-looking, isolationist and unconcerned about the common good, their schools will neither deserve nor attract the support of a wider society.'
12 See Grace (2002) chapter 3.
13 For one case study of a Catholic secondary school with significant achievements in citizenship education see Grace (2001).

References

Arthur, J. (1995) *The Ebbing Tide: Policy and Principles of Catholic Education* (Leominster, Gracewing Publications).

Astley, J. and Francis, L. (Eds) (1994) *Critical Perspectives in Christian Education* (Leominster, Gracewing Publications).

Bryk, A., Lee, V. and Holland, P. (1993) *Catholic Schools and the Common Good* (Cambridge MA, Harvard University Press).

Catholic Education Service (1997) *The Common Good in Education* (London, CES).

Chadwick, P. (1997) *Shifting Alliances: Church and State in English Education* (London, Cassell).

Cibulka, J., O'Brien, T. and Zewe, D. (1982) *Inner City Private Elementary Schools* (Milwaukee, Marquette University Press).

Coleman, J., Hoffer, T. and Kilgore, S. (1982) *High School Achievement: Public, Catholic and Private Schools Compared* (New York, Basic Books).

Convey, J. (1992) *Catholic Schools make a Difference: Twenty Five Years of Research* (Washington DC, National Catholic Educational Association).

Dawkins, R. (2001) No faith in the absurd, *Times Educational Supplement,* 23 February.

Dearing, R. (2001) *The Way Ahead: Church of England Schools in the New Millennium* (London, Church House Publishing).

Feheney, M. (Ed.) (1998) *From Ideal to Action: The Inner Nature of a Catholic School Today* (Dublin, Veritas).

Feheney, M. (Ed.) (1999) *Beyond the Race for Points: Aspects of Pastoral Care in a Catholic School Today* (Dublin, Veritas).

Flannery, A. (1998) *Vatican Council II: The Conciliar and Post-Conciliar Documents Vol I.* New revised edition (New York, Costello Publications and Dublin, Dominican Publications).

Flynn, M. and Mok, M. (2002) *Catholic Schools 2000* (NSW Australia, Catholic Education Commission).

Francis, L. and Thatcher, A. (Eds) (1990) *Christian Perspectives for Education* (Leominster, Gracewing Books).

Francis, L. and Lankshear, D. (Eds) (1993) *Christian Perspectives on Church Schools* (Leominster, Gracewing Books).

Francis, L. and Kay, W. (1995) *Teenage Religion and Values* (Leominster, Gracewing Books).

Francis, L., Kay, W. and Campbell, W. (Eds) (1996) *Research in Religious Education* (Leominster, Gracewing Books).

Gallagher, A. M. (1992) Education in a divided society, *Psychologist,* 5, 353–356.

Gallagher, M. (1997) New forms of cultural unbelief. In P. Hogan and K. Williams (Eds) *The Future of Religion in Irish Education* (Dublin, Veritas).

Goldstein, H. (2001) Catholic schools and achievement: a critical response (unpublished paper) (London, Institute of Education).

Grace, G. (2001) St Michael's Roman Catholic Comprehensive School. In M. Maden (Ed.) *Success Against the Odds: Five Years On* (London, Routledge Falmer).

Grace, G. (2002) *Catholic Schools: Mission, Markets and Morality* (London, Routledge Falmer).

Grace, G. (2003) 'First and foremost, the Church offers its educational service to the poor': class, inequality and Catholic schooling in contemporary contexts, *International Studies in Sociology of Education* (forthcoming).

Greeley, A., McCready, W. and McCourt, K. (1976) *Catholic Schools in a Declining Church* (Kansas City, Sheed and Ward).

Greeley, A. (1982) *Catholic High Schools and Minority Students* (New Brunswick, NJ, Transaction Books).

Greeley, A. (1989) Catholic schools: a golden twilight, *Catholic School Studies*, 62 (2), 8–12.

Greeley, A. (1998) Catholic schools at the crossroads: an American perspective. In J.M. Feheney (Ed.) *From Ideal to Action: The Inner Nature of a Catholic School Today* (Dublin, Veritas).

Greer, J. (1993) Viewing 'the other side' in Northern Ireland. In L. Francis and D. Lankshear (Eds) *Christian Perspectives on Church Schools* (Leominster, Gracewing Books).

Halpin, D. (2001) Utopianism and education: the legacy of Thomas More, *British Journal of Educational Studies*, 49 (3), 299–315.

Halstead, J. (1995) Voluntary apartheid? Problems of schooling for religious and other minorities in democratic societies, *Journal of Philosophy of Education*, 29 (2), 257–272.

Hewer, C. (2001) Schools for Muslims, *Oxford Review of Education*, 27 (4), 515–527.

HMSO (1973) *Northern Ireland Constitutional Proposals* (White Paper, Cmnd 5259) (London, HMSO). Quoted in M. McGrath (2000) *The Catholic Church and Catholic Schools in Northern Ireland: The Price of Faith* (Dublin, Irish Academic Press).

Hornsby-Smith, M. (1978) *Catholic Education: The Unobtrusive Partner* (London, Sheed and Ward).

Hornsby-Smith, M. (Ed.) (1999) *Catholics in England 1950–2000: Historical and Sociological Perspectives* (London, Cassell).

Hornsby-Smith, M. (2000) The changing social and religious content of Catholic schooling in England and Wales. In M. Eaton, J. Longman and A. Naylor (Eds) *Commitment to Diversity: Catholics and Education in a Changing World* (London, Cassell).

Humanist Philosophers' Group (2001) *Religious Schools: The Case Against* (London, British Humanist Association).

Kay, W. (1996) Religious education and assemblies: pupils' changing views. In L. Francis *et al.* (Eds) *Research in Religious Education* (Leominster, Gracewing Books).

Lauder, H. and Hughes, D. (1999) *Trading in Futures: Why Markets in Education don't Work* (Buckingham, Open University Press).

McDonagh, J. (1991) Catholic education and evaluation. In N. Brennan (Ed.) *The Catholic School in Contemporary Society* (Dublin, Conference of Major Religious Superiors).

McLaughlin, T. (1996) The distinctiveness of Catholic education. In T. McLaughlin, J. O'Keefe and B. O'Keeffe (Eds) *The Contemporary Catholic School: Context, Identity and Diversity* (London, Falmer Press).

Miller, H. (2001) Meeting the challenge: the Jewish schooling phenomenon in the UK. *Oxford Review of Education*, 27 (4), 501–513.

O'Donnell, E. (1977) *Northern Ireland Stereotypes* (Dublin, College of Industrial Relations).

O'Keefe, J. (1996) No margin, no mission. In T. McLaughlin, J. O'Keefe and B. O'Keeffe (Eds) *The Contemporary Catholic School: Context, Identity and Diversity* (London, Falmer Press).

O'Keeffe, B. (1997) The changing role of Catholic schools in England and Wales: from exclusiveness to engagement. In J. McMahon *et al.* (Eds) *Leading the Catholic School* (Victoria NSW, Spectrum Publications).

O'Keeffe, B. (1999) Reordering perspectives in Catholic schools. In M. Hornsby-Smith (Ed.) *Catholics in England 1950–2000: Historical and Sociological Perspectives* (London, Cassell).

O'Sullivan, D. (1996) Cultural exclusion and educational change: education, Church and religion in the Irish Republic, *Compare,* 26 (1), 35–49.

Paterson, L. (2000) Catholic education and Scottish democracy, *Journal of Education and Christian Belief,* 4 (1), 37–49.

Pittau, G. (2000) Education on the threshold of the third millennium: challenge, mission and adventure, *Catholic Education,* 4 (2), 139–152.

Raudenbush, S. and Bryk, A. (1986) A hierarchical model for studying school effects, *Sociology of Education,* 59, 1–17.

Rudduck, J. and Flutter, J. (2000) Pupil participation and pupil perspectives, *Cambridge Journal of Education,* 30 (1), 75–89.

Soros, G. (1999) *The Crisis of Global Capitalism* (London, Little, Brown).

Sullivan, J. (2001) *Catholic Education: Distinctive and Inclusive* (Dordrecht, Kluwer Academic Publishers).

Valins, O., Kosmin, B. and Goldberg, J. (2001) *The Future of Jewish Schooling in the United Kingdom* (London, Institute for Jewish Policy Research).

Vitullo-Martin, T. (1979) *Catholic Inner-City Schools: The Future* (Washington, DC, US Catholic Bishops' Conference).

Walford, G. (2000) *Policy, Politics and Education: Sponsored Grant-maintained Schools and Religious Diversity* (Aldershot, Ashgate).

Walford, G. (2001) Evangelical Christian schools in England and the Netherlands, *Oxford Review of Education,* 27 (4), 529–541.

Chapter 7

Making connections for future directions

Taking religion seriously in the sociology of education

International Studies in Sociology of Education, 2004, 14(1), 47–56.

This article argues that a problem for the contemporary sociology of education is that it has operated within a 'secularisation of consciousness paradigm'. This has limited both the depth and the scope of its intellectual enquiries. Sociological analysis which elides a religious dimension not only presents an over-simplified view of social relations in 'the modern West', but it also fails to make an authentic engagement with many socio-cultural and educational situations internationally, where God is far from dead. The article suggests various ways forward for a reorientation of sociological writing and research.

Sociology of education and secular marginalisation

The Jesuit writer Michael Paul Gallagher (1997) has argued that contemporary intellectual culture in the West is characterised by 'secular marginalisation'. This phenomenon has replaced eighteenth- and nineteenth-century polemics against religion by a cultural form of marginalisation and silence. The outcome is that, as Gallagher asserts, 'especially in the academic and media worlds, a secular culture reigns with the result that religion is subtly ignored as unimportant' (p. 23).

The validity of this observation for the sociology of education is immediately obvious. A detailed scrutiny of the current literature on globalisation and education, on educational policy studies, on school effectiveness and school leadership will show that major studies proceed as if the existence of religion and of faith-based schooling systems is marginal to the central questions being investigated. All contemporary sociological writers and researchers are expected to be sensitive to the importance of class, race and gender analysis in their accounts of educational cultures and practices internationally, and yet it seems that the cultures of religion and faith can be, as Gallagher puts it, 'subtly ignored as unimportant'.

Given the contemporary impact of religious cultures in international politics and globalisation outcomes across the world, this lacuna of the religions is difficult to understand. There are thousands of faith-based schools worldwide in which the messages of Catholic Christianity, of Evangelical

Christianity, of Islam and of Judaism are in sharp contradiction to the messages of international capitalism.

A number of credible reasons may explain the failure of sociologists of education to take religion seriously in their work, but the most important is the dominance of Western secular insularity within the intellectual culture of the discipline. Peter Berger in *The Social Reality of Religion* (1973) noted that the development of secularisation in 'the modern world' represented a denial of the validity of the sacred and of its associated cultures and their replacement by logical, rational, empirical and scientific intellectual cultures in which notions of the transcendent and the divine have no place.

Secularisation, with its 'death of God' thesis, implies that religious concepts, religious discourse and religious practices are irrelevant to the conduct of socio-political, economic and cultural relations in liberated, post-Enlightenment societies. Secularisation not only changes intellectual, culture and power relations but it also operates to affect the world view of many individuals. This is what Berger (1973) refers to as 'a secularisation of consciousness': 'put simply, this means that the modern West has produced an increasing number of individuals who look upon the world and their own lives without the benefits of religious interpretation' (p. 113).[1]

The problem for the sociology of education has been that it has operated within a 'secularisation of consciousness' paradigm which has limited both the depth and scope of its intellectual enquiries. Sociological analysis which elides a religious dimension not only presents an oversimplified view of social relations in 'the modern West', but also fails to make an authentic engagement with many socio-cultural and educational situations internationally where God is far from dead.

Just as Marx believed that ultimately the state would 'wither away', so too many sociologists of education have conducted their scholarly and research activities as if religion has withered away and therefore does not need analytical attention. While this perspective is an understandable (although flawed) sociological view of the 'modern West', in international terms it is blind to contemporary socio-cultural and political realities. As globalisation studies become more prominent in the sociology of education, the need to take religion and faith seriously in our studies becomes more urgent. Secular marginalisation needs to be replaced by a renewed sensitivity to the role of religion in educational, social, economic and political relations.

Sociology and the role of religion

To 'bring religion back into' sociological consciousness requires us to rediscover the classical texts of the discipline and to interpret these in the light of contemporary circumstances. In what might be called the historical canon of sociology, i.e. the founding scholarship of Emile Durkheim (1858–1917), Max Weber (1864–1920) and Karl Marx (1818–1883), the role of religion in social and economic relations is clearly recognised. As McLellan (1995) argues, Marx did not write much directly about religion because he saw it as a conservative ideology of alienation that impeded the development of class struggle and revolutionary consciousness. It was in this sense 'the opium of the people'. While this phrase has come to define *the* Marxist position on religion, McLellan points out that Marx also characterised religion as 'the sigh of the oppressed creature, the feeling of a heartless world and the soul of soulless circumstances' (p. 79). While Marx was clear that the religious cultures and ideologies of his time and place were legitimating agencies for an unjust distribution of economic resources, this is not necessarily the last word on the subject. Marx also recognised that 'religious suffering is at the same time an expression of real suffering and a protest against real suffering.' Since the time of Marx, it is possible to trace transformations in the role of *some* religions from that of social opium to that of social protest and action.[2]

Contemporary sociological writing in education would benefit from closer engagement with major texts which articulate these transformations, such as Gustavo Gutierrez's *A Theology of Liberation* (1974) and *The Power of the Poor in History* (1983). Paulo Freire's writings, particularly his texts *Pedagogy of the Oppressed* (1973), *Education for Critical Consciousness* (1990) and *Pedagogy of Hope* (1994) express some of the educational implications of what Freire (1984) described as a reformed and 'Prophetic Church'. Religion in certain cultural locations has become, if not part of the class struggle, at least part of the struggle for educational and human liberation.[3] The extent of these religious transformations and their educational implications and consequences internationally could provide the sociology of education with a significant agenda for research in the future.

A similar agenda is likely to emerge in revisiting the writings of Durkheim on the role of religion. For Durkheim, both in *The Elementary Forms of the Religious Life* (1971) and in *The Evolution of Educational Thought* (1977), there could be no meaningful sociological analysis which was not founded upon a prior investigation of religious values and practices. In *The Elementary Forms* he made a sustained attempt, from the standpoint of religious sociology, to understand the nature of the sacred and of its relation to the profane in human societies. The sacred was a representation of the Other in human existence, 'something added to and above the real', that which was holy, ineffable and mysterious. Religion, for Durkheim, was the social and cultural form which regulated relations with the sacred but which also had other profound social and intellectual functions in being constitutive of categories of thought, of the nature of the person and of society and of constructs of a possible ideal world. Durkheim argued, in the conclusion of his study:

> We have established the fact that the fundamental categories of thought . . . are of religious origin . . . Nearly all of the great social institutions have been born in religion . . . If religion has given birth to

all that is essential in society, it is because the idea of society is the soul of religion.

(p. 419)

Durkheim's own sociological project and his conceptions of an ideal educational system and an ideal society were entirely secular, but he recognised the powerful formative influences of religion in socio-cultural terms and of its possible continuing influence.

While Durkheim was concerned, among other things, to analyse the essence of religion as culture, particularly relating to conceptions of the sacred and the profane, Weber in both *The Protestant Ethic and the Spirit of Capitalism* (1965) and *The Sociology of Religion* (1966) was more interested in its social consequences. His sociology was an analysis of the social effects of religion on economic and political development. Particularly in *The Protestant Ethic,* Weber argued that Protestant asceticism performed a crucial role in the rise of Western rationality and in the rise of capitalism in Europe. He wanted to show how certain types of Protestantism provided a cultural milieu which encouraged the development of economic enterprise. Weber also pursued the relation of religion's cultures to different forms of economic development in his later studies of Islam[4] and Judaism.

The formation of many sociologists of education in the 1960s and 1970s involved some encounter, at least in advanced programmes, with the classic sociological discourses in which religion was implicated in various ways with social institutions and social processes. This grounding in 'grand theory' became progressively weaker in the 1980s and 1990s as sociology of education as a discipline became marginalised and reduced to technical service functions in the 'training' of teachers. A larger analytical vision of the historical and religious cultures of educational activity was lost at this time. In weakening its connection with the historical canon of sociology in this way, sociology of education reduced its opportunities to take religions seriously in educational analysis.

However, the connection with Durkheim was not entirely lost, but rather reconstituted in creative ways in the sociological writings of Basil Bernstein. In *Pedagogy, Symbolic Control and Identity* (1996) he declared:

> I shall start where Durkheim left off in his discussion of the Trivium/ Quadriviuum and carry his analysis a stage further. I shall propose that the Trivium is not simply about understanding the word, the principles of which lie behind it, the mechanics of language and reasoning, but is concerned to constitute a particular form of consciousness, a distinct modality of the self . . . To constitute that self in the Word, yes, but the Word of God. A particular god. The Christian God.

(p. 84)

The mature work of Bernstein made visible connections between the surface structures of educational and sociological phenomena and the deep structures of religious cultures, doctrines and practices. It set in place an intellectually stimulating theoretical framework for studying pedagogic and curricular transformations in a socio-historical sequence, that is, from transcendent religious principle, to humane secular principle, to marketised secular principle. His observation, that in contemporary settings 'we are experiencing a truly secular concept of knowledge' (p. 4), presents in condensed form the dilemmas facing all faith-based educational systems.[5]

An important agenda for writing and research thus becomes available, in which sociologists of education internationally can monitor the rise of a marketised secular curriculum and its associated pedagogy and educational social relations, while analysing the counter-cultural response of various faith-based schooling systems to this new phenomenon. It may be argued that the great countervailing force to global capitalism and its educational consequences is no longer international Marxism but rather certain forms[6] of religious culture and practice, in various parts of the world.

Understanding Islam

At this particular historical juncture, there is clearly a need for sociologists of education to deepen their understanding of the cultures of Islam and of the educational, social and political relations which arise from these different manifestations of faith. As Turner (1999) argues:

> Believing that the modern world on a global scale is going through a process of secularisation would be odd, given the central place of religion in many forms of political change in the world order. The rise of fundamentalist Islam is the most obvious example and its involvement in the modern politics of Iran, Iraq and Pakistan is clear . . . Islamic fundamentalism has been important in mobilising urban and peasant opposition to western secularisation and consumerism.
>
> (pp. xx–xxi)

Making connections between sociology of education and the cultures of Islam will not be easy, for many reasons. For example, Edward Said (2003), in his magisterial book *Orientalism,* has pointed out that Western perceptions of Islam are frequently distorted by prejudice, polemic and stereotypes. Said cautions against the use of Western classic writings on Islam for some of these reasons and points serious students of Islam and economic relations to Maxime Rodinson's (1974) text *Islam and Capitalism.*

Sociologists of education who want to understand the educational institutions and cultures of Islam will not only have to rise above the dominant stereotypes of historical and contemporary discourses, but will have to make connections with valid scholarship beyond the confines of sociology *per se*. Edward Said's *Orientalism* is an obvious starting point, with its extensive scholarship and its stark warning:

> Books and articles are regularly published on Islam and the Arabs that represent absolutely no change over the virulent anti-Islamic polemics of the Middle Ages and the Renaissance. For no other ethnic or religious group is it true that virtually anything can be written and said about it, without challenge or demurral.
>
> (p. 287)

Much contemporary discussion of Islam and of its social, educational and political relations is dominated by concepts of 'Islamic fundamentalism'. It is forgotten that such fundamentalism represents only one face of Islam and it is also forgotten that religious fundamentalism is itself a universal phenomenon. As Karen Armstrong (2001a, 2001b) reminds us, in her impressive socio-historical analyses of religious cultures, 'Fundamentalism is a global fact and has surfaced in every major faith in response to the problems of our modernity. There is fundamentalist Judaism, fundamentalist Christianity, fundamentalist Hinduism . . . ' (2001a, p. 140).[7]

If globalisation and education are to become a central research theme for the sociology of education, then it is clear that sociologists must come to a deeper understanding of the various forms of religious fundamentalism as cultural responses to a threatened hegemony of secularism and Western capitalism. Such fundamentalism has significant educational implications. However, the educational consequences of *fundamentalism* must not be confused with the mainstream educational cultures of the various faith communities. Within each religious community there are internal theological and social struggles which result in different approaches to educational issues.[8]

Making connections

If Durkheim's observation that 'the idea of society is the soul of religion' has any validity, then making connections between sociological study and religious study would seem to be a potentially valuable development.[9] The sociological imagination could be enriched by such a conjunction, not to mention substantial areas of study such as globalisation and education. Faith schools internationally constitute a significant and ever-growing sector of educational provision. If sociologists of education are to gain any useful research insight into the educational cultures and outcomes of these schools, they will require some understanding of the various faiths which have generated them.

One of the few writers to make these crucial connections in a sustained way is Michael Apple in his important text, *Educating the 'Right' Way: markets, standards, God and inequality* (2001). This is a model of the type of scholarship which is needed at this time.

Apple's specific focus is to examine the growing power of the 'Christian Right' (evangelicals and fundamentalists) in the USA and their impact upon social, economic and political relations and 'the growing influence of authoritarian, populist religious conservatism on education' (p. 27). The agenda of the 'Christian Right' includes attempts to influence state policy by 'bringing God back into the schools'; advancing particular views on gender issues, sexuality and the family and, crucially, by shaping ideas about what is to count as legitimate knowledge in the schools. This whole agenda is based upon a conservative and inflexible reading of the Bible as the revealed truth of God. At the same time, the 'Christian Right' pursues a conservative position on socio-political and economic issues. As Apple makes clear, 'By and large, evangelicals do not question the larger structures of the economy' (p. 132). The evangelical position is that individual enterprise, pursued with moral probity, will generate economic relations blessed by God. Here we have *The Protestant Ethic and Spirit of Capitalism* renewed and resurgent in the contemporary United States.

The agenda of the 'Christian Right' in the USA is powerful because of the commitment of its activists, its large financial backing and its creative and extensive use of the mass media to propagate its messages. In noting this, Apple alerts us to the international mission potential of Christian evangelical groups. Evangelicals are active in Latin America, in Eastern Europe, in Africa, India and many parts of Asia. The 'Christian Right', in other words, is not simply a phenomenon of the USA; it has worldwide implications. Here is an important field for research and critical writing in the sociology of education. What impact are evangelicals having upon educational policy and practice in these various contexts?

However, Apple is careful not to imply that religion *per se* is a conservative force in social relations. He recognises another face of religious commitment: 'I tend to believe that in many nations it would be impossible to develop larger liberatory movements without religious mediation as one of the major dynamics' (p. 28). The impact of liberation theology and the growth of progressive Christian base community movements in Latin America are cited as examples of this.[10] Apple's analysis of the activities of the 'Christian Right' internationally needs to be balanced by studies of the 'Christian Left' and its involvement in educational policy and practice.

While the 'Christian Left' does not have the resources available to the 'Christian Right' in either political or financial terms, it does have significant cultural resources in the writings of liberation theologians and associated texts in critical pedagogy.[11] From this perspective, much more research attention needs to be given to educational developments in Latin America.[12] Here, in particular, the impact of the Christian evangelicals is increasing, in the cultural settings in which liberation theology and 'education as liberation' has been most active in practice. Michael Apple (2001) makes the pertinent observation that 'One should never underestimate the power of religion in the United States' (p. 102). This observation may be generalised to many other cultural contexts. Religious relations, despite their formal pursuit of the spiritual and the transcendent, are at the same time power relations. As such they are an appropriate focus for sociological analysis and research.

None of this implies that sociologists have to be either religious believers or particularly sympathetic to faith-based educational provision. What is required is a disinterested and judicious scholarship which can rise above prejudice, polemic and stereotypes. It should be remembered that some of the most profound insights into the nature of Christian religious thought and its associated pedagogy and curricula were produced by Emile Durkheim, a secular Jew. Philip Wexler (1997, p. 11) has called for 'the resacralization of social understanding'. This is a radical call and perhaps it is asking too much at this juncture. This article is not calling for 'resacralization' (which may imply a conversion experience), but for more serious attention to religious and faith cultures in the future work of the sociology of education.

Acknowledgement

I thank the two anonymous referees of this journal for their valuable suggestions in developing the first draft of this article.

Notes

1 I interpret Berger to mean intellectual benefits as well as personal ones.
2 The role of liberation theology in South America and other settings in a clear example of this.
3 The part played by Catholic educators in the struggle against apartheid in South Africa has been analysed by Pam Christie (1990).
4 See Turner (1974).
5 This argument was first used in Grace (2001).
6 It is important to distinguish among different forms of religious culture and practice in their relation to social and political issues. The radicalism of Catholic forms of liberation theology can be contrasted with the conservatism of some forms of Christian evangelical and fundamentalist religion.
7 The scholarly work of Karen Armstrong provides a rich resource upon which sociologists of education can draw. Armstrong is, for instance, a valuable source for examining the status of women in fundamentalist Christianity, Islam and Judaism and of the various distortions of religious practice which have resulted from the domination of patriarchy in these major faiths.
8 I have attempted to show this in relation to Catholic Christianity in Grace (2003).
9 For similar arguments, see Wilson (2002).
10 See Van Vught (1991).
11 For example, Oldenski (1997).
12 See Ball et al (2003).

References

Apple, M. (2001) *Educating the 'Right' Way: markets, standards, God and inequality*. New York: RoutledgeFalmer.

Armstrong, K. (2001a) *Islam: a short history*. London: Phoenix.

Armstrong, K. (2001b) *The Battle for God: a history of fundamentalism*. New York: Ballantine Books.

Ball, S., Fischman, G. & Gvirtz, S. (Eds) (2003) *Crisis and Hope: the educational hopscotch of Latin America*. New York: RoutledgeFalmer.

Berger, P. (1973) *The Social Reality of Religion*. London: Penguin.

Bernstein, B. (1996) *Pedagogy, Symbolic Control and Identity*. London: Taylor & Francis.

Christie, P. (1990) *Open Schools: racially mixed Catholic schools in South Africa 1976–1986*. Johannesburg: Raven Press.

Durkheim, E. (1971) *The Elementary Forms of the Religious Life: a study of religious sociology*. London: Allen & Unwin (original publication 1912).

Durkheim, E. (1977) *The Evolution of Educational Thought*. London: Routledge & Kegan Paul (original publication 1938).

Freire, P. (1973) *Pedagogy of the Oppressed*. London: Penguin.

Freire, P. (1984) Education, Liberation and the Church, *Religious Education*, 79(4), pp. 524–545.

Freire, P. (1990) *Education for Critical Consciousness*. New York: Continuum.

Freire, P. (1994) *Pedagogy of Hope*. New York: Continuum.

Gallagher, M. (1997) New Forms of Cultural Unbelief, in P. Hogan & K. Williams (Eds) *The Future of Religion in Irish Education*. Dublin: Veritas.

Grace, G. (2001) Bernstein and Catholicism: relationships visible and invisible, in S. Power, P. Aggleton, J. Brannen, A. Brown, L. Chisholm & J. Mace (Eds) *A Tribute to Basil Bernstein*. London: Institute of Education.

Grace, G. (2003) 'First and Foremost the Church offers Its Educational Service to Poor': class, inequality and Catholic schooling in contemporary contexts, *International Studies in Sociology of Education*, 13(1), pp. 35–53.

Gutierrez, G. (1974) *A Theology of Liberation*. London: SCM Press.

Gutierrez, G. (1983) *The Power of the Poor in History*. London: SCM Press.

McLellan, D. (1995) *Karl Marx: a biography*. London: Macmillan.

Oldenski, T. (1997) *Liberation Theology and Critical Pedagogy in Today's Catholic Schools*. New York: Garland.

Rodinson, M. (1974) *Islam and Capitalism*. New York: Pantheon.

Said, E. (2003) *Orientalism*. London: Penguin.

Turner, B. (1974) *Weber and Islam: a critical study*. London: Routledge.

Turner, B. (1999) *Religion and Social Theory*. London: Sage.

Van Vught, J. (1991) *Democratic Organisations for Social Change: Latin American Christian base communities*. New York: Bergin & Garvey.

Weber, M. (1965) *The Protestant Ethic and the Spirit of Capitalism*. Boston: Beacon Press (original publication 1904).

Weber, M. (1966) *The Sociology of Religion*. Boston: Beacon Press (original publication 1920).

Wexler, P. (1997) *Holy Sparks: social theory, education and religion*. London: Macmillan.

Wilson, B. (2002) *Religion in Sociological Perspective*. Oxford: Oxford University Press.

Chapter 8

On the international study of Catholic education

Why we need more systematic scholarship and research

International Studies in Catholic Education, 2009, 1(1), 6–14.

There is a considerable contradiction in the field of Catholic education. On the one hand, the Catholic educational system is the largest faith-based educational mission in the world, having almost 200,000 schools and over 1000 universities and colleges, while on the other hand, very little systematic scholarship and research exist to assist, evaluate and professionally develop this great enterprise as it faces the many challenges of the contemporary world. This article argues for more systematic study of and research in Catholic education in all its forms and suggests an agenda for future investigation.

An international perspective on Catholic education

The publication of the *International Handbook of Catholic Education* (*IHCE*) in two volumes (Grace and O'Keefe 2007) marked the first ever international survey of the challenges facing Catholic school systems in over 30 societies across the world. *IHCE* was the outcome of five years' work in forming a team of international scholars, researchers, school leaders and teachers to give a major impetus to the serious study of Catholic education and to establish it as a distinctive academic and policy-related field.

IHCE consists of 45 chapters, with six from North America; five from Latin America; 15 from Europe; five from Africa; eight from Asia; four from Australasia; and one from the Holy Land. Professor Joseph O'Keefe, SJ and I as the Editors, contributed an overview chapter entitled, 'Catholic schools facing the challenges of the 21st Century'.

This extensive analytical investigation revealed 10 major challenges facing Catholic schools in the contemporary world. These may be stated in summary form as follows:

1 The impact of secularisation upon the work of Catholic education (see Aristimuño 2007).
2 The influence of global capitalism and its associated materialist values (see Klaiber 2007).
3 The authenticity of the mission integrity of Catholic schools that, 'first and foremost the Church offers its educational services to the poor'

(Sacred Congregation for Catholic Education 1977, 44) (see Martinic and Anaya 2007; Toppo 2007).

4   Issues of faith formation for both teachers and students.

5   Moral and social formation in changing cultural situations.

6   Maintaining the educational mission as religious congregations declined in numbers.

7   Problems of recruitment, formation and retention of school leaders and teachers in Catholic education.

8   Responding to changing expectations for the education of girls and women.[1]

9   Understanding contemporary students' attitudes towards, and experiences of, Catholic schooling.

10 The finance, economics of schooling and politics of schooling (Church–state relations) in various societies.

Many of these challenges are interconnected and therefore Catholic schools, universities and colleges are located in a complex matrix of social forces which, taken together, present considerable obstacles to the integrity and effectiveness of the Catholic educational mission in the world. There are obvious connections for instance between secularisation and globalisation; between the mission to the poor and the decline of religious teaching congregations; and between faith, moral and social formation issues and the attitudes of contemporary youth and of their parents.[2]

In his contribution to the *IHCE* (Grace and O'Keefe 2007), Archbishop Michael Miller, CSB, then Secretary of the Congregation for Catholic Education in Rome, argued that in the face of these major challenges, Catholic universities and colleges should devote serious attention to them, not only to understand the nature of the challenges but also to formulate, cooperatively, appropriate educational responses to them. In other words, a clear call was made for a stronger scholarly, research-based and policy-related approach to Catholic education in the faculties of Catholic universities:

> Since research should serve the human person, it is altogether fitting that the Church's institutions of higher education take up the pressing challenge of fostering serious studies that further the common good of Catholic schooling. This research should include longitudinal, cross-cultural and interdisciplinary studies that would enable educators to gain a more international and empirically based perspective on the strengths, weaknesses, opportunities and challenges faced by Catholic schools across the globe.
>
> (Miller 2007, 475–476)

My five years' involvement with Catholic universities internationally revealed that many could not respond easily to an invitation to contribute a chapter for the *IHCE*, either because the university did not possess a Faculty of Education or Pedagogy,[3] or because, if they did, they reported that the systematic study of Catholic schooling was not well developed in the university. What was largely absent in many cases was any extensive research into the effectiveness of Catholic schooling. There were, of course, some exceptions to this lacuna. Both the United States and Australia had strong profiles of academic writing and research in the field[4] but what was lacking, even in these developed fields, was a strong comparative and international perspective in analysis.

What this amounts to is a considerable contradiction in the context of Catholic education. On the one hand, the Catholic educational system is the largest faith-based educational mission in the world, having almost 200,000 schools and over 1000 universities and colleges, while, on the other hand, very little systematic scholarship and research attempts to assist, evaluate and develop this great enterprise as it faces the many challenges of the contemporary world. As Archbishop Miller argued in 2007, this situation cannot continue if the mission integrity and effectiveness of Catholic education worldwide is to be maintained and improved.

Why we need more systematic scholarship and research

There are at least three major reasons why the serious study of Catholic education in all its forms (schooling, higher education, community and parish-based education (adult education), seminary education) should be more extensively developed.

First and foremost the intention of such study should be to provide ideas, inspirations, evaluations, empirical data, theoretical reflections and pedagogic suggestions which will assist Catholic educators to improve the integrity and effectiveness of the various forms of educational work in which they are engaged. As Archbishop Miller stated, 'research should serve the human person', and therefore the intention of those writing in this field should be an act of service to the common good of Catholic education. While such writing must observe the usual canons of systematic and objective scholarship, it must at the same time be presented in a language and style which is accessible to all Catholic educators, and indeed to the wider Catholic community and the secular world.

The second reason is to realise the rich potential of international cross-cultural learning which is present in the Catholic educational mission. When I surveyed the existing fields of Catholic educational research as the background for the study, *Catholic Schools: Mission, Market and Morality* (Grace 2002a), I found that most published research was nationally focused, i.e., it was written with little comparative on international cross-referencing. Here was another contradiction of this field of studies. While located in the largest cross-cultural educational enterprise in the world, most writers and researchers adopted only a national-cultural focus in their analysis.[5]

In March 2003 a new journal was launched with the title, *Globalisation, Societies and Education* (Dale and Robertson 2003). In the first issue, the Editors, Roger Dale and Susan Robertson argued that:

> the most important reason for establishing the journal is that in current analyses of globalisation in contemporary societies, education has suffered from considerable neglect.
>
> (2003, 6)

The new journal was intended to make stronger links between educational scholarship and the phenomenon of globalisation. What applies in the secular academic world, clearly applies in the field of Catholic educational studies. We work in the context of globalisation. We need to investigate the impact of globalisation upon Catholic educational systems and in doing so we need to draw upon the global scholarship and resources of Catholic educational studies. There is a great potential for international networking, partnerships and cross-cultural learning in the worldwide Catholic system but it is a potential yet to be fully realised.

Finally, a more systematic scholarly and research-based approach to Catholic education will provide a necessary intellectual and cultural defence against the challenges of secularisation in contemporary societies. While secularisation manifests itself in various ways, one of its current manifestations is what Cardinal Cormac Murphy O'Connor has called 'aggressive secularism'.

In Western societies at least, we are witnessing powerful attacks upon religious ideas and religious institutions from those who have been styled 'the new atheists'. These include widely read writers such as Richard Dawkins, Chris Hitchens, A.C. Grayling and Daniel Dennett.[6]

The Catholic Church is a frequent target for these polemical attacks which are given considerable amplification by mass media agencies and journals. Catholic educational institutions it is claimed are characterised as indoctrination centres, marked by social selection and exclusivity, and institutional hypocrisy, and as having the effect of being deleterious to community and social cohesion. These claims are based, in general, upon ideological assertions and polemical arguments having no basis in reliable evidence (see Grace 2003a). The need for a strongly developed field of scholarship and research from the international missions of Catholic education is very clear. This is not a case for developing research as a form of apologetics but rather as a resource for reliable evidence-based argument in the public arena.

There will be cases where systematic inquiry will reveal that some of the charges of the critics of Catholic education do have a basis in fact. In these cases such evidence will provide the basis for necessary reforms in the policies and processes of Catholic education. We can and must learn from our critics.

A fully developed and integrated field of Catholic education scholarship will need to draw upon interdisciplinary perspectives, as Archbishop Miller has suggested. It cannot be undertaken simply by Faculties of Education and Pedagogy but will need the support of Faculties of Theology, Philosophy, History, Economics and Social Science. It is to be hoped that Catholic universities, colleges, diocesan education offices and major religious congregations with missions in education will contribute to the construction of this new interdisciplinary and international field.

However, this cannot be a project internal to the Catholic academic and professional world. Its academic integrity requires that contributions should be made by those external to the Catholic community. It is for this reason, that this new journal, *International Studies in Catholic Education* will positively invite academic and research writing from other faith perspectives and from secular analysts, including critics of Catholic education.

An international agenda for Catholic educational studies

The 10 major challenges indicated at the beginning of this article provide a comprehensive agenda for future writing and research. We need sustained investigations in different international settings of the ways in which these challenges are manifested and of the ways in which Catholic educators are responding to them.

For this writer, a reading of the *IHCE* (Grace and O'Keefe 2007) suggests that among the 10 identified, two are particularly salient as suggested below.

The impact of secularisation and globalisation

The most dominant challenge, which is identified in almost all the chapters of the *IHCE* is that constituted by the conjunction of secularisation and the materialist values of global capitalism as an expression of globalisation.[7] The development of secularisation in the modern world from the Enlightenment (so-called) to the twenty-first century, presents the agencies of sacred knowledge and culture with a powerful and sharp challenge. Secularisation represents the denial of the validity of the sacred and the transcendental, and of the institutions (churches and schools) which exist to renew spiritual culture and practice. Secularists work to replace this 'redundant' culture with 'modern', 'logical', 'empirical' and 'scientific' intellectual cultures in which notions of the transcendent have no place. For many individuals in the West, religious concepts, religious discourse and religious sensitivities are regarded as simply irrelevant to the everyday business of life. This is what Peter Berger (1973) in his influential study *The Social Reality of Religion* refers to as 'a secularisation of consciousness'. Steve Bruce (2003) in his provocative book *God is Dead: Secularisation in the West* argues that 'widespread indifference' characterises the attitudes of most people in the West towards religion.

The economist, Kamran Mofid (2002) has suggested that one dimension of globalisation (the extension of capitalist consumer values to every part of the world) is contributing to the growth of commodity worship internationally even in those countries which still possess a strong religious culture. Mofid presents a powerful argument:

> Today, in place of the one God that I was encouraged to believe in, we have been offered many global gods to worship. For many people, today's gods are Nike, Adidas, Levi, Calvin Klein, American Express, Nokia . . . Today's global churches are the shopping malls, the super-stores and factory outlets, many of them open twenty-four hours a day for maximum worship.
>
> (Mofid 2002, 8)

The impact of materialist consumer culture upon young people was a concern for the Congregation for Catholic Education in 1988 when it called for a counter-cultural response from the Catholic schooling system internationally to these challenges:

> Many young people find themselves in a condition of radical instability. They live in a one-dimensional universe in which the only criterion is practical utility and the only value is economic and technological progress . . . Young people unable to find any meaning in life . . . turn to alcohol, drugs, the erotic, the exotic. Christian education is faced with the huge challenge of helping these young people discover something of value in their lives.
>
> (Congregation for Catholic Education 1988, 8–10)

Catholic schools across the world continue the struggle to bring young people to a knowledge and experience of God, especially in the person of Jesus Christ, and seek to be counter-cultural to the powerful materialist forces of secularisation and globalisation. We need to investigate the various ways in which an increasingly secularised and globalised international culture is affecting the consciousness and behaviour of children and youth. Case studies of the ways in which Catholic educational institutions and educational initiatives are able to be counter-cultural in practice would be valuable for international learning and evaluation.[8]

Mission integrity[9] and the preferential option for the poor

While the challenges of secularisation, globalisation and formation of the young in faith, morality and social responsibility emerge as dominant concerns for Catholic educators internationally, these are closely followed by dilemmas relating to mission integrity and service to the poor and the powerless. Catholic educators are very conscious of a Vatican II re-emphasis upon the preferential option for the poor in Catholic schooling. As the foundational document, *The Catholic School* expressed it in 1977:

> First and foremost, the Church offers its educational services to the poor, or those who are deprived of family help and affection or those who are far from the faith. Since education is an important means of improving the social and economic condition of the individual and of peoples, if the Catholic school was to turn attention exclusively or predominantly to those from wealthier social classes it could be contributing towards maintaining their privileged position and could thereby continue to favour a society which is unjust.
>
> (Sacred Congregation for Catholic Education 1977, 44–45)

Financing the Catholic educational mission in changing circumstances emerges as a major problem for Catholic schooling internationally. In the past, the many religious congregations and teaching brotherhoods provided, what I have called, 'a strategic subsidy' (see Grace 2002a, 87), especially for the Catholic education of the poor in every country. This strategic subsidy consisted of providing the physical plant, the personnel, the cultural, spiritual and financial capital to facilitate the mission, and above all, the inspirational ideology and vocational role models which constituted a distinctive Catholic educational habitus. As this strategic subsidy has declined over time, and as many secular governments will not fund faith-based schools, there has been an inevitable increase in the costs of providing Catholic schooling as more lay people have to be employed at higher salary levels. The consequences of this are very serious for Catholic schooling in general but especially for the Church's commitment that 'first and foremost the Church offers its educational services to the poor'.[10]

The researches of Joseph O'Keefe, SJ and his team (2004) at Boston College have brought into sharp focus how this situation is threatening the Catholic education mission in poor inner-city areas in the USA. In an update of this research, reported as chapter 2 in the *IHCE* (Grace and O'Keefe 2007), there is evidence of an increasing rate of Catholic school closures in the areas of greatest educational and social need. In this journal, O'Keefe and Scheopner (2007) continue to document this trend, concluding that action must be taken to reverse this disturbing situation.

This threat to the 'preferential option for the poor' in Catholic education exists wherever religious congregations are declining and where there is inadequate financial support from the state. Those Catholic systems which do receive this support, such as England and Wales, Scotland, Ireland, Belgium, The Netherlands, Germany, Australia and New Zealand have relative financial protection (but the declining presence of the religious threatens to weaken the religious ethos and vocational culture of the schools). However, for schools in Africa, India, South East Asia and Latin America, and in European states such as France, Spain and Italy serious problems exist in terms of an authentic mission to the poor.

The *IHCE,* while reporting these serious threats to the mission integrity of Catholic schooling, also reports examples of imaginative and progressive developments in relation to these challenges. An inspirational chapter by Cardinal Telesphore Toppo, President of the Catholic Bishops' Conference of India shows the ways in which the church's educational concern for the poorest and most marginalised sectors of Indian society remains strong (Grace and O'Keefe 2007, chapter 33). Similarly, the chapters from Brazil (9), Peru (10) and Chile (11) show what Streck and Segala (2007) call 'a new way of being school' in Latin America. This new way of being school has been influenced by liberation theology, by the educational writing of Paolo Freire (1973, 1984, 1994) and by a post-Vatican II commitment of many priests and religious to a greater solidarity with the poor in Latin America. However, it is also clear from the contributions from other national settings that many Catholic schools and religious congregations are very much in the service of the 'wealthier social classes'. Secularists and atheist critics of Catholic schooling make much of this relation in their attacks upon Catholic education and in their calls for its abolition.[11]

Here is a situation where fundamental research in Catholic education must be integrated with a responsible politics of education. Research has established (Greeley 1982; Convey 1992; Bryk, Lee, and Holland 1993) that Catholic schools provide considerable educational, moral and social benefits for poor and marginalised students and thereby make important contributions to the common good of the societies in which they are located. Those states which provide financial support to faith schools are recognising a principle of economic equity in access to such schooling and are recognising the contribution to the common good which Catholic schools achieve. Those states which deny such financial support restrict this option in practice mainly to those who can afford to pay the fees and thereby constitute these schools as being 'in the service of the wealthier social classes'. This clear distortion of the authentic mission of Catholic education makes it essential that Catholic school leaders (both clerical and lay) should draw upon such research findings to advance evidence-based advocacy for state financial support for Catholic schools in the service of deprived populations and commitments. Research in this case becomes the engine for potential educational transformations in society.

Learning from each other internationally

The *IHCE* (Grace and O'Keefe 2007) has been a first step in the development of the systematic study of Catholic schooling systems across the world.

International Studies in Catholic Education marks a second step which widens the focus of writing and analysis to include Catholic higher education[12] and adult education, not only in institutional settings but also in community and parish-based settings.

In the last analysis, the work of Catholic education is crucial to the renewal of the faith and of the Church itself. We need to know more about its present mission integrity and education and spiritual effectiveness in challenging circumstances. To do this we need more research, evaluation and serious scholarship and more international communication among Catholic educators of various backgrounds, cultures and disciplines.[13]

Notes

1 See Mary Darmanin (2007, chapter 22) in *IHCE* and also in this journal.
2 The Congregation for Catholic Education in its 1998 publication took a sombre view of the attitudes of many pupils and parents:

> (Of pupils) 'In an increasing number of instances they are not only indifferent and non-practising but also totally lacking in religious or moral formation. To this, we must add – on the part of numerous pupils and families – a profound apathy where ethical and religious formation is concerned, to the extent that what is in fact required of the Catholic schools is a certificate of studies or, at the most, quality instruction and training for employment'.
>
> (pp. 37–38)

Much more research is needed into the attitudes and motivations of contemporary youth and their parents in opting for a Catholic education. How valid and general are the assertions made in the above quotation?
3 Of the eight Pontifical Universities in Rome, only the Pontifical Salesian University has a Faculty of Education.
4 Notable examples would be the work of Greeley et al. (1966, 1976, 1982, 1998), Convey (1992) and Bryk et al. (1993) in the USA and of Marcellin Flynn et al. (1975, 1985, 1993, 2002) in Australia. See also Brian Croke (2007).
5 To try to counter this tendency an International Network of Catholic Education Research and Scholarship (INCERS) will be launched in 2009.
6 Richard Dawkins' book, *The God Delusion* (2006) has made an international impact and has been widely amplified in the mass media. In back cover endorsements, Philip Pullman argues that 'children deserve to read it as well as adults. It should have a place in every school library – especially in the library of every "faith" school'.
  We need to know how Catholic school educators are responding to this challenge. See also the writings of Dennett (2006), Hitchens (2008) and Grayling (2007).
7 For a recent statement on this conjunction see 'The Cultural Challenges of Secularism Spreading through Globalisation', an address to the Pontifical Council for Culture by Archbishop Gianfranco Ravasi (President), July 2008.
8 These issues are particularly addressed in the *IHCE* in the chapters for Uruguay (8), Scotland (21), Poland (26), South Africa (29), India (35), Philippines (37), Thailand (38, 39) and Japan (41).
9 For a development of the concept of 'mission integrity', see Grace (2002b, 427–449).
10 For a more developed argument, see Grace (2003b).

11 The charge of 'institutional hypocrisy' is made in these cases.
12 For a recent study of Catholic and other faith-based colleges and universities in relation to secularisation, see Arthur (2006).
13 The Editors of this journal hope to receive contributions from theologians, philosophers, historians, economists and social scientists as well as from Education Faculties and school system leaders and teachers.

References

Aristimuño, A. 2007. Secularization: challenges for Catholic schools in Uruguay. In *International handbook of Catholic education,* ed. G. Grace and J. O'Keefe, 149–163. Dordrecht: Springer.

Arthur, J. 2006. *Faith and secularisation in religious colleges and universities.* London: Routledge.

Berger, P. 1973. *Social reality of religion.* London: Penguin.

Bruce, S. 2003. *God is dead: Secularisation in the West.* Oxford: Blackwell Publishing.

Bryk, A, V. Lee, and P. Holland. 1993. *Catholic schools and the common good.* Cambridge, MA: Harvard University Press.

Congregation for Catholic Education. 1988. *The religious dimension of education in a Catholic school.* Vatican City: Liberia Editrice Vaticana.

Congregation for Catholic Education. 1998. *The Catholic school on the threshold of the third millennium.* Vatican City: Liberia Editrice Vaticana.

Convey, J. 1992. *Catholic schools make a difference: Twenty-five years of research.* Washington, DC: National Catholic Educational Association.

Croke, B. 2007. Australian Catholic schools in a changing political and religious landscape. In *International handbook of Catholic education,* eds. G. Grace and J. O'Keefe, 811–833. Dordrecht: Springer.

Dale, R., and S. Robertson. 2003. Editorial introduction. *Globalisation, Societies and Education* 1, no. 1: 3–11.

Darmanin, M. 2007. Catholic schooling and the changing role of women: Perspectives from Malta. In *International handbook of Catholic education,* eds. G. Grace and J. O'Keefe, 407–434. Dordrecht: Springer.

Dawkins, R. 2006. *The God delusion.* London: Bantam Press.

Dennett, D. 2006. *Breaking the spell: Religion as a natural phenomenon.* London: Viking.

Flynn, M. 1975. *Some Catholic schools in action.* Sydney: Catholic Education Office.

Flynn, M. 1985. *The effectiveness of Catholic schools.* Homebush, NSW: St Paul Publications.

Flynn, M. 1993. *The culture of Catholic schools.* Homebush, NSW: St Paul Publications.

Flynn, M., and M. Mok. 2002. *Catholic schools 2000: A longitudinal study of Year 12 students in Catholic schools: 1972–1982–1990–1998.* Sydney: Catholic Education Commission.

Freire, P. 1973. *Pedagogy of the oppressed.* Harmondsworth: Penguin Books.

Freire, P. 1984. Education, liberation and the Church. *Religious Education* 79, no. 4: 524–545.

Freire, P. 1994. *Pedagogy of hope.* New York: Continuum.

Grace, G. 2002a. *Catholic schools: Mission, markets and morality.* London: RoutledgeFalmer.

Grace, G. 2002b. Mission integrity: Contemporary challenges for Catholic school leaders. In *Second international handbook of educational leadership and administration*, eds. K. Leithwood and P. Hallinger, 427–449. Dordrecht: Kluwer Academic Publishers.

Grace, G. 2003a. Educational studies and faith-based schooling: Moving from prejudice to evidence-based argument. *British Journal of Educational Studies* 51, no. 2: 149–167.

Grace, G. 2003b. First and foremost the Church offers its educational services to the poor: Class, inequality and Catholic schooling in contemporary contexts. *International Studies in Sociology of Education* 13, no. 1: 35–53.

Grace, G. and J. O'Keefe, eds. 2007. *International handbook of Catholic education* (2 vols). Dordrecht: Springer.

Grayling, A. 2007. *Against all Gods*. Ottawa: Oberon Books.

Greeley, A. 1982. *Catholic high schools and minority students*. New Brunswick, NJ: Transaction Books.

Greeley, A. 1998. Catholic schools at the crossroads: An American perspective. In *From ideal to action: The inner nature of a Catholic school today*, ed. J.M. Feheney, 181–189. Dublin: Veritas.

Greeley, A., and P. Rossi. 1966. *The education of Catholic Americans*. Chicago: Aldine.

Greeley, A., W. McCready and K. McCourt. 1976. *Catholic schools in a declining Church*. Kansas City: Sheed and Ward.

Hitchens, C. 2008. *God is not great*. London: Atlantic Books.

Klaiber, J. 2007. Catholic schools in Peru: Elites, the poor and the challenge of Neoliberalism. In *International handbook of Catholic education*, eds. G. Grace and J. O'Keefe, 181–193. Dordrecht: Springer.

Martinic, S. and M. Anaya. 2007. The Catholic school in the context of inequality: The case of Chile. In *International handbook of Catholic education*, ed. G. Grace and J. O'Keefe, 195–209. Dordrecht: Springer.

Miller, M. (Archbishop). 2007. Challenges for Catholic schools: A view from Rome. In *International handbook of Catholic education*, eds. G. Grace and J. O'Keefe, 449–480. Dordrecht: Springer.

Mofid, K. 2002. *Globalisation and the common good*. London: Shepherd-Walwyn.

O'Keefe, J., E. Goldschmidt, J. Green, and S. Henderson. 2004. *Sustaining the legacy: Inner-city Catholic elementary schools in the United States*. Washington, DC: National Catholic Educational Association.

O'Keefe, J. and A. Scheopner. 2007. No margin, no mission: Challenges for Catholic urban schools in the USA. In *International handbook of Catholic education*, ed. G. Grace and J. O'Keefe, 15–35. Dordrecht: Springer.

Ravasi, G. (Archbishop). 2008. *Address to the cultural challenges of Secularism spreading through globalisation*. Pontifical Council for Culture, Vatican City.

Sacred Congregation for Catholic Education. 1977. *The Catholic school*. London: Catholic Truth Society.

Streck, D. and A. Segala. 2007. A theological–pedagogical turning point in Latin America. A new way of being school in Brazil. In *International handbook of Catholic education*, eds. G. Grace and J. O'Keefe, 165–179. Dordrecht: Springer.

Toppo, T. (Cardinal). 2007. Catholic education and the Church's concern for the marginalised: A view from India. In *International handbook of Catholic education*, eds. G. Grace and J. O'Keefe, 653–663. Dordrecht: Springer.

Part 4

Concepts of educational leadership and concepts of educational 'effectiveness' in Catholic schooling

Chapter 9

The dilemmas of Catholic headteachers

School Leadership: Beyond Educational Management, 1995, (Ed). G. Grace, 159–79, Falmer.

Bryk *et al.* (1993), in a major study of the culture of Catholic schooling in the USA, have argued that such schools are informed by 'an inspirational ideology' (p.301) which makes them qualitatively different from public (state) schools. This inspirational ideology celebrates the primacy of the spiritual and moral life; the dignity of the person; the importance of community and moral commitments to caring, social justice and the common good. Vatican II, in the view of Bryk *et al.*, produced not only a new role for the Church in the modern world, but a new conception of the Catholic school and of Catholic education in which enhanced importance has been given to respect for persons, active community and a strong social ethic of citizen responsibility in a national and an international sense. The argument of *The Catholic School and the Common Good* is, among other things, that Catholic schools are culturally and morally distinctive as educational institutions:

> Two important ideas shape life in Catholic schools, making them very different from their organizational counterparts in the public sector: Christian personalism and subsidiarity. Christian personalism calls for humaneness in the myriad of mundane social interactions that make up daily life . . . it signifies a moral conception of social behaviour in a just community . . . subsidiarity means that the schools reject a purely bureaucratic conception of an organization . . . Decentralization of school governance is not chosen purely because it is more efficient . . . rather decentralization is predicated in the view that personal dignity and human respect are advanced when work is organized in small communities where dialogue and collegiality may flourish.[1]

These at least are the commitments of the formal inspirational ideology of the new Catholic schooling in America, although the extent to which these virtues are actually realized will, it is acknowledged, vary from school to school.

The critical agents for the translation of these formal commitments into lived school experience are, in the view of Bryk *et al.*, the school principals. Catholic school principalship in American has been strongly influenced by the spiritual and moral capital of the various religious orders which have provided most of the leadership positions until recently.[2] There are therefore also qualitative differences in the nature of school leadership:

> Although much of the work of Catholic school principals is similar to that of their public school counterparts, we conclude that the nature of school leadership has a distinctive character here. Both public and Catholic school principals value academic excellence and students' educational attainment. For principals in Catholic schools, however, there is also an important spiritual dimension to leadership that is apt to be absent from the concerns of public school administrators. This spirituality is manifest in the language of community that principals use to describe their schools and in their actions as they work to achieve the goal of community.[3]

Although lay Catholics are increasingly taking over school leadership positions, such lay principals are the heirs of a tradition of spirituality established by religious orders and it is not uncommon for them to have received their own education and professional formation in institutions provided by such orders.

The distinctiveness of Catholic schooling culture and of its educational leadership has been commented on, in a variety of contexts, by Hornsby-Smith (1978), Flynn (1985), Egan (1988), Angus (1988), O'Keeffe (1992) and McLaren (1993). In all cases these analyses have noted the tensions and dilemmas that occur when Catholic schooling values (which are themselves in a process of change) encounter situations of rapid social, cultural and ideological change. The Catholic schooling system has been historically relatively insulated in various ways from the changes in secular culture in America, Australia and Britain. Catholic schools in these societies were constructed as defensive citadels for minority communities anxious to preserve the transmission of the faith and of its spiritual and moral codes and symbols. How this relatively insulated educational tradition is responding to the challenges of individualism, competitiveness, new managerialism, market culture and the commodification of knowledge is a matter of considerable research interest. For McLaren (1993) the issues are clear:

> It is crucial that we continue to explore how Catholic schooling, by virtue of its ineffably vast and unique universe of signifying structures, plays a fundamental role in the socialization of students[4] . . . A pedagogy that is not grounded in a preferential option for the disempowered and disenfranchised – 'the wretched of the earth' – only transforms students into vessels for the preparation of new forms of fascism and a grand epic of destruction.[5]

In referring here to the preferential option for the poor, McLaren is emphasizing the historical commitment of Catholic schooling to the service of poor immigrant and ethnic minority communities and to its particular mission in inner city localities in a number of societies. However, the Catholic population in various contexts has become more prosperous and socially differentiated over time so that the mission of Catholic schooling is less focused and unitary than it once was. As Catholic schools respond to contemporary market values in education and to the issues of institutional survival which they generate, a conflict of values is likely to result. Stated in the starkest form, it could be argued that there is little market yield or return for schools which continue to operate a preferential option for the poor. In a market economy for schooling the imperatives of visible and measurable success, financial balance and good public image all combine against commitment to 'customers' who are lacking in both cultural and economic capital. How will the leaders of Catholic schools respond to this dilemma? Will headteachers and school principals work to maintain the integrity of Catholic schooling values and commitments in the new market place for education? Will they be able to balance moral purpose and institutional survival?

In examining the British Government's 1992 White Paper, *Choice and Diversity*, Richard Pring (1993) has argued that its philosophy is incompatible with the distinctive Catholic idea of the nature and purpose of schools. In particular, in placing the market and individual self-interest at the centre of educational arrangements, the reforms undermine Catholic educational values and practices which emphasize the importance of community and of concern for the common good:

> The point is that the market model of individuals all pursuing their own respective interests leads not to an improvement of the general good but only to an improvement of the positional good of some vis-à-vis other competitors and also to a deterioration of the overall situation . . .
>
> (p.8)

The thirty-four Catholic headteacher accounts which were generated during the fieldwork for this study represented the responses of fifteen headteachers in the north-east region and nineteen working in other regions. These headteachers were asked, with varying degrees of explicitness, to indicate their responses to the changing culture of English schooling in relation to the 'special mission' of the Catholic school. In order to provide the appropriate value framework in which these responses could be located, the participants were first invited to make explicit, as school leaders, their understanding of the distinctive objectives and commitments of Catholic schooling.

The special mission of the Catholic school

Writing of Catholic schooling, Bryk *et al.* (1993) have asserted that 'the underlying values of the institution – shared by its members – provide the animating force for the entire enterprise' (p.279). This formal position was endorsed by all of the Catholic headteachers but from a research viewpoint what was more significant was the way in which these Catholic school leaders articulated and defined 'the underlying values'. The predominant view was that the special mission of Catholic schools was expressed in three interrelated features, i.e., Gospel values, the teachings of Christ and the nurture of community. These features were articulated by primary and secondary school headteachers:

- We represent the only 'face of Christ' for many pupils. We are the new Church – and possibly the Hope of tomorrow . . . [against] a vast depressive value-for-money culture being focused on our pupils. Catholic schools are about evangelization and mission. They are about community . . . 'our' school is a protector of the real values. RC schools must uphold such commitment. *(Male Secondary Head) (63)*＊

- The special mission of a Catholic school is to have Christ at the centre of all we do in school and to give the pupils in our care opportunities to take part in spiritual growth . . . in a living, worshipping community . . . I firmly believe it is my prime responsibility to keep God at the heart of our school, permeating everything. *(Female Primary School Head) (64)*

- To change and challenge society's norms and ideals based on Christ's teaching and example . . . To work with Catholic parents and the parish to provide an education compatible with Christian principles. *(Female Primary School Head) (68)*

- To demonstrate that Christian values and beliefs are relevant and of use in the modern world. To help young people have a sense of justice, rights and responsibilities which transcends pragmatism . . . To help them towards a knowledge that there is a God who loves them and gives them worth. *(Male Secondary Head) (71)*

In these terms, the underlying values of Catholic schooling were defined formally by many of the headteachers in this inquiry. However, all of them recognized that this was a *discourse of mission*. The realization of this mission was not straightforward but dependent upon: their own leadership qualities; support from parents, governors and the parish; the commitments of teachers, not all of whom were Catholics; and, the response of pupils, many from nominally Catholic homes and an increasing proportion from non-Catholic backgrounds. At the same time some of the headteachers believed that wider social, cultural and ideological changes in English society were antithetical to the special mission of Catholic schools.

In addition to the prime value commitments already indicated, many of the participants saw a social ethic of 'serving others' as central to the mission of the Catholic school. In many accounts this social ethic was implicit in the strong discourse and imagery of educational community and wider community. In other accounts, it was explicitly referred to:

- To find God in all things and to serve others are at the heart of what we try to do. *(Male Secondary Head) (72)*
- To provide an overtly Christian education within an overtly Christian environment and with particular concern for the 'poor' [of all types]. *(Male Secondary Head) (76)*
- The total development of individuals to full potential – spiritual, intellectual, social, moral, physical. It is not self-fulfilment but the development and use of our gifts to serve God through others. *(Male Secondary Head) (73)*

There was a division of opinion among the Catholic headteachers participating in this study as to whether or not the realization of the special mission of the Catholic school was becoming more difficult to achieve in contemporary conditions. Some headteachers took the view that the challenges that Catholic schools faced had resulted in more explicit discussion and clarification of underlying values and mission and that the schools were stronger in their identity from these processes. An enhanced culture of partnership with governors, parents and the parish was also seen to have reinvigorated and empowered the schools in respect to their spiritual and moral purposes. A sense of confidence existed among some of these Catholic school leaders who believed that the defined spiritual and moral commitments of Catholic education were attractive to a wide constituency of parents, i.e., not only to Catholic parents. Other headteachers were less confident that their schools were actually realizing their special mission in terms of real effects upon the beliefs and practices of their pupils. They recognized considerable contemporary impediments to the successful translation of formal mission into lived practice. For these headteachers such impediments were located both within Catholic schools and in the wider society. The participants, however, whether confident or less confident on this issue, were largely in agreement that Catholic school leaders faced a whole range of moral, ethical and professional dilemmas of a kind not encountered by their predecessors. These dilemmas ranged from the specifics of individual moral behaviour to wider cultural, structural and political issues. Taken together they provided considerable challenges to Catholic headteachers as school leaders.[6]

Catholic school leadership and changing moral codes

Referring to a new culture of religious and moral teaching in Catholic schools, Bryk *et al.* (1993) have argued that:

> The spirit of Vatican II has softened Catholic claims to universal truth with a call for continuing public dialogue about how we live as

people . . . This principle implies a very different conception of religious instruction. In contrast to the pre-Vatican II emphasis on indoctrination in the 'mind of the Church', contemporary religion classes now emphasise dialogue and encounter. Drawing on systematic Christian thought, teachers encourage students to discuss and reflect on their lives . . .

(p.302)

While many liberal Catholic educators and school leaders have welcomed this greater openness about religious and moral questions, this new culture also generates its own problems and dilemmas. In a pluralist and secular society, the existence of an absolute and clear-cut religious and moral credo provides an anchor for teaching and for moral decisions. Where the credo is less absolute and clear cut, the dilemmas for teachers and parents become more challenging. This situation is no longer about the application of an absolute moral code to a given human situation. School leaders, teachers and parents have to engage in principled moral reasoning about different human dilemmas in which some degree of personal autonomy and situational adjustment is expected by the participants.

At the level of the Catholic school, leadership on these complex issues is looked to from the headteacher, among others. The headteachers in this study had encountered dilemmas of moral behaviour relating to pupils, parents and teachers. They were aware that some form of moral leadership was expected from them but they were now more uncertain than in the past about the nature and direction of that moral leadership.

Many of the dilemmas which the headteachers faced arose from a disjuncture between official Catholic moral teaching and the mores of contemporary society:

- The gap between traditional Catholic images of 'the family' and the reality of children's experience of single parents, violence, abuse, crime. *(Female Primary School Head) (66)*
- Increasingly, Catholic staff are divorced, separated or living together. As a leader of a Catholic community where do I draw the line between the church's teaching and my compassion as a Christian? *(Female Infant School Head) (75)*
- Trying to reason with 6th formers who are active sexually – trying to give any moral teaching when the answer comes back, 'My mother can have her boyfriend at home but won't let me bring mine home.' The double standards of parents who expect us to preach morality but do not give the example. *(Female Secondary Head) (80)*
- The church's teaching on sexual behaviour and values is promulgated within the school so that contraception, as discussed openly in society in general, is not really addressed. Inevitably, youngsters at the school become pregnant – and some have abortions. Others go on to produce

more children (in or out of marriage) without consideration of the long-term demands of parenting and often beyond their capacity to cope. *(Male Secondary Head) (77)*

While it was open to these Catholic headteachers to try to displace such sharp moral dilemmas to the school governors, the priest or school chaplain or to religious education teachers and pastoral care staff, their own professional conception of school leadership prevented this from being an easy way out. The community of school parents who might have been looked to as a source of support in coming to a reasoned and consensual position on these moral dilemmas was not an unproblematic ally. Parents' own double standards and disagreements about the appropriate 'Catholic' response to particular situations were complicating factors. In particular, some headteachers noted that community, partnership and dialogue approaches to trying to resolve difficult moral and behavioural situations were being threatened by parents' more assertive use of legal procedures:

- Parents' knowledge of, and awareness of, their legal rights is in conflict with the concept of working together and ideas of mutual support and reconciliation. *(Female Primary School Head) (66)*
- Parents who have become aware of legal procedures and approach solicitors without first attempting dialogue with the school – increasing in respect of racial issues and serious behavioural issues. *(Female Secondary Head) (69)*

It became apparent during the course of this study that 'community' as a central value and symbol of Catholic schooling was under attack from the ethic of possessive individualism, from market forces and from a customer culture reinforced by quick recourse to legal procedures.[7]

In his ethnographic study of the conservative Catholic school of St Ryan, McLaren (1993) noted that:

In essence, the teacher defined – in fact, *created* – a moral order. The parameters that defined Catholic behaviour were thus drawn up and the students now had a criterion with which to judge subsequent behaviour as right [Catholic] or wrong [non-Catholic].

(p.107)

These certainties were no longer available to the Catholic headteachers participating in this study. Both the spiritual and moral orders of the schools were now open to discussion and dialogue among pupils, parents and teachers. For most of the research participants, who were lay Catholics rather than priests, or religious leaders, spiritual and moral leadership in these circumstances was demanding. They were aware of their own professional needs for staff development and support in dealing with changing moral codes and such support was looked for in courses provided by the Diocese, the Catholic Education Service and professional organizations such as The Association of Catholic Schools and Colleges.[8] The headteachers also recognized the strategic importance of 'good priests' and 'good school chaplains' in assisting them to find a basis for dealing with the moral dilemmas of school leadership. In these cultural support networks, Catholic headteachers had access to resources for dealing with the challenges of moral leadership and in this sense they were in a relatively stronger position than their colleagues in state schools.

Bernstein (1990) has suggested that 'Christianity is less a religion of certainty [faith cannot be taken for granted, it must be continuously won] than a religion of ambiguity and paradox' (p. 149). The culture of traditional Catholicism had been constructed to reduce ambiguity and paradox by the strong framing of its teaching. Post-Vatican II Catholicism has resulted in greater realizations of ambiguity and paradox in moral codes. Leadership in Catholic schools has therefore involved headteachers in a continuing struggle with these ambiguities.

Catholic schools and community: admissions and exclusions

> As Christians we aim to create a loving, worshipping community where joys and sorrows, successes and set-backs will be shared . . . We aim to provide a curriculum permeated by the Gospel spirit . . .

This statement, taken from the mission document of one of the participating Catholic schools in this inquiry,[9] represents important elements of the 'inspirational ideology' of Catholic schooling. A high aspiration for the creation of a loving and worshipping community is set forth as the educational ideal to be worked for.

On trying to realize this ideal in their particular school settings, Catholic headteachers had to face many impediments and dilemmas. Among these were the difficult issues of school admissions and exclusions. Such issues were fundamental to the constitution and nature of the Catholic school as a community. Admission decisions regulated who might be allowed to join the community and to benefit from its academic, spiritual and moral culture. Exclusion involved painful decisions about temporary or permanent 'excommunication' from the school community.

Dilemmas of admission related to conflicts in wishing to be 'open' to the Catholic communities and to other faith communities in the locality without weakening the Catholic ethos of the school.[10] While this was the ostensible issue, it also encoded a whole range of other issues relating to the social class and ability characteristics of pupils and issues of race and ethnicity. In other words, a tension existed between a relatively open and comprehensive policy on school admissions and an awareness that certain amounts of selectivity by faith commitment, social class and ability level would be in the long-term interests of the school in a competitive market for schooling.

The disjunctures between the principles of formal mission statements and the realities of admissions policies were clear to a number of the participants:

- When rejecting admissions applications are we displaying Gospel values? *(Male Primary School Head) (67)*
- Coping with increasing numbers of SEN pupils in mainstream school (especially behavioural/emotional needs) creates much tension and moral dilemma. We are under-resourced and inappropriately trained and skilled to cope. The mission is under threat. *(Female Secondary Head) (82)*
- Preference in admissions at Year 7 is sometimes given to the most able rather than the most deserving, in order to maintain good results. *(Male Secondary Head) (77)*

If dilemmas of admissions exercised the moral and professional conscience of Catholic school leaders, issues of exclusion from school were even sharper. Catholic headteachers could find themselves torn between a 'prodigal son/ daughter' imperative with its implications of forgiveness and reconciliation and a responsibility to the whole community imperative with implications for firm discipline and hard decisions if necessary. The act of exclusion has powerful symbolic and cultural meanings within Catholic schooling. To the extent that such schools explicitly represented themselves as loving and caring communities permeated by Gospel values, the act of pupil exclusion, as an act of apparent rejection, was discordant with this value culture.

Bernstein (1977) and McLaren (1993) have pointed to the significance of consensual rituals of various types in constituting and renewing the moral and social orders of schools and in reaffirming the idea of the school as a community of shared values and practice. Catholic schools in general have an educational culture strongly marked by ritual and symbolic forms derived from the symbolic capital of Catholicism as a religion. Permeating such schools in the practice of the faith is a discourse and an imagery of fall and reconciliation, of sin and forgiveness, and of justice and mercy. But just as the Catholic Church has rituals of inclusion and acceptance as well as rituals of exclusion and rejection, so too do Catholic schools. The modern and enlightened practice of both the church and the schools has been to place the emphasis upon the former, but the latter still exists and may be used if the circumstances require it.

Some of the Catholic headteachers in this study were finding that the circumstances in their school and localities were requiring the serious consideration of exclusion despite the negative spiritual, moral and cultural associations which it carried. With the removal of certain forms of traditional disciplinary sanction in Catholic schools, the act of exclusion had taken on a new significance but at the same time challenged school leaders who claimed that community informed by Gospel values was a defining feature of Catholic education. Because such headteachers had a keen awareness of this dissonance and because they realized that most cases for the exclusion of individual pupils arose out of wider interpersonal and social difficulties in the life of such pupils, they encountered moral and professional dilemmas. These dilemmas were sometimes compounded by pressure brought to bear upon headteachers by groups of parents or groups of teachers who claimed that the exclusion of certain pupils was necessary for the common good of the school. In these circumstances such headteachers felt a leadership responsibility as the guardian of the school's moral and spiritual integrity in making judgments about individual deviance and the common good:

- Exclusions are a very difficult area especially for Roman Catholic schools because by exclusion we put a child out of our pastoral care and the Church itself is 'opportunity for forgiveness'. However there is also the claim of Justice and Peace for others in the community, other pupils and the staff. Staff feel that we don't support them if we hold on to their problems. *(Female Secondary Head) (82)*
- There is a danger of casting a child adrift. Those excluded often lack parental support/control in any case. *(Male Secondary Head) (78)*
- The dilemma is care for the individual pupil versus showing the pupil that there must be boundaries . . . There is the dilemma of the racial imbalance in exclusions (e.g., black pupils are 10 per cent of the school population but 20 per cent of exclusions). *(Male Secondary Head) (76)*

It was noted in Chapter 8 that even within the confidential and confessional context of the research inquiry, headteachers were silent on some issues which were known to be real problems in their schools and localities. For the sample of schools in the north-east region, drug-taking was a paradigm case of headteacher silence. The sample of Catholic schools was a national one *(albeit* small) including major metropolitan areas as well as small town and rural areas. Despite this wider social and cultural constituency it is remarkable that very few references were made to racial or ethnic issues as those which posed dilemmas for Catholic school leaders. The explicit acknowledgment of the racial imbalance in pupil exclusions in an urban Catholic school, given in account 76 above, broke this culture of silence.

The culture of silence on racial issues in the participating Catholic schools might be explained in various ways, including the stance that for Catholic headteachers there is 'no problem here'.[11] However, as O'Keeffe (1992) notes:

> The demographic changes which have taken place in British society are manifested in all aspects of British life including the pupil population of Catholic schools . . . Catholic schools face the need for development of good practice in multicultural education, the adoption of anti-racist stances and the demands of a multi-faith intake.
>
> (pp.42–3)

It seems improbable that Catholic urban schools are insulated from problems of locality racism or institutional racism and therefore another explanation for the silence on these issues might be that Catholic headteachers find it a discomforting issue. Official Catholic teaching is quite clear that racism, in all its forms, offends against Christian values, ideas of community and respect for persons, and Catholic schools have been exhorted to generate an educational ethos which resists racism. The relative silence of the Catholic school leaders on this issue does, however, suggest that there must be more than exhortation if an effective anti-racist stance is to become a priority commitment for Catholic headteachers. Mukherjee (1984) in a challenging statement to all white educators has stated that 'your racism has been your silence . . . ' (p.6).[12] To the extent that such an observation is true for this present study it would imply that Catholic school leaders (and other school leaders) must be prepared to 'give leadership' in breaking the culture of silence about racism.

Catholic schools and community: grant-maintained status

> The Education Reform Act 1988 and Education (Schools) Act 1992 have set in train a transformation of our school system. They have created more choice and wider opportunities as a springboard to higher standards. Central to this has been the development of school autonomy, both within schemes of local management and increasingly as GM (grant-maintained) schools outside local government.[13]

The official discourse of the government White Paper, *Choice and Diversity: a new framework for schools* (1992), made it quite clear to all governors, parents and headteachers that a strong political imperative existed to encourage maintained schools to opt-out of local government jurisdiction and to choose 'autonomous', grant-maintained status. To add economic incentives to these political imperatives, parents and governors were assured in 1993 that the grant-maintained school 'received extra money to reflect its particular circumstances and responsibilities compared with other schools'[14] and in 1994 large scale newspaper advertising was undertaken by the Department for Education with headings such as 'Three-quarters of grant-maintained secondary schools have employed additional teachers'[15] and 'The majority of grant-maintained schools have increased spending on books and equipment'.[16]

For Catholic school governors and parents, the financial incentives associated with the option for grant-maintained status constituted a particular form of educational temptation. As Simon and Chitty (1993) noted:

> The most decisive of financial inducements so far offered lies in capital grants (for new buildings etc.). Several years' experience have now made it abundantly clear that schools becoming GMS have been treated far more generously than county schools. In 1991 for instance GMS schools got an average four times as much in the way of capital grants than mainstream county schools . . .
>
> (p.44)

As the Catholic community in England and Wales had significant financial responsibilities for the capital costs of the Catholic schooling system, the grant-maintained option became a major focus for debate in the 1990s. For some Catholics, the grant-maintained option appeared to be a form of manna from heaven, providing extra resources to build upon and expand the excellences of Catholic education. For other Catholics, the financial inducements were the equivalent of thirty pieces of silver,[17] encouraging Catholic schools to abandon community values for individual self-interest. In other words, the Catholic educational community in England was deeply divided as to what course of action would be in the best interests of the pupils, the future of Catholic schooling and of the integrity of its special mission.

In order to give educational leadership in this contested situation, the Catholic hierarchy through the agency of the Catholic Education Service gave its formal response to the White Paper. This response took up the moral and professional dilemma of common good versus individual self-interest and implicitly criticized the GMS option for advancing the latter:

> We do not in principle oppose increased independence and self management for schools. However, the GM option is more than this. It intensifies financial and curricular inequalities between schools and creates new inequalities. It also supposes that schools derive their strength from their own autonomy, without any sense of having a wider responsibility (the common good). Moreover there is no reason to believe that the growth of the GM sector will do other than undermine the financial viability and reputation of those schools which remain outside the GM sector.[18]

The official discourse of the Catholic hierarchy, although coded in diplomatic forms, made it clear that they had grave reservations about the autonomous advantages of grant-maintained schools and perceived serious moral dilemmas arising from conflicts between Catholic community values and the values of the GMS option.[19] However, as James Arthur (1994a and 1994b) has demonstrated, Catholic parents and school governors in England were not prepared to accept the voice of the hierarchy as the definitive voice on this issue. Some parents and governors took the view that it was for Catholic parents by a democratic process of balloting to adjudicate the GMS option in particular localities and for particular schools. The ideology of parent power had produced some significant transformations within Catholic schooling culture. In a culture which had been historically characterized by deference to the teachings and advice of an ecclesiastical hierarchy on matters spiritual, moral and social, the 1980s and 1990s had produced a more assertive and differentiated Catholic community.

The headteachers of Catholic schools were caught up in this struggle between hierarchical counsel and parental assertion, and in the dilemmas arising from conflicts between a construct of special mission as community values and a construct of special mission as providing the best educational resources for Catholic pupils. The most characteristic response of the participants was a recognition of the moral and professional dilemmas posed by the GMS option without much indication of how they, as school leaders, thought that these dilemmas should be resolved:

- The option of GMS presents a major philosophical dilemma. If a school opts out, does it benefit to the detriment of others; if the school stays with the LEA are the pupils not receiving their due desserts? *(Male Secondary Head) (40)*

There were few robust condemnations of the GMS option by these Catholic headteachers and where indications of personal disapproval were given, they were signalled in a qualified and tentative way:

- I feel there is a danger of enjoying and capitalizing on the different image and possible more elite image which GMS would probably bring with it. This would be giving in to and going along with an essentially competitive rather than cooperative approach. *(Male Secondary Head) (78)*
- Grant-maintained status has my gut reaction of, no way! However, faced with the question, would I resign as head if there was a vote to opt-out, I have to admit that I would stay. *(Female Primary School Head) (64)*
- My beliefs are opposed to GM status but I realize that if and when other schools in the locality opt for GM status, I will be left with no alternative. *(Male Primary School Head) (67)*

It seems clear from these responses that many of the Catholic headteachers, while fully recognizing the moral dilemmas posed in the option for grant-maintained status, also recognized the power relations in which such a decision was structurally located. If the authority of the Catholic hierarchy had been opposed by groups of parents and governors on this issue, then the authority of the headteacher as school leader could similarly be challenged if the head was explicitly opposed to such a change. The dilemma for the headteachers was that they were aware of expectations for leadership on this major policy issue and yet they were cautious about giving such leadership if this meant expressing an authoritative professional and moral stance. Formally, this was a decision for the parents and therefore it was possible to say that constitutional leadership involved facilitating the correct procedures for parental decision making rather than articulating a personal professional preference.

In a difficult policy dilemma position such as this, Catholic intellectual and cultural capital could provide resources for headteachers in a mode of analysis popularly designated as Jesuitical reasoning. This cultural resource was used, to good effect, by one participant who not only recognized the dilemmas of the grant maintained option but wished to resolve them in terms of valid Catholic practice:

- The major criticism of GMS must be that it can only be introduced into an individual school by disadvantaging some other part of the service. This must represent a serious moral dilemma – particularly when there are significant funding and educational advantages on offer to the school that successfully obtains grant-maintained status – and those advantages must be at another school's expense . . . There is also, of course, a moral dilemma for the Bishop of a Diocese in terms of grant-maintained schools because, in Canon Law, it is incumbent upon him to provide for the Catholic community education which is at least as good, or better than, alternative education that is available in the area. A criticism of the grant-maintained principle has been (or is) that it creates a two tier system – presumably based on one tier being better than the other. If the better education is provided by grant-maintained schools and if, under Canon Law, it is incumbent upon the Bishop to provide education comparable with the best, then he would appear to be obliged to support grant-maintained schools – despite the damage that it might cause to other parts of the service. *(Male Secondary Head)* (77)

This argument, that the prime responsibility of Catholic educational leaders (bishops, school governors and headteachers) was to ensure that the best possible educational resources were available for the education of Catholic pupils, was echoed by those headteachers who saw no dilemma in the grant-maintained option. Although a minority of the participants in this inquiry, such headteachers took the view that the Catholic schooling system in England included independent and private schools and therefore, by logical extension, the creation of 'state independent schools' in the GMS option presented no major moral or professional dilemmas for Catholic educators.

Catholic educational leadership in the 1980s and 1990s in England has had to face, once again, fundamental dilemmas between notions of the common good and of autonomous advantage. These dilemmas have been crystallized particularly by the specific policy issue of grant-maintained status and by a general increased salience of market values in schooling. The Catholic community appears to have been as divided on these issues as the non-Catholic constituency. In the most recent review of these divisions, James Arthur (1994a) concludes:

> The Church's dispute with both government and some of its own members can be located in the differing interpretations of parental rights. The government's stress on parental involvement and choice gives predominance to 'the market' and emphasises individual rights over the rights of the community as a whole. By contrast, the Church's distinctive mission places greater emphasis on the right of the whole Catholic community in determining the future of Catholic schools. The Church does not recognize that the rights of parents and pupils already placed in Catholic schools can override the rights of the whole Catholic community.
>
> (p.188)

There are considerable theoretical paradoxes and contradictions which are generated by this situation. On the one hand, an essentially authoritarian and hierarchical leadership claims to speak for the good of the whole Catholic community on educational policy matters. On the other hand groups of school governors and parents claim, through the process of a ballot, to be the democratic voice of the community on a key issue such as grant-maintained status. Objections to the validity and legitimacy of both sets of claims can be made. What is missing in this contested area of educational policy is the active democratic involvement of the whole Catholic community,[20] informed by a balanced representation of the arguments. Without such involvement, Catholic headteachers as school leaders find themselves, in general, trapped in a network of contradictions.

Catholic values and market values

Bryk *et al.* (1993) have argued that Catholic schools in the USA have historically been engaged in a cultural struggle to balance market concerns (critical to survival) with Catholic values (critical to mission). In other words, Catholic schooling in America has been powerfully shaped both by the influence of market forces and by the influence of an inspirational ideology of Catholic schooling. The sensitivity of American Catholic schools to market values has been the inevitable result of receiving no financial support from public funds. American Catholic schools, unlike their English counterparts, have not been culturally and financially insulated from the market and they have had to demonstrate a responsiveness to clients in a competitive situation. However, Bryk *et al.* (1993) concluded in their major research inquiry:

> Even so, the control of Catholic school operations involves considerably more than market responsiveness to clients. Many important observations about these schools cannot be reconciled in these terms. Market forces cannot explain the broadly shared institutional purpose of advancing social equity or account for the efforts of Catholic educators to maintain inner-city schools (with large non-Catholic enrolments) while facing mounting financial woes. Likewise, market forces cannot easily explain why resources are allocated within schools in a compensatory fashion in order to provide an academic education for every student. Nor can they explain the norms of community that infuse daily life in these schools.
>
> (p.300)

The detailed research reported in *Catholic Schools and the Common Good*, while it celebrates the balance achieved between market and mission in Catholic schooling, concludes in sombre terms. Contemporary conditions in America are beginning to demonstrate that market forces, market values and the inexorable circumstances for institutional survival and financial solvency are threatening the historical mission and values of Catholic schooling.

For English Catholic schools in the maintained sector of education this encounter with market forces and market values is a much more recent phenomenon, an experience of the 1980s and 1990s. Previously insulated to a large extent from market forces by state and Diocesan funding, by the historical loyalty of local Catholic communities, and by large pupil enrolments resulting from large Catholic families, Catholic schools were the possessors of a relatively autonomous zone of influence. Within this autonomous zone, Catholic school leaders could articulate a distinctive mission and set of Catholic values independently of market culture and market values. Bernstein (1990) has pointed to the crucial importance of structural and cultural boundaries and insulations in the maintenance of a distinctive mission or voice for cultural institutions and their agents. However, such boundaries and insulations are in a constant process of change and:

> It follows that, as the strength of the insulation between categories varies, so will the categories vary in their relation to each other and so will their space, their identity and 'voice'.
>
> (p.24)

This precisely describes, in formal theoretical terms, the changing relation between Catholic schools and the market place. These two categories, previously with strong insulations from each other in English schooling have, as a result of the education reforms of the 1980s, been brought into a much closer relationship. With local management of schools, open enrolments, a more differentiated Catholic community, and a lower Catholic birth-rate, such schools have to operate in a competitive market in education. In other words, the space, identity and voice of contemporary Catholic schooling is now more directly challenged by market values then ever before in its history. In these circumstances the critical question for Catholic school leaders is, can a balance be found between Catholic values and market values, or will market forces begin to compromise the integrity of the special mission of Catholic schooling? Can Gospel values survive in the face of a more direct relationship with the market place?

McLaughlin (1994) has argued that there are important moral limits to the extension of market culture into schooling. Among these are considerations about the generation of civic virtue and about the provision of fair educational entitlements for all pupils. In short, McLaughlin is arguing that central elements of market culture are in conflict with Catholic values in education. However, a minority of the Catholic headteachers involved in this inquiry were confident that, with appropriate school leadership, the integrity of Catholic values in education could not only be maintained but extended in its range of influence:

- Heads of Catholic Aided schools might experience fewer dilemmas here than County colleagues . . . The apparent decline of moral and spiritual functions in schools might explain why Church schools are quite attractive to a wide community. *(Male Secondary Head) (40)*
- There is support from parents for a stance which is overtly counter to the prevailing market values. Parents do want good exam results but not at all costs and an education which is balanced and Christian has attractions. *(Male Secondary Head) (72)*
- The voluntary aided sector is prominent here and still under the control of the Diocese, so most headteachers in this sector are aware of a need for moral controls. *(Male Secondary Head) (37)*

This confident minority of headteachers took the view that not only were the spiritual and moral resources of Catholic schooling strong enough to resist possible corruption or pollution by market values in education but that, ironically, these moral resources were being recontextualized as potent market assets in the competitive appeal for parental choice of schools in a wider constituency. In other words, demonstrable moral leadership would ensure the success of Catholic schooling in the new conditions of the educational market place.

While not denying that Catholic schools had moral and spiritual strengths which could be viewed as assets in a competitive situation of parental choice, the majority of the headteachers had reservations and dilemmas about the impact of market values upon the special mission of their schools:

- Catholic values and market values appear to be ever in conflict – an obvious example is the funding available for religious education and for spiritual and moral experiences, e.g., residential courses. *(Female Secondary Head) (69)*
- I would rather see the school shrink in size but remain true to its ideals and faith commitment. I do not see a child as a £1000 through the school gate. *(Male Primary School Head) (42)*
- Catholic schools really must keep the explicit link between Christ and person-centred education . . . How do we square our vocational vision of pupils as persons, with the market vision of economic units? How does this affect our treatment of special educational needs? How does this affect our admissions policy? *(Female Secondary Head) (82)*

For the Catholic headteachers who took seriously those aspects of the special mission of Catholic schools which related especially to service to the poor and the disadvantaged, there were dilemmas. Such headteachers realized that a new set of strategies known as 'playing the market' was emerging among some school leaders in their localities. In essence, playing the educational market[21] involved selecting the most able pupils from the most educationally supportive homes in order to maximize the output of measurable success on league tables of performance. In this way, a public image of an 'excellent', 'successful' or 'effective' school could be constructed and the cultural capital of success once acquired could be further strengthened. Failure to engage in this market strategy could lead to a school's decline and to the creation of a 'sink school' image.[22] The moral dilemma for educational leaders (as opposed to simply managers), however, was constituted by a recognition that 'playing the market' made it much more difficult to serve the poor and the powerless. Success could be achieved with the poor and the powerless but at a greater cost in terms of time, resources, staff commitment and educational support. It was precisely the questions of 'cost' and 'cost effectiveness' which were preoccupying all headteachers in the market conditions for schooling.

Challenges for contemporary Catholic school leaders

Catholic school principals and headteachers are being exhorted to defend the historical commitment of Catholic schooling to the service of disadvantaged communities in America and in Britain. McNamee (1993), in reviewing the challenges for Catholic schools in the USA, concludes:

> What can Catholic schools do to meet current and future challenges presented by Hispanics, new immigrants and the poor? First, the Church must make a commitment to increase the access of these special populations to Catholic schools.
>
> (p.17)

As this study has shown, the growing influence of market culture upon Catholic schooling makes the realization of this educational ideal more difficult than in the past. Also, as a result of wider cultural and religious change, it is much less certain that 'the Church' as an entity can make such a commitment in an era of devolved school-site management and of increased parental choice and assertion. In a similar way, O'Keefe (1993) argues that:

> The rationale and current status of Catholic schools for the poor in the United States present a powerful challenge to the Catholic community.
>
> (p.14)

Despite an analysis which calls for a new belief in education for the common good, O'Keefe is forced to acknowledge 'the reluctance of white, middle class suburban Catholics to see themselves in communion with poor, urban minorities.'

In Britain, John Haldane (1993) has asserted that:

> Catholic education must establish a social conscience as well as one concerned with individual well-being . . . the first task for a Catholic philosophy of education is to identify the good. The social good is only a part of that but it is a sufficiently large and central part to justify making it a focus of attention . . .
>
> (pp.11–12)

At the same time as he sets this mission for Catholic education, Haldane recognizes that liberal individualism is politically and ideologically in the ascendant in Britain and elsewhere rather than forms of social communitarianism with commitments to the social good.

These are the fundamental dilemmas and challenges for Catholic school leaders in contemporary conditions. While there have always been tensions between the educational pursuit of the common good and the educational pursuit of individual interest, these tensions have at least been held in a position of ideological balance. There has been an educational settlement or compromise based upon a recognition that both common good and individual interest have their legitimate claims in educational theory and practice. The ideological changes of the 1980s and 1990s, in particular the influence of New Right agencies in both America and Britain, have broken that historical settlement by, in effect, denying the existence of constructs such as 'society' or of 'common good'.

The apparent triumph of liberal individualism as a decisive political, economic and cultural doctrine and its implementation in terms of educational policy and practice provided the majority of Catholic headteachers in this study with the greatest challenge they had yet faced in their careers as school leaders. These headteachers might look for guidance or leadership to 'the Church' on these contested matters, but in a post-modern age what 'the Church' was and what its voice on these issues might be lacked the definition and certainties of the past. There were therefore no *ex cathedra* statements or absolute moral codes which could give instant guidance on these social, cultural and professional dilemmas.[23]

Notes

* *Note* Numbers in brackets used after quotations refer to the code numbers of the headteachers' accounts.
1 Bryk *et al.* (1993, pp.301–2).
2 Bryk notes that 'the majority of principalships in Catholic high school (61 per cent in 1988) still come from religious orders, an arrangement that provides schools with some distinct benefits' (p.157).
3 *Ibid.*, p.156.
4 McLaren (1993, p.254).
5 *Ibid.*, p.290.
6 It must be noted here that the participating headteachers represented a very limited sample of the Catholic school system in England and Wales which consists of 1886 primary schools and 407 secondary schools. Catholic provision is approximately 10 per cent of the public education service (Catholic Education Service data).
7 However, it is important not to romanticize concepts of community in schooling. Community can be appropriated for oppressive and unjust processes and recourse to legal and bureaucratic procedures may be necessary in the interests of justice for individuals.
8 It can be noted that all of these agencies are giving much more attention in the 1990s to courses on school leadership rather than simply school management and that such courses are addressing spiritual, moral and value issues in Catholic schooling.
9 See Headteacher, Account 39.
10 This major dilemma permeated many of the headteacher accounts. Demographic changes were affecting Catholic schools and school closures were becoming a feature of the system (356 schools closed between 1978 and 1991). The percentage of Catholic teachers in Catholic secondary schools has fallen from 66 per cent in 1978 to 58 per cent in 1991. Non-Catholic pupils have increased from 3 per cent of the school population to 14 per cent in 1991 (Catholic Education Service data).
11 The 'no problem here' response is characteristically given in schools and localities which have no significant ethnic diversity or in situations where it is claimed that racism may feature in the community but not in the school.

12 Mukherjee, quoted in Troyna (1993, p.92).
13 White Paper, 1992, p.19, para. 3.1.
14 *Grant Maintained Schools: Questions Parents Ask,* DFE booklet, November 1993, p.5.
15 *The Guardian,* 4 February 1994.
16 *The Times Educational Supplement,* 4 February 1994.
17 This classic phrase was used by some headteachers during the course of this inquiry.
18 Catholic Education Service: *A Response to the White Paper,* 24 September 1992, p.7.
19 The Catholic response can be compared with the much stronger criticism of grant-maintained policy emanating from the Muslim community in Britain. The *Times Educational Supplement* for 1 July 1994 carried a front page report under the heading 'Muslims condemn "unfair" GM Policy'. Leading Muslim educators argued that 'it's not acceptable and it's not Islamic to disadvantage the majority for the benefit of the privileged minority'.
20 Despite a Vatican II discourse of involvement of the 'whole people of God' in the life of the Church, active democratic involvement is radically at odds with the hierarchical and authoritarian traditions of Catholicism.
21 These strategies are indicated by a growing discourse in education using constructs such as 'the major players' or 'the stakeholders'.
22 As one head noted, 'once a school is on a downward spiral it is going to be much more difficult than in the past to build it up'. His argument was that the removal of LEA support and greater dependence on market forces would cause this difficulty. See account (10).
23 The categorical teaching of Catholicism on the regulation of sexual behaviour can be contrasted with a much greater degree of ambiguity on social, economic and political matters.

Bibliography

Angus, L.B. (1988) *Continuity and Change in Catholic Schooling,* London, Falmer Press.

Arthur, J. (1994a) 'Catholic responses to the 1988 Education Reform Act: problems of authority and ethos', in L. Francis and D.W. Lankshear (Eds) *Christian Perspectives on Church Schools,* Leominster, Fowler Wright Books.

Arthur, J. (1994b) 'Parental involvement in Catholic schools: A case of increasing conflict', *British Journal of Educational Studies,* XXXXII, 2, June, pp. 179–90.

Bernstein, B. (1977) 'Aspects of the relations between education and production', in B. Bernstein *Class, Codes and Control: Vol.3. Towards a Theory of Educational Transmissions* (2nd edn), London, Routledge.

Bernstein, B. (1990) *The Structuring of Pedagogic Discourse: Vol. IV. Class, Codes and Control,* London, Routledge.

Bryk, A., Lee, V. and Holland, P. (1993) *Catholic Schools and the Common Good,* Cambridge, Mass., Harvard University Press.

Department for Education (1992) *Choice and Diversity: A New Framework for Schools* (July 1992), Cm.2021. London, HMSO.

Egan, J. (1988) *Opting Out: Catholic Schools Today,* Leominster, Fowler Wright Books.

Flynn, M. (1985) *The Effectiveness of Catholic Schools,* Homebush, St Paul Publications.

Haldane, J. (1993) 'A prolegomenon to an unwritten philosophy of education: Catholic social teaching and the common good', paper presented to the 'Contemporary Catholic School and the Common Good' Conference, St Edmund's College, Cambridge, July 1993.

Hornsby-Smith, M. (1978) *Catholic Education: The Unobtrusive Partner*, London, Sheed and Ward.

McLaren, P. (1993) *Schooling as a Ritual Performance: Towards a Political Economy of Educational Symbols and Gestures*, London, Routledge.

McLaughlin, T. (1994) 'Politics, markets and schools: The central issues', in D. Bridges and T. McLaughlin (Eds) *Education and the Market Place*, London, Falmer Press.

McNamee, C. (1993) 'Catholic Schools in the US: Perspectives and Developments', paper presented to the 'Contemporary Catholic School and the Common Good' Conference, St Edmund's College, Cambridge, July 1993.

Mukherjee, T. (1984) 'I'm not blaming you – an antiracist analysis', *Multicultural Teaching*, 2, pp.5–8.

O'Keefe, J. (1993) 'Catholic schools for the poor: rationale and current status', paper presented to the 'Contemporary Catholic School and the Common Good' Conference, St Edmund's College, Cambridge, July 1993. (Boston, Boston College.)

O'Keeffe, B. (1992) 'Catholic schools in an open society: The English challenge', in V.A. McClelland (Ed.) *The Catholic School and the European Context*, Hull, University of Hull.

Pring, R. (1993) 'Markets, education and Catholic schools', paper presented to the 'Contemporary Catholic School and the Common Good' Conference, Cambridge, July 1993. (Oxford, Department of Educational Studies.)

Simon, B. and Chitty, C. (1993) *SOS: Save Our Schools*, London, Lawrence and Wishart.

Troyna, B. (1993) *Racism and Education*, Buckingham, Open University Press.

Chapter 10

Realizing the mission

Catholic approaches to school effectiveness

School Effectiveness for Whom? 1998, (Eds). R. Slee, G. Weiner,
S. Tomlinson, 117–127, Falmer.

The field of school effectiveness research (SER) is currently marked by a lively debate and by conflicting evaluations of its own significance and effectiveness. For Reynolds (1995, p. 53) this 'infant discipline' has already achieved many positive results in that:

> . . . it has helped to combat pessimism about the importance of the school system, to build professional self esteem and to provide a knowledge base that can act as a foundation for the development of improved practice . . .

Reynolds emphasizes the important role which SER has played in overcoming earlier notions of structural and cultural determinism (the school as relatively ineffective against existing social divisions) and against feelings of powerlessness for educational practitioners which could arise from such an analysis. In short, against pessimistic forms of sociological pre-destination along the lines of 'abandon hope, all you who work in capitalist school systems', SER has offered a measure of hope and a form of empowerment for education professionals.

For Hamilton (1996, pp. 54–6), however, school effectiveness research is not an infant discipline but 'an international industry' engaged in 'peddling feel-good fictions' among educators by generating research and writing which is 'technically and morally problematic'. The problematic nature of its research and writing, according to Hamilton, is that it oversimplifies both the concept of 'effectiveness' and the comprehensive range of methodological approaches needed to appreciate it. Above all, it offers to New Right ideologues in education policy an apparently scientific legitimation for placing *all* of the blame for educational underachievement upon 'failing' schools and 'incompetent' teachers, while 'winning' schools and 'successful' teachers can celebrate the virtues of self-improvement. Such debates, as that represented here, are important for a field of research which has risen to prominence in only the last 20 years. For all his positive credo in praise of school effectiveness research, Reynolds (1995, pp. 54–9) does recognize that it is characterized by: 'many controversies concerning epistemological issues, methodological concerns and more theoretical matters'. He also recognizes that: 'we have been instrumental in creating a quite widespread popular view that schools do not just make *a* difference but that they make *all* the difference'. The value of these exchanges is that they draw the attention of all those working in the field of SER to some of its vulnerabilities as well as to some of its strengths.

This chapter is intended as a contribution to the debate. It will argue that despite the progressive origins of school effectiveness research in attempts to improve the schooling of the urban poor[1] and despite some positive and impressive achievement in the last 20 years (see Sammons, Hillman and Mortimore, 1995), the field remains vulnerable to the twin dangers of technical reductionism on the one hand and of ideological appropriation on the other. Most attention will be given to an examination of technical reductionism because arguments about ideological appropriation of research results are well known in the social sciences.

Technical reductionism in school effectiveness research

As I have argued elsewhere, research in the social sciences runs the constant risk of becoming constituted as policy science rather than as policy scholarship (Grace, 1995). Policy science abstracts a given social phenomenon from its historical, cultural, ideological, socio-economic and political relations and then subjects it to close, technical analysis which has immediate policy consequences. Policy scholarship, on the other hand, recognizes that the social entity under investigation can only be understood and evaluated in the complexity of those social relations. Policy science marginalizes history, culture and economic and political relations – they are reduced to 'externalities'. Policy scholarship recognizes that a social institution, for instance, is crucially constituted by its history, its culture and its socio-political relations and that no in-depth or valid assessment of it can take place in abstraction from what are in fact 'centralities' for social science research. Part of current controversies about SER is related to a belief among its critics that it has not given sufficient attention to this distinction in research paradigms and that it has become largely the prisoner of policy science and of its conceptual and methodological limitations in technical reductionism.

A scrutiny of the available literature of SER (see Scheerens, 1992; Reynolds and Cuttance, 1992; and Creemers, 1994; among other studies) shows that technical reductionism in this sector of educational inquiry has two dimensions which may be called *Contextual reductionism* and *Mission reductionism*. Contextual reductionism involves a process of abstracting the scholarly and measurable performance indicators of a school from its own history and cultural formation, from its social and economic community setting and from its relation with the wider society.[2] Mission reductionism involves abstracting scholarly performance indicators per se from the whole integrated matrix of school outcomes and effects which constitute the educational mission of the school such that measures of academic performance are taken to be the 'real' measures of what a school is about.

There are many reasons why these forms of reductionism have become prevalent in school effectiveness research. Insofar as SER has become legitimated and funded by governments and state agencies looking for quick fire solutions and bullet point answers to complex educational situations, research contracts and publication prescriptions may circumscribe the intellectual freedom and autonomy of scholars. Governments and state agencies in general are not prepared to pay for research which shows that their own social and economic policies have contributed significantly to crises in the schools. They would rather pay for research which shows that some schools have been able to overcome these created impediments more successfully and 'effectively' than other schools. Thus the ideological and political focus is shifted from analysis of the policies themselves to analysis of the differential ability of schools to cope with these policies.

This form of analytical reductionism arises wherever research is closely tied to policy prescription, wherever a 'bidding culture' for government controlled research funds is dominant and wherever relatively autonomous sources of research money for 'fundamental' research are limited. School effectiveness is one of a number of fields which now have to operate largely under these constraints.

Methodological issues are also implicated in what I have called mission reductionism. In an early critique of the Effective Schools Movement (ESM), Lauder and Khan (1988, p. 53) argued that:

> Part of the responsibility . . . must rest with the quantitative research methodology employed by the ESM. For example, outcome measures like exam results or rates of truancy lend themselves to quantification and it may be for this reason that the ESM has placed such a heavy emphasis on exam results. In contrast, other educational aims and processes whose outcomes may be no less important . . . are ignored.'[3]

The reduction of a school's educational mission to an assessment of its academic results and of its truancy and delinquent rates seemed not unreasonable in a research culture in which scientific objectivity was equated with certain kinds of measurement and in which assertions were made that this was the sort of information that most parents and citizens wanted to know. These two assumptions have shaped much of the work in school effectiveness research in the past. However, both of these assumptions are now subject to critical scrutiny. As qualitative inquiry matures and sophisticates itself as a research approach and with a growing recognition that a wider range of school outcomes must be evaluated, a more comprehensive and catholic paradigm for school effectiveness research can be established. Objectivity does not have to be the prisoner of a particular methodological approach.

The second assumption, that parents and citizens are concerned with school effectiveness only as measured by academic results, has been shown to be false by the research of Gewirtz, Ball and Bowe (1995) and by that of Vincent (1996). Parents show more interest in the social and affective outcomes of schooling, in its human and community faces, than many state agencies allow for. There is now an encouraging recognition in SER that mission reductionism must be overcome. Sammons, Hillman and Mortimore (1995, p. 4) in their review of research conclude that: 'studies which focus on only one or two outcomes may give only a partial picture of effectiveness' and they call for research which focuses on 'a broad range reflecting the aims of schooling'. Reynolds (1995, p. 65) concludes that: 'we are not at the moment tapping the school variables (climate? emotional tone? relationships?) necessary' and the implications here are that school effectiveness research must look more closely at the *cultural* features of schooling, e.g. the ethos and values climate of a school, the quality of interpersonal relations within it, etc.

As other chapters in this book address in detail issues to do with contextual reductionism in SER, the remainder of this chapter will suggest some approaches to transcending mission reductionism in future research.

A Catholic approach to school effectiveness research

The notion of a catholic approach to school effectiveness is used here in two senses. In the first place an argument is made that school effectiveness literature and research needs to be more catholic in the sense of being more comprehensive, universal and inclusive in the range of school outcomes which are taken seriously. While there can be general agreement with statements, such as that of Sammons, Hillman and Mortimore (1995, p. 3), that 'an effective school adds extra value to its students' outcomes in comparison with other schools serving similar intakes', a catholic approach to SER requires an elaboration of what these outcomes might be and of how 'extra value' assessment or appreciation[4] can be attempted in relation to those outcomes which do not have obvious performance indicators. Similarly, when Reynolds and Creemers (1990, p. 1) assert that: 'schools matter . . . schools do have major effects upon children's development . . . schools do make a difference', a catholic approach has to ask (in detail), 'difference to what?'

The difficult question which these considerations generate is how can school effectiveness research concentrate more systematically and seriously upon 'a broad range (of outcomes) reflecting the aims of schooling'?[5] The rhetoric of catholic assessment is relatively easy, its practical applications in research are much more challenging. One way forward would be to take school mission statements as the fundamental basis for school effectiveness research in the future.

Mission statements have many catholic virtues. They constitute a principled and comprehensive articulation of what a school claims to be its distinctive educational, social and moral purposes. They characteristically, therefore, specify a range of desired outcomes which are often the result of consultation exercises involving teachers, the pupils, parents and governors and sometimes members of the wider community. They are published to the community as a statement saying 'this is what this school is about' and (implicitly) saying 'this is the basis upon which you can judge us'. A research paradigm based upon school mission statements would therefore have the virtue of working with school and community generated 'desired outcomes agendas' rather than imposing only those generated by state agencies or by the formal research community. This could be the beginning, for English schooling culture at least, of a more democratic, more flexible, more sensitive and more humane practice of school effectiveness research. School effectiveness research could then become a report to the community on 'realizing the mission' and upon what aspects of the mission were being realized and what aspects were being impeded and why. This would be a catholic approach to SER in the sense of being inclusive of the range of school outcomes and inclusive of both school and community members in the processes of assessment and evaluation.

Catholic schooling culture as a research field

It is perhaps hardly surprising that the mission statements of Catholic schools provide a particularly rich source of material relevant to this argument, given that the Catholic school system has long claimed to have a distinctive educational culture and mission. There can be some value therefore in looking at a Catholic approach, in the second sense, i.e. that which is represented in the mission statements of the Catholic system and of Catholic primary and secondary schools.

The aspirations of Catholic education are constituted at two levels, i.e. that of formal ecclesiastical authority and that of individual school communities. At the formal level, the Sacred Congregation for Catholic Education, in publications such as *The Catholic School* (1988), defines 'the Catholic school's fundamental reasons for existing' (p. 8). These are stated at a high level of generality but nevertheless set the broad parameters for Catholic educational activity in the following way:

- 'Catholic schools [should] . . . provide a service which is truly civic and apostolic' (p. 9);
- 'This is the basis of a Catholic school's educational work. Education is not given for the purpose of gaining power but as an aid towards a fuller understanding of and communion with man (sic), events and things.

Knowledge is not to be considered as a means of material prosperity and success but as a call to serve and be responsible for others' (p. 43);

- 'First and foremost the Church offers its educational service to "the poor or those who are deprived of family help and affection or those who are far from the faith"' (p. 45).

Such statements provide a broad and universal rationale for the Catholic educational system. Within these guidelines, individual Catholic primary and secondary schools are expected to formulate their own mission statements which relate these general principles to the particular circumstances of their own locations and socio-cultural settings.

As part of a larger study of Catholic schools in deprived urban areas, I have recently undertaken an analysis of the mission statements of 25 secondary schools located in various parts of England.[6] The purpose of this analysis was to clarify the range of educational, spiritual, social and moral outcomes which such schools sought to achieve and how these related to the needs and challenges of their specific urban locations. I believe that the study of Catholic schools has much to offer to the general field of SER, in part because these schools characteristically link academic outcomes with wider spiritual, moral, personal, social and community outcomes, and their notions of individual good with that of common good.[7] This is not to imply that County schools and those of other religious faith communities are less significant for SER – it is simply to assert that strong claims for Catholic school distinctiveness have resulted in rich and comprehensive mission statements as a basic data source for SER.

The expectation that all schools will have produced formal mission statements has been important for Catholic schools in urban poverty areas in a number of ways. It has stimulated new thinking about the pastoral and educational mission of Catholic schools in situations of high educational, social and economic challenge. It has encouraged, in many cases, dialogue and participation involving school governors, teachers, parents, community members and pupils in the process of formulating an agreed statement of aims. It has caused people to think about the distinctiveness of the Catholic educational mission in changing circumstances (see McLaughlin, O'Keeffe and O'Keefe, 1996). While the emphasis of each mission statement reflected the 'desired outcomes agenda' of each specific educational community, it was possible to discern across the 25 statements a fundamental set of aspirations which extended well beyond academic performance indicators alone. The first of these replicated the findings of Bryk, Lee and Holland (1993) in their major study of Catholic schooling in the USA, that Catholic schools emphasize 'the primacy of the spiritual and moral life as realised in Catholic religious culture' (p. 301). Effectiveness for Catholic schools has to be about:

- [developing] 'love for and commitment to Jesus Christ, the Catholic Church and the Gospel message of love, peace, truth and justice';[8]

- 'establishing a community based on love and care for the individual in which the Faith of the Church gives ultimate meaning to all the community's activities';
- 'developing the spiritual awareness of pupils';
- 'promoting the spiritual growth of all members of our community through prayer, the celebration of the Mass and the work of the Chaplaincy'.

These statements are important in placing spiritual and moral awareness on the 'desired outcomes agenda'. While there are those who would not wish to accept the particular Catholic expression of these ends as desirable, it seems likely that a large constituency would endorse the desirability of spiritual and moral awareness and sensitivity, broadly conceived, as an aim for schooling. School effectiveness research must then face the challenge of how such enhancement can be sensitively appreciated and reported.[9] This will not be easy because such appreciation will require some *extended* fieldwork participation in the life and culture of the school, in observations of classrooms and teacher–pupil interactions, discussions with pupils on spiritual and moral issues and some involvement with the wider community.

A second emphasis in the mission statements of the schools was focused upon 'the dignity of the person'. This fundamental aim can be interpreted in a variety of ways. The dignity of a person is enhanced by the acquisition of knowledge and skills and by the fulfilment of intellectual, physical, artistic and creative potential.[10] All objectives relating to academic and personal achievement and attainment can be subsumed within this aim, which has the advantage also of relating achievement measures to issues to do with equal educational opportunities, to multicultural and anti-racist commitments, and to statements about respect for persons regardless of their social class, race, gender or ability status. In other words, 'dignity of the person', as an aim for schooling, includes measures of academic and personal achievement but places these in a more complex and sensitive matrix of respect and justice for all school members, i.e. a learning culture which is also a humane culture. From this perspective, effectiveness for Catholic schools has to be about:

- [creating] 'a place where children and staff feel valued – where children and staff are given individual support – where there is respect and trust for all';
- 'in addition to national curriculum and academic demands, [setting] out to create a happy atmosphere in which the dignity and worth of everyone is recognised, developed and safeguarded';
- 'encouraging, promoting, recognising and celebrating all aspects of achievement within the school';

- [creating] 'an environment which enables and encourages all members of the community to reach out for excellence in every sphere of academic, pastoral, social, moral, physical and spiritual activity';
- 'the distinctive Catholic ethos of our school which is distinguished by the quality of care extended to all its members regardless of race, gender, background or ability'.

(CES, 1997, pp. 35–56)

Such statements are important because they encourage school effectiveness researchers to go beyond one dimensional 'value added' measures of pupil academic achievements, important though these are, to the more complex assessment of the culture of learning and the culture of pupil and teacher respect and dignity within each school.[11]

A third emphasis in the mission statements of the Catholic schools related to 'the importance of community' (Ibid). Almost every school claimed that the generation of community values, community support, community spirit and community commitment was an important educational aim. As statements relating to 'community' were also integral to spiritual and moral aims and to 'dignity of the person' aims, it can be said that Catholic schools have very strong aspirations for the educational realization of social bonding and solidarity and therefore that any evaluation of their effectiveness would have to engage seriously with these issues. These aspirations were expressed as:

- 'To create a multicultural community in which all the talents of both students and staff are recognized, valued and encouraged'; (Ibid)
- 'access for parents to counselling, advice and school facilities – the community is recognized as the world of the pupil, links are encouraged with the local community';
- 'the school aims to foster an active partnership between home, parishes and school which enhances our involvement in the wider community';
- 'to develop in members of the school community that sense of personal responsibility . . . which is essential as a preparation for active citizenship';
- 'We are proud of our reputation as a community caring for all children in a warm and friendly manner and seeking out ways of supporting the most vulnerable at any time. This will remain at the heart of our mission'.

The analysis of the nature of community has long been a challenge to the social sciences. The analysis of 'community effectiveness' therefore presents SER with many difficulties which it is tempting to ignore in favour of more individualistic and measurable performance indicators. However, to do so is to marginalize what many schools proclaim to be a major educational objective.

The fourth and final emphasis in the mission statements was closely related to the earlier aspirations of Catholic schooling but distinct from them in the discourse and imagery utilized. Some schools moved beyond a general discourse of 'community' to employ a more specific focus upon social justice, the common good[12] and notions of service. This was expressed as:

- 'To implant and foster in the pupils' minds an awareness of their duty to carry on their economic and social activities in a Christian manner';
- 'We recognise that our school has a special responsibility for meeting the needs of the poor . . . we offer our Catholic community as a radical alternative to a materialistic society';
- 'Our mission is to contribute . . . to the development of Christian women who are confident, can think for themselves, who understand the concepts of equality and justice and who can play a full and responsible part in a changing and multicultural society';
- 'The school aims to nurture an awareness of, and a response to, our brothers and sisters throughout the world'[13]

In general, it can be said that the aspirations of these Catholic school mission statements provided an integrated matrix of desired school outcomes and of pupil outcomes. Catholic schooling culture is, by its comprehensive and inclusive nature, resistant to policy science atomization and commodification. It continues to assert the interrelatedness of educational aims. This is powerfully expressed by one headteacher in another context as:

> The total development of individuals to full potential – spiritual, intellectual, social, moral, and physical. It is *not* self-fulfilment but the development and use of our gifts to serve God through others.

> (Grace, 1995, p. 163)

While we cannot expect SER to bring God into the equation, we can expect that future research will be more sensitive to the complex and interrelated nature of school outcomes and therefore more innovative in its conceptual analysis and in its methodological approaches.[14] **This could be achieved by extending the important concept of 'value-added' research to include the equally important concept of 'values-added' inquiry[15] – a more catholic paradigm.**

Acknowledgment

I would like to thank Harvey Goldstein, Peter Mortimore, Kate Myers, Louise Stoll and Paddy Walsh for comments received on the draft version. They are not responsible for the final text but where I have taken their advice it has improved the analysis.

Notes

1 For a review of early school effectiveness studies in the USA, see Firestone (1991). Studies by Edmonds (1979) and Goodlad et al. (1979) are foundation texts in the field.

2 This tendency was classically referred to by C. Wright Mills (1973) as 'abstracted empiricism'. Angus, reviewing the field, (1993) notes:

> The school, the process of schooling, the culture of pupils, the nature of community, the society, the economy, are not seen in relation to each other. It is particular school practices and their direct connection with particular outcomes which is important. All else is 'simply' context and needs to be statistically controlled.
>
> (p. 341)

3 Harvey Goldstein and Kate Myers (1996, p. 15) have called for the use of a principle of multiple indicators in school effectiveness research: 'Multiple indicators should be presented rather than a single or summary one. This is intended to avoid over-concentration on one aspect of performance.' Goldstein also takes the view that a wide range of school outcomes are *potentially* quantifiable.

4 In less tangible categories of school and pupil outcomes, notions of critical appreciation or illuminative evaluation seem more appropriate than those of assessment and measurement. The use of triangulation of accounts may be helpful. For an example, see Grace, Bell and Browne (1996).

5 It should be noted that some studies have attempted this, e.g. Mortimore et al. (1988). *School Matters* included in its outcome measures pupils' attitudes to schooling and issues to do with pupils' self-concept. In other words, serious attention was given to some of the social outcomes of schooling.

6 These schools are located in major urban centres such as London, Birmingham, Manchester, Liverpool and in smaller urban centres in Lancashire, Merseyside and Yorkshire.

7 For a discussion of the relation of Catholic schools to notions of the common good (in the USA) see Bryk et al. (1993).

8 All quotations are taken from the mission statements of the participating schools.

9 At present, the spiritual and moral culture of schools is commented on in reports of the Office for Standards in Education (OFSTED) and, additionally for Catholic schools, in Section 13 Reports by Diocesan inspectors. However, more needs to be known about the evidential basis of these reports and about the methodologies used in the collection of evidence.

10 There is evidence that Catholic schools are effective, in the main, in providing good standards of academic education. See Bryk et al. (1993) for the USA and CES (1995) for England and Wales.

11 Much more use could be made of accounts gathered from pupils and teachers about their experiences of the 'effectiveness' of cultures of learning and of personal respect in schools. Pupils, in particular, are well placed to comment upon the extent to which mission statement commitments are actually realized in practice.

12 A recent statement from the Catholic Bishops' Conference for England and Wales (1996) has given salience to discussions about the common good and its implications for the work of Catholic institutions.

13 This school (as with many other Catholic schools) had a serious and sustained commitment to fund-raising for the relief of poverty and famine in Africa and elsewhere. This was related to an educational programme which tried to clarify

the causes of poverty and famine arising from colonialism and the current operation of the global economy. This raises the question, 'to what extent is world citizenship awareness a feature of the "effective" school?'

14 For a recent powerful argument in support of this view, see 'Evaluate what you value', Chapter 11 in Stoll and Fink (1996).

15 Such research would attempt to evaluate the relative effectiveness of a school's ethos and culture in contributing towards the social, moral and spiritual development of young people. This research would require an initial assessment and a final assessment. As Goldstein has pointed out (private communication, 1997) 'to judge whether a school has promoted "community values" you need to know where the students started from'.

References

Angus, L. (1993) 'The sociology of school effectiveness', *British Journal of Sociology of Education*, **14**, 3, pp. 333–45.

Bryk, A., Lee, V. and Holland, P. (1993) *Catholic Schools and the Common Good*, Cambridge, Mass.: Harvard University Press.

Catholic Bishops' Conference (1996) *The Common Good and the Catholic Church's Social Teaching*, Manchester: Gabriel Communications.

Catholic Education Service (1995) *Quality of Education in Catholic Secondary Schools*, London: CES.

Catholic Education Service (1997) *A Struggle for Excellence: Catholic Secondary Schools in Urban Poverty*, London: CES.

Creemers, B. (1994) 'The history, value and purpose of school effectiveness studies', in Reynolds, D., Creemers, B., Stringfield, S., Teddlie, C., Schaffer, E. and Nesselrodt, P. (eds) *Advances in School Effectiveness Research and Practice*, Oxford: Pergamon.

Edmonds, R. (1979) 'Effective schools for the urban poor', *Educational Leadership*, **37**, 1, pp. 15–27.

Firestone, W. (1991) Chapter 1 (Education, researchers & the effective schools movement) in Bliss, J. et al. (eds) *Rethinking Effective Schools*, New Jersey: Prentice Hall.

Gewirtz, S., Ball, S. and Bowe, R. (1995) *Markets, Choice and Equity in Education*, Buckingham: Open University Press.

Goldstein, H. and Myers, K. (1996) 'Towards a code of ethics for performance indicators', *British Educational Research Association Newsletter*, No. 57.

Goodlad, J., Sirotnik, K.A. and Overman, B.C. (1979) *A Study of Schooling*, Indiana: Phi Delta Kappa.

Grace, G. (1995) *School Leadership: Beyond Education Management: An Essay in Policy Scholarship*, London: Falmer Press.

Grace, G., Bell, D. and Browne, B. (1996) 'St Michael's Roman Catholic Comprehensive School', in National Commission on Education (eds) *Success Against the Odds: Effective Schools in Disadvantaged Areas*, London: Routledge.

Hamilton, D. (1996) 'Peddling feel-good fictions', *Forum*, **38**, 2, pp. 54–6.

Lauder, H. and Khan, G. (1988) 'Democracy and the effective schools movement', *International Journal of Qualitative Studies in Education*, **1**, pp. 51–68.

McLaughlin, T., O'Keeffe, B. and O'Keefe, J. (eds) (1996) *The Contemporary Catholic School: Context, Identity and Diversity*, London: Falmer Press.

Mortimore, P., Sammons, P., Stoll, L., Lewis, D. and Ecob, R. (1988) *School Matters: The Junior Years,* Wells: Open Books.

National Commission on Education (1996) *Success Against the Odds: Effective Schools in Disadvantaged Areas,* London: Routledge.

Reynolds, D. (ed.) (1995) 'School effectiveness', *Evaluation and Research in Education,* **9,** 2, Special Issue.

Reynolds, D. and Creemers, B. (1990) 'School effectiveness and school improvement: A mission statement', *School Effectiveness and School Improvement,* **1,** 1, pp. 1–3.

Reynolds, D. and Cuttance, P. (eds) (1992) *School Effectiveness Research, Policy and Practice,* London: Cassell.

Sacred Congregation for Catholic Education (1988 version) *The Catholic School,* Homebush NSW: St Paul's Publications.

Sammons, P., Hillman, J. and Mortimore, P. (1995) *Key Characteristics of Effective Schools: A Review of School Effectiveness Research,* London: Institute of Education.

Scheerens, J. (1992) *Effective Schooling: Research, Theory and Practice,* London: Cassell.

Stoll, L. and Fink, D. (1996) *Changing Our Schools: Linking School Effectiveness and School Improvement,* Buckingham: Open University Press.

Vincent, C. (1996) *Parents and Teachers: Power and Participation,* London: Falmer Press.

Wright Mills, C. (1973) *The Sociological Imagination,* Harmondsworth: Penguin Books.

Chapter 11

Faith school leadership

A neglected sector of in-service education in the United Kingdom

Professional Development in Education, 2009, 35(3), 485–494.

This paper argues that the professional development and in-service educational needs of faith school leaders have been neglected by mainstream providers of continuing professional development programmes in the United Kingdom. Given the substantial presence of Church of England and Roman Catholic schools and colleges in the UK system and current plans for an increased number of Muslim, Jewish and Christian Evangelical schools, some positive response is necessary. The distinctive needs of faith school leaders (Christian, Muslim and Jewish) require the provision of continuing professional development and in-service courses that look seriously at the specific challenges of faith school leadership in contemporary conditions.

Introduction

Despite the considerable growth of school leadership research, publication, public discussion and course provision in the past three decades, the professional and in-service needs of faith school leaders have been almost entirely neglected. Just as the feminist critics of school leadership studies and practice, such as Jill Blackmore (1989), Jenny Ozga (1993) and Valerie Hall (1994), were able to argue that school leadership studies and continuing professional development (CPD) programmes were blind to significant gender differences, so it is possible to argue that such studies and programmes are still blind to religious differences in the philosophies, practices and challenges of faith school leadership.

Given the substantial presence of Church of England and Roman Catholic schools in the United Kingdom[1] and the fact that other faith communities representing the Jewish, Islamic, Hindu and Sikh faiths have current plans for the expansion of their schools, this neglect is remarkable. It is all the more surprising when the scale of faith-based school provision internationally is examined, as will become apparent in the forthcoming *International Handbook of Catholic Education*, *International Handbook of Jewish Education* and *International Handbook of Muslim Education*.[2] CPD for faith school leaders is an international need and not simply a UK need.

The Catholic school system – as the largest faith-based system in the world, including as it does about 200,000 Catholic schools serving over 50 million students (Miller, 2007) – seems to justify more systematic attention than it has so far received, either from educational researchers or from school leadership writers and in-service course providers The school leaders of this system and the school leaders of Anglican, Christian Evangelical, Jewish, Muslim, Hindu and Sikh schools are the forgotten constituency of both academic researchers and of programme providers in education.

Why has this neglect occurred? Michael Paul Gallagher (1997) has argued that contemporary intellectual culture in the West is characterised by 'secular marginalisation'. This phenomenon has replaced eighteenth-century and nineteenth-century polemics against religion by a cultural form of marginalisation and silence. The outcome is that 'especially in the academic and media worlds, a secular culture reigns with the result that religion is subtly ignored as unimportant' (Gallagher, 1997, p. 23).

The validity of this observation for school leadership studies and continuing professional course provision is immediately obvious. Mainstream school leadership writing and CPD programme design is undertaken within a limited secular paradigm. The assumptions of the field are relatively blind to the various cultural differences of race, class, gender and religion that permeate school leadership contexts, concepts and professional practice. The distinctive educational cultures of faith schools and the distinctive challenges that their leaders face have been sidelined within this secular worldview.

With the growing significance of faith-based schooling in the United Kingdom and internationally, this situation obviously cannot continue. The needs of faith school leaders from both a research perspective and a professional development perspective have to be met more adequately in the future.[3]

A further limitation of the field has been the widespread assumption that the specific needs of faith school leaders will be met and should be met entirely within the resources of their own faith communities. This assumption is mistaken on a number of grounds. In the first place it is premised on the view that religion in the modern age is a private matter and that it should be attended to in private contexts. This denies religious perspectives and religious discourse their legitimate place in the public settings of higher education and educational agency programmes. Secondly, it overestimates the resources of the various faith communities in being able to provide academically valid and professionally well-supported programmes of research, study and development for their school leaders. Thirdly, it results in a situation where research and professional development work is undertaken largely by members of the faith community. Thus Catholics tend to study Catholic school leadership, Jews study Jewish school leadership, Muslims study Muslim school leadership, and so on. As Geoffrey Walford (2003) has argued, it is necessary in the interests of academic and professional objectivity that such research and course provision should also be undertaken by those outside a particular faith community.

The time has surely come when universities, colleges, professional development agencies and bodies such as the National College for School Leadership (NCSL) should recognise the needs of the faith schools sector and, in particular, the needs of its school leaders.[4] These needs include involvement in and access to research investigations of their schools and involvement in and access to programmes of professional development for leaders and teachers that take faith seriously in its implications for school culture, organisation and learning.[5] I outline below some possible areas and issues for future development.

The future: research and in-service agendas for faith-based school leadership

Working on the assumption that the best work in school leadership and in-service provision is always research based or evidence based, there are a number of crucial issues awaiting investigation in the faith school sector. However, the difficulties involved in this project are fully recognised. While it is the case that mainstream educational study and research has largely ignored the relevance of faith-based educational culture (until recently), it is also the case that the various faith communities have not given much priority to researching the leadership, cultures and outcomes of their particular school systems. Just as there can be an uneasy relation between faith and reason, there can also be an uneasy relation between faith and research. Research can produce results that are disturbing to the faithful, and for this reason some religious authorities have not encouraged systematic and rigorous investigations of their own schooling systems

Future research that intends to cast more light on the leadership and educational cultures of faith schools must recognise these historical and religious sensitivities and take them into account in the planning and design stages of any empirical projects. Given that research into faith school leadership issues will be another form of cross-cultural research (linking a secular research culture with a faith-based culture), then the protocols and sensitivities of the projects will need to be observed. Clearly this will involve an obligation upon the researcher to come to an informal understanding of the faith and of its religious and social teaching. It will also require a partnership mode of educational inquiry in which members of the faith are actively involved in the process of inquiry, without prejudice to objective procedures of analysis and reporting. If such cooperative and partnership relationships can be negotiated, then important projects into faith school leadership can proceed with great potential benefit both to the faith communities themselves and to the wider field of educational research. The outcomes of such research could then provide the necessary substantive inputs and contents for the creation of professional development programmes for faith school leaders and teachers.

A possible research agenda for the future is suggested, which could include some of the following main areas for investigation.

Faith school leadership and community relations

At present, given the expansion of the faith school sector as an outcome of both government policy in the United Kingdom and of the aspirations of the various faith communities in Britain, the leaders of such schools are faced by public and political criticism that such schools lead to community and social divisiveness. Thus, in a special issue of the *Oxford Review of Education* (December 2001) devoted to the faith school question, Harry Judge argued that:

> . . . any further extension of state aid to faith-based schools is likely to lead to an unwelcome fragmentation of society . . .
>
> (2001, p. 463)

These claims are widely made, and faith schools, it is asserted, are responsible for the generation of community conflict in Northern Ireland, in Bradford and in other northern cities and are implicated in the rise of racism in certain communities. It is unfortunate that so much critical and even hostile commentary on the existence of faith schools and on their supposed consequences should have emerged at precisely the time when the Islamic community in Britain has plans for the establishment of more Muslim schools (Parker-Jenkins *et al.*, 2005).

What characterises all of this commentary, however, is that it is based upon assertion and ignorance of the internal educational cultures of faith schools. Large claims are made without reference to empirical research evidence about faith schools.[6]

Faith school leaders – Anglican, Catholic, Jewish and Muslim – can be expected to welcome research and in-service provision that investigates this crucial area of community relations. All of the major faiths proclaim missions of love, peace, harmony, forgiveness and reconciliation (often formally expressed in school mission statements). It is important, therefore, to evaluate the extent to which these principles are realised in practice in the educational cultures of their schools. It is important for such school leaders to know to what extent the faith, in educational terms, leads young people to an open, caring and integrated relationship with others beyond their immediate community or to what extent it results in closure. The different ways in which faith schools are integrated with their local communities by admissions procedures, involvement in community work and partnership arrangements with other schools are also significant areas of inquiry.

With appropriate research assistance and continuing professional development, faith school leaders will be able to strengthen those features of their educational cultures that enhance community relations and seek to minimise those aspects that may work against these goals.

Faith school leadership, liberal education and democratic culture

Critics of faith-based schools often imply that the pedagogical culture of such organisations has more to do with indoctrination than education *per se*; that it does not accord with liberal educational principles and does not contribute towards the formation of democratic citizenship in the context of the British state.

Such assumptions may be based upon out-dated and distorted understandings of a particular faith community. It seems likely that faith school leaders, in the context of a liberal, pluralistic and democratic state, will want to demonstrate that faith-based schooling is an alternative form of liberal education and not a form of indoctrination. Terence McLaughlin (1996) has argued that modern forms of religious schooling are compatible with a liberal and democratic education, especially if they are characterised by what has been described as 'openness with roots' that is, 'providing a particular substantial starting point for the child's eventual development into autonomous agency and democratic citizenship' (McLaughlin, 1996, p. 147).

The concept of 'openness with roots' is itself derived from an extensive and rigorous empirical research undertaken by Tony Bryk and his colleagues into the educational cultures of Post-Vatican II Catholic secondary schools in the USA. Published as *Catholic Schools and the Common Good* (Bryk *et al.*, 1993), this work demonstrated that these faith schools provided a dialogic and open encounter with religious teaching that was in no sense an indoctrination experience. If modern Catholic schools have moved from a pedagogy of faith indoctrination (pre-1960s) to a pedagogy of faith encounter and dialogue, it seems likely that they are not alone.

Given that 'openness with roots' represents an alternative and defensible approach to teaching and learning in faith schools in liberal and democratic societies, then it becomes important to know how widespread such an educational culture is across the whole range of faith schooling. Educational researchers and CPD providers could assist faith school leaders in evaluating the extent to which their particular school culture realises this ideal in practice. Difficult questions will arise of course if the faith school is founded upon a fundamentalist interpretation of religious belief. Karen Armstrong (2001, 2002) has pointed out that, despite a current preoccupation with Islamic fundamentalism, religious fundamentalism as a defensive reaction against secularist, relativist and materialistic values in the contemporary world is a widespread phenomenon:

> Fundamentalism is a global fact and has surfaced in every major faith in response to the problems of our modernity. There is fundamentalist Judaism, fundamentalist Christianity, fundamentalist Hinduism . . .
>
> (Armstrong, 2002, p. 140)

Religious schools of a fundamentalist kind will, by definition, be more closed off and insulated from what are seen to be the corrupting features of secular liberal states. However, it does seem important that the services of educational researchers and programmes of leadership development should be offered to such schools to try to offset tendencies to the ghettoisation of a sector of faith schooling.[7]

Faith school leadership, market values and mission integrity

In the early 1990s I undertook research into the moral, ethical and professional dilemmas encountered by a sample of head teachers (primary and secondary), most of whom were located in the north-east of England. This research was published as *School Leadership: Beyond Education Management* (Grace, 1995). Of the 88 head teachers who participated in this research, 34 were leaders of Catholic schools; and in Chapter Nine I analysed the dilemmas experienced by these Catholic school leaders. Among these dilemmas the tension between Catholic values in education and market values in education emerged very clearly. As I expressed these at the time:

> Such headteachers realized that a new set of strategies known as 'playing the market' was emerging . . . In essence, playing the market involved selecting the most able pupils from the most educationally supportive homes in order to maximize the output of measurable success on league tables of performance . . . The moral dilemma for educational leaders (as opposed to simply managers) was constituted by a recognition that 'playing the market' made it much more difficult to serve the poor and the powerless. Success could be achieved with the poor and the powerless but at a greater cost in terms of time, resources, staff commitment and educational support.
>
> (Grace, 1995, pp. 176–177)

This was a serious dilemma for Catholic school leaders because, following the reforms of the Second Vatican Council (1962–1965), the Church had formally declared that 'First and foremost the Church offers its educational services to the poor'.

In subsequent research with 60 Catholic secondary head teachers in inner London, inner Liverpool and inner Birmingham (Grace 2002a), I was able to demonstrate how these dilemmas had become sharper over time.

It could be argued that the 1990s was unduly preoccupied by the organisational, logistical and technical aspects of education management, with the result that the values dimension of school leadership (i.e. its moral, ethical and spiritual responsibilities) were relatively neglected. Mike Bottery, in his crucial texts *Education, Policy and Ethics* (Bottery, 2000) and *The Challenges of Educational Leadership: Values in a Globalized Age* (Bottery, 2004), has been able to 'bring values back' into a field of studies that in some senses had lost its educational and philosophical vision. As a contribution to this reorientation of the field, the concept of 'mission integrity' (Grace, 2002b, 2003) can be a powerful construct for the analysis of faith schooling (but not only faith schooling). Defined as 'fidelity in educational practice and not just in public rhetoric to the distinctive and authentic principles of a faith-based schooling' (Grace, 2003, p. 162), mission integrity becomes a useful lens through which school self-evaluation exercise can be undertaken.[8]

All faith-based schools are vulnerable to *mission drift* over time, especially when the secular political and public worlds offer such schools extra resources, status and the accolades of 'excellence', 'successful' and 'effective' if they meet the requirements of the state. Faith schools have a dual mission to serve 'God and Caesar', and a major challenge for faith school leadership is to keep that mission in an appropriate balance. It is here that educational research, consultancy and CPD provision can help to meet the needs of such school leaders as these dilemmas become sharper for Anglican, Catholic, Jewish and Muslim school leaders.

The future: providing programmes of professional development for faith school leaders

There is no shortage of CPD programmes designed to help faith school leaders with what might be described as their secular professional needs. Thus leadership for learning, information and communications technology literacy, financial literacy, performance management, target setting, marketing the school, parent relations and preparing for OfSTED are all currently on offer.

However, provision for the religious, spiritual and moral responsibilities of faith school leaders is much less extensive. For such leaders, concepts such as theological literacy are just as important as information and communications technology literacy. This is another situation in which it is expected that the various faith communities must be responsible for the development of such literacy. The Catholic community in both the USA and the United Kingdom has recognised this need and responded to it. The USA, with its extensive provision of Catholic universities and colleges, has been a leader in this field. The situation in the United Kingdom is more modest but St Mary's

University College, Strawberry Hill has been a pioneer in offering an MA in Catholic School Leadership, with a significant theological component. Various Catholic dioceses offer short courses for this purpose and a recent text to assist professional development in this area has been published (Weeks, 2007). The Anglican, Jewish and Muslim communities have also provided some courses for their school leaders.[9]

Valuable as these programmes are for the school leaders concerned, they also have some potential disadvantages. This form of 'in house' provision confirms the idea that religion and faith-related views on values, morality and social teaching is part of a private realm within the secular modern state and its higher educational system. While CPD providers cannot be expected to provide theological literacy resourcing *per se*, such programmes in the future could make more space for the discussion of religious, spiritual and moral issues as viewed from the perspectives of the various faiths and of the secular world. This could have advantages for all concerned. The benefits for state school leaders would be that they would gain more insight into the religious cultures that will be represented in their own multi-faith school populations. The benefits for faith school leaders will be that they will gain more inter-faith understanding and understanding of secular perspectives. Overall, such programmes at their best will be contexts for secular professionals and religious professionals to engage in productive dialogue that may help to reduce stereotypes and misrepresentations based upon ignorance of the other.[10]

The potential of the Anglican community in the United Kingdom to provide research and evidence-based programmes of CPD for faith-school leaders has greatly increased. With universities of Anglican heritage now existing at Canterbury, Chester, Chichester, Gloucestershire, Winchester and York, there is an enhanced opportunity for the provision of systematic programmes to meet the needs of faith school leaders. York St John University, for instance, has established the Centre for Church School Education, which offers programmes of study for faith school leaders. The Leo Baeck College in London, through its Department of Education and Professional Development, now offers school leaders in the reform and liberal tradition of Judaism programmes including an Advanced Diploma and an MA in Jewish Education, as well as various short courses. The Muslim community is making CPD programmes available through the agency of the Association of Muslim Schools in the United Kingdom.

However, it is the major thesis of this article that the 'in-house' provision of programmes and research by the various faith communities in the United Kingdom must be complemented by and integrated with mainstream and public provision by secular agencies. The key to greater social, educational and cultural cohesion is not the abolition of faith schooling, as radical secularists demand, but rather the development of dialogue to generate greater mutual understanding and appreciation of the varieties of faith and secular schooling in a multi-faith democracy.

There are some encouraging signs that this is beginning to happen. In recent years, the NCSL has begun to focus upon themes particularly relevant for faith school leaders, such as 'the leadership of faith schools', 'leadership and spirituality' and 'developing leadership for faith schools'. A national survey of leadership needs has been conducted by NCSL, the Catholic Education Service and the Church of England Education Division across Anglican and Roman Catholic dioceses.

In spring 2005, the NCSL commissioned a report from Ibrahim Lawson of the Association of Muslim Schools in the United Kingdom, with the title *Leading Islamic Schools in the UK: A Challenge for us All.* As Lawson concluded:

> The context of the research was the social, cultural and political challenges presented by the growing Muslim population of the UK . . . Given that this is an entirely new situation . . . my report proposes that we all look for new ways of thinking together that offer the possibility of resolving what appear to be potentially serious conflicts.
>
> (2005, p. 21)

This is a wise recommendation. It takes us beyond the negativity of radical secularists (abolish the faith schools) and the limited vision of mainstream academe (faith schools as marginal) to propose an educational future that engages with the existence (and expansion) of faith schools in a responsible and mature way and the construction of better working relations with secular schools and communities. This situation requires imaginative new proposals for in-service and CPD programmes that meet the needs of the neglected sector of faith school leadership.[11]

Acknowledgements

The author would like to thank the following for assistance received in the writing of this article: Dr Helena Miller, Leo Baeck College, London; Ibrahim Lawson, Association of Muslim Schools in the United Kingdom; Sister Maria Supavai, SPC; Professor Geoff Southworth, Di Morton and Susan Beer, National College for School Leadership; and Matt Urmenyi and Diego Santori, CRDCE, London.

Notes

1 There are 4843 Church of England schools and 3154 Catholic schools in the United Kingdom. For recent analysis of Anglican schools, see Chadwick (2001) and Dearing (2001). For Jewish schools, see Miller (2001) and for Muslim schools see Hewer (2001). For Evangelical schools, see Walford (2001).
2 To be published in the series *International Handbooks of Religion and Education* by Springer Publications of the Netherlands in the period 2007–2010.

3 This is argued in more detail in Grace (2002b).
4 This need has been recognised in the USA where many Catholic universities and colleges offer CPD programmes for faith school leaders.
5 See, for instance, Alford and Naughton's (2001) *Managing as if Faith Mattered* for an application of Christian social principles to modern organisations.
6 See Grace (2003) for a more detailed argument.
7 A conceptual problem in the field is the undifferentiated use of 'faith schools' as if these were a single category. Quite apart from the fact that there are significant cultural and demographic differences in the populations of Church of England, Catholic, Jewish and Muslim schools, there are also major differences depending upon liberal or fundamentalist interpretation of the faiths.
8 For state secular schools, 'mission integrity' evaluation would relate to the extent to which the principles of the school's mission statement were actually present in its educational practice.
9 These courses have been part of 'the secret garden' of faith schooling. This article attempts to bring them to the notice of mainstream CPD providers.
10 Many of the controversies associated with the faith schools sector arise because there are not sufficient opportunities for faith school leaders and secular school leaders to engage in dialogue.
11 Useful material can be found in Grace and O'Keefe (2007).

References

Alford, H. & Naughton, M. (2001) *Managing as if faith mattered* (Notre Dame, University of Notre Dame Press).

Armstrong, K. (2001) *The battle for God: a history of fundamentalism* (New York, Ballantine Books).

Armstrong, K. (2002) *Islam: a short history* (London, Phoenix Press).

Blackmore, J. (1989) Educational leadership: a feminist critique and reconstruction, in: J. Smyth (Ed.) *Critical perspectives on educational leadership* (London, Falmer Press), pp. 3–129.

Bottery, M. (2000) *Education, policy and ethics* (London, Continuum).

Bottery, M. (2004) *The challenges of educational leadership: values in a globalized age* (London, Paul Chapman).

Bryk, A., Lee, V. & Holland, P. (1993) *Catholic schools and the common good* (Cambridge, MA, Harvard University Press).

Chadwick, P. (2001) The Anglican perspective on church schools, *Oxford Review of Education,* 27(4), 475–487.

Dearing, R. (2001) *The way ahead: Church of England schools in the new millennium* (London, Church House Publishing).

Gallagher, M. (1997) New forms of cultural unbelief, in: P. Hogan & K. Williams (Eds) *The future of the religion in Irish education* (Dublin, Veritas).

Grace, G. (1995) *School leadership: beyond education management* (London, Falmer Press).

Grace, G. (2002a) *Catholic schools: mission, markets, and morality* (London, Routledge Falmer).

Grace, G. (2002b) Mission integrity: contemporary challenges for Catholic school leaders, in: K. Leithwood & P. Hallinger (Eds) *Second international handbook of educational leadership and administration* (Dordrecht, Kluwer Academic Press).

Grace, G. (2003) Educational studies and faith-based schooling: moving from prejudice to evidence-based argument, *British Journal of Educational Studies,* 51(2), 149–167.

Grace, G. & O'Keefe, J. (Eds) (2007) *International handbook of Catholic education* (Dordrecht, Springer Publications).

Hall, V. (1994) Making it happen: a study of women headteachers, paper presented at the AERA Conference, New Orleans, LA, April 1994.

Hewer, C. (2001) Schools for Muslims, *Oxford Review of Education,* 27(4), 515–527.

Judge, H. (2001) Faith-based schools and state funding: a partial argument, *Oxford Review of Education,* 27(4), 463–474.

Lawson, I. (2005) *Leading Islamic schools in the UK: a challenge for us all* (Nottingham, NCSL).

McLaughlin, T. (1996) The distinctiveness of Catholic education, in: T. McLaughlin, J. O'Keefe & B. O'Keeffe (Eds) *The contemporary Catholic school* (London, Falmer Press).

Miller, H. (2001) Meeting the challenge: the Jewish schooling phenomena in the UK, *Oxford Review of Education,* 27(4), 501–513.

Miller, M. (2007) Challenges facing Catholic schools: a view from Rome, in: G. Grace & J. O'Keefe (Eds), *International handbook of Catholic education* (Dordrecht, Springer Publications), Chapter 24.

Ozga, J. (Ed.) (1993) *Women in educational management* (Buckingham, Open University Press).

Parker-Jenkins, M., Hartas, D. & Irving, B. (2005) *In good faith: schools, religion and public funding* (Aldershot, Ashgate Publishing).

Walford, G. (2001) Evangelical Christian schools in England and The Netherlands, *Oxford Review of Education,* 27(4), 529–541.

Walford, G. (2003) Review article, *British Journal of Sociology of Education,* 24(1), 113–115.

Weeks, N. (2007) *Theological literacy and Catholic schools* (London, CRDCE Publications).

Part 5

Mission integrity

Chapter 12

The State and Catholic schooling in England and Wales

Politics, ideology and mission integrity

Oxford Review of Education, 2001, 27(4), 489–500.

Changing relations between the English State and the Roman Catholic Church in the sphere of education policy are examined in two historical periods. Between the 1870s and the 1970s, despite initial anti-Catholic prejudice, the Catholic hierarchy was able to negotiate a favourable educational settlement in which substantial public funding was obtained without serious loss of autonomy and mission integrity for the Catholic schooling system. The existence of a liberal State, a voluntarist tradition in schooling and the relative social and political unity of the Catholic community all contributed towards this settlement.

The inauguration of an ideologically 'Strong State' in the 1980s and 1990s, pursuing an interventionist strategy in education driven by New Right market doctrines, threatened the whole basis of this settlement. The Catholic hierarchy had to develop new strategies to respond to this situation, complicated by the fact that the Catholic community was now more socially differentiated and more divided on key education policy questions.

When St Thomas More at the moment of his execution in 1535 declared himself to be 'the King's good servant, but God's first', he expressed in a powerful but condensed form the Catholic view of legitimate Church–State relations.[1] This involves an understanding that Catholics, the Catholic Church and all its associated agencies are in the service of lawfully established secular authorities insofar as these authorities do not threaten the necessary autonomy and mission integrity of the Catholic Church.

This classic understanding was elaborated by Christopher Dawson in his 1935 reflections upon 'The Catholic Doctrine of the State' when he wrote:

> To the Catholic . . . the State is itself the servant of a spiritual order which transcends the sphere of political and economic interests. Nor has it any right to absorb the whole of human life or to treat the individual simply as a means to its ends. The individual, the family, the Church

and the religious community all have their own autonomous spheres of activity and their independent rights.

(p. 136)

In both the 19th and 20th centuries the Roman Catholic hierarchy in England and Wales, in their negotiations with state agencies on the provision and nature of education for Catholic communities, had sought to maintain these principles of necessary autonomy and of mission integrity.[2] This paper will review the political and ideological struggles around these themes, with special reference to Church–State relations in the 1980s and 1990s, a time of particularly high levels of tension in those relations. Before engaging with the substantive detail of these relations it is necessary to clarify the central concepts used in this analysis, i.e. that of 'State' and of 'Church'.

Dale (1989, p. 57) in his much quoted text *The State and Education Policy* has pointed out that 'the State is not a monolith'. He goes on to argue that what is called 'the State' is an internally differentiated entity which includes the elected government, bureaucratic agencies of various kinds and ideological agencies internal to state mechanisms or closely related to particular projects of influential ministers of state. Given this situation, it is quite possible for state action to be limited by internal conflicts and power struggles among its various elements or to be unusually dynamic if an alliance is formed between a powerful government leader and a set of ideological agencies. In relation to education policy, Britain saw a particular manifestation of the latter phenomenon in the 1980s and early 1990s in what has come to be called 'Thatcherism'.

The Church, in this case the Roman Catholic Church, is similarly not a monolith (despite popular perceptions to the contrary). Distinctions may be made, especially since the reforms of the Second Vatican Council (1962–1965) between the institutional Church (represented by the Papacy, the Hierarchy, the Priesthood and Religious Communities) and the Church, understood as 'the people of God' (represented by parish communities of practising Catholics). While the whole ensemble of the Catholic Church is expected by its founding mission to work together in a spirit of harmony and unity, in practice (given the fallen nature of its members) internal struggles and conflicts do occur over various controversial issues.

Church–State relations in educational policy and practice matters are not therefore the meeting of two monoliths either in conflict or in alliance on specific questions. They are rather a more complex manoeuvring of interest groups located within both the structures of the State and the structures of the Church. Although in the following substantive analysis the terms Church and State are used in summary form, the crucial question of internal differentiation must always be borne in mind when considering any given policy struggle.

State and Church: early struggles and strong settlements[3]

In 1870, Archbishop (later Cardinal) Manning wrote to the British Prime Minister, William Gladstone, a letter pointing out that:

> the integrity of our schools as to (i) Doctrine, (ii) religious management and the responsibility of the Bishops in these respects, cannot be touched without opening a multitude of contentions and vexations.[4]

The Catholic hierarchy in England and Wales in the 19th and 20th centuries was guided in all its negotiations with the state on educational policy and practice by these three foundational principles, i.e. doctrinal integrity, religious management integrity and the primacy of episcopal jurisdiction on educational matters.

Throughout the 19th and early 20th centuries a whole series of issues had to be fought to preserve the integrity of these principles. These included the nature of religious instruction and of the texts to be used in supporting it, the notion of a Catholic curriculum as opposed to a secular curriculum, the nature of school inspection, the authority of religious and diocesan authorities in school management as opposed to the authority of secular School Boards and later of secular Local Education Authorities. A central issue in extending Catholic schooling to every Catholic child and young person in England and Wales was the struggle to obtain government grants for Catholic schools on a scale which matched those available to Church of England schools. While the Catholic bishops were forced to make some compromises on specific administrative questions in their negotiations with state agencies, they were not prepared to compromise on anything which, in their view, threatened the religious integrity of Catholic schools. Even on an issue as vital as government grants, Priscilla Chadwick (1997, p. 8) makes it clear that:

> Roman Catholic bishops were prepared to jeopardize government grants for Catholic schools rather than meet the State's wish to have the Authorized Version [of the Bible] used in Catholic classrooms.

For the Catholic bishops it had to be the Douay Version. This strong stance of the bishops, supported by priests and laity, proved to be successful over time and government grants in support of Catholic schooling progressively increased without a proportionate increase in the state's influence over religious teaching and curriculum provision in Catholic schools. Compared with many Catholic systems of schooling internationally, the Catholic bishops of England and Wales were able to obtain a very favourable educational settlement with the English State from the 1870s to the 1970s.

The most remarkable achievements of this period were that the Catholic bishops were able to negotiate state funding for new school buildings, rising from 50% in 1936 to 85% in 1975, with the state meeting the running costs of all Catholic maintained schools in England and Wales. At the same time, but especially after the 1944 Education Act, the Catholic Church, through its educational agency, the Catholic Education Council, enjoyed partnership status with the Church of England, the Local Education Authorities and the state in educational decision-making at national and local levels. Bernadette O'Keeffe (1999, p. 244) has summarised the position in these terms:

> The restructuring of education culminating in the 1944 Education Act was a landmark in the development of the Catholic school system in England and Wales. For the Catholic Church, in its educative role, it signified a shift from the margins of educational endeavour towards a more pivotal role in an enhanced partnership with the state in a publicly funded education system . . . It is significant that the expansion of school development at that time was undertaken with a minimum of encroachment on the church's autonomy.

What the Catholic bishops had achieved in their negotiations with the English State between the 1870s and the 1970s was a substantial public underwriting of the costs of Catholic education and a partnership status in educational decision-making without compromising the three regulative principles of the educational mission, i.e. religious and doctrinal integrity, religious management integrity and episcopal jurisdiction. Catholic schools, supported by public funds, taught the Christian message as realised within Catholic religious culture and practice, gave first priority to the admission of Catholic pupils and the appointment of Catholic teachers, appointed head-teachers only from a professional constituency of practising Catholics, had governing bodies with a majority representation of Catholics (appointed by the bishops) and taught a curriculum shaped and permeated by Catholic religious teaching and Catholic values. Access to Catholic schools having the status 'Voluntary Aided' meant that Catholic primary and secondary schools were an integrated (although distinctive) part of universal free education in Britain and were not associated with concepts of private schooling or fee-paying educational provision which characterised Catholic school systems in the USA and elsewhere.

From an international perspective this Church–State educational settlement for Catholic schooling is exceptional and the reasons for it need close examination. It is suggested here that this distinctive settlement for Catholic schooling arose in England and Wales as a result of the conjunction of two crucial factors.

The first of these relates to the process of state formation. Green (1990), in his important text *Education and State Formation: the rise of education systems in England, France and the USA*, has argued that British state formation was 'relatively gradual, protracted and delayed' (p. 34), with a greater emphasis upon the role of voluntarism than was the case with the more intensive forms of state formation in France, Prussia and the USA. Thus the central state in Britain was much slower to act decisively in the realm of education, leaving initial provision of schooling to religious interests. Throughout the 19th century, therefore, the Protestant churches in England and Wales were major providers of elementary education and as such received funding support from the State. Once this notion of state support for Protestant schooling provision had been established and, after 1870, the concept of a 'Dual System' of church and state schools was developed, the Catholic bishops could argue that the precedents were there to legitimate the extension of state funding to Roman Catholic schools. The privileged role of the Church of England as the Established Church meant in practice that it was the major provider of church schooling and the major recipient of government grants. The strategy adopted by the Catholic bishops was to focus upon the extent of differential funding of Anglican schools compared with Catholic schools. In the early part of the 19th century, when both English state agencies and English society were still influenced by religious bigotry and anti-Catholic prejudice,[5] such arguments made little progress. With the weakening of such prejudice over time it became increasingly difficult for the English State to resist such arguments, especially as more of the Catholic community were becoming enfranchised citizens and voters.

The second factor relates to the existence of political organisation and decisive leadership in education from the Catholic bishops, coupled with a very clear sense of the importance of the Catholic education mission in England. At the first Synod of the restored Catholic hierarchy in 1852 the bishops placed schooling provision at the top of the agenda:

> The first necessity . . . is a sufficient provision of education adequate to the wants of our poor. It must become universal . . . to prefer the establishment of good schools to every other work. Indeed, wherever there may seem to be an opening for a new mission, we would prefer the erection of a school, so arranged as to serve temporarily for a chapel, to that of a church without one.[6]

To achieve this aim, Catholic bishops, priests and religious shaped a strategy for organising the laity on this issue. The maintenance and extension of 'our Catholic schools' became a rallying cry for the Catholic community in England and Wales and impressive sums of money were raised despite the largely working-class and poor socio-economic profile of Catholics in Britain at that time. However, more important than this over time was the creation of a strong political alliance between the Catholic bishops and Catholic lay people on educational policy issues. Especially in the 20th century, the negotiations of the Catholic hierarchy with the elected government of the day were backed by a mutual understanding that behind the bishops' requests for more funding and more autonomy for Catholic schools was the 'Catholic vote'. For Labour Party administrations in particular and for members of parliament representing urban constituencies, the 'Catholic vote', and especially the Irish Catholic vote, could not lightly be ignored.

It was in these ways that the Catholic Church obtained from the English state an exceptional educational settlement between the 1870s and the 1970s in which public funding was obtained without loss of religious and mission integrity. A particular combination of circumstances including the existence of a liberal state formation, a strong voluntarist culture, precedents for state-supported religious schooling, strong leadership from the Catholic bishops and a degree of political organisation and unity which produced a 'Catholic vote' on education matters all contributed to this successful outcome.

The educational settlement between the Catholic Church and the English state depended upon the existence of this particular socio-political and cultural matrix. If any part of it was radically changed then it could be expected that the settlement would be radically changed. To the dismay of the contemporary Catholic hierarchy and of Catholic educators in England and Wales such radical changes were to occur in the 1980s and 1990s.

The Catholic Church and the 'strong State': education policy struggles in the 1980s and 1990s

Reviewing the educational changes of this period, Whitty, Power and Halpin (1998, p. 18) have noted that:

> After the Conservative general election victory of 1979, the Thatcher and Major governments set about trying to break the LEA monopoly of public schooling through the provisions of a series of Education Acts passed in the 1980s and 1990s.

While a major struggle between the central state and the local state in education was part of the educational reforms inaugurated at this time, the full nature of the educational transformations being attempted was even more radical. As Whitty (1989) argued in an earlier paper, the power of a strong, interventionist state was being mobilised to enforce an entirely new conception of the nature of education and of its cultural, social and political significance.

What occurred in England and Wales during these decades was nothing less than the demise of the liberal pluralist state and its gradual replacement by the ideological strong state. In relation to education policy and provision, a liberal, voluntarist tradition was decisively replaced by a strong state interventionist strategy significantly influenced by New Right ideologies of various kinds, and especially by doctrines of the beneficial effects of market values and market competition in all sectors of economic and social activity.

Gamble (1988), in his study *The Free Economy and the Strong State*, noted that in the attempted transformation of the socio-economic, cultural and political cultures of a number of societies, an evident strategy involved the initial use of 'strong state' legislative intervention in order to overcome potential sources of resistance to free market forces as a reforming mechanism in society. This was certainly the case in England and Wales and the 'strong state' was particularly active in the realm of education. The strong state in education, particularly as constituted by the personal political commitments of Mrs Thatcher[7] (and later John Major), reinforced by the programmes of various New Right agencies in England, intended to establish a radical, market-driven, educational settlement which, it was believed, would celebrate choice, improve performance and enhance Britain's competitive position in the world economy.

This radical programme of educational transformation was to be implemented by a 'strong state' series of Education Acts (1980, 1986, 1988, 1992, 1993, 1994, 1996) which would have the effect of overpowering alternative programmes. Roger Dale (1989, pp. 116–117) has provided a comprehensive account of the ideological intentions of the first stages of this process:

> The cornerstone of the new settlement is the market. The market is to achieve more effectively . . . all that the Welfare State . . . it is argued, failed to achieve . . . Ministers want to extend freedom of choice but only if they can first make sure that the right choices will be made. They no longer seek to liberate society from the embrace of the central state. They seek to use the central state to re-fashion society . . . they are determined to tame, indeed if necessary to dismantle, the intermediate institutions . . . between the state and the citizen . . . The Secretary of State will determine the programmes of study needed to implement the curriculum which all schools will be obliged to teach.

In these ways, the Catholic hierarchy and its educational advisers faced an entirely new configuration of power and ideological relations in educational policy in England and Wales during the 1980s and 1990s. The situation presented major challenges to its three regulative principles of educational provision, i.e. religious integrity, management integrity and episcopal jurisdiction.

The introduction of a National Curriculum with specified 'core subjects' threatened the integrity of notions of a relatively autonomous Catholic curriculum shaped by Catholic educational principles. The fact that religious education was not defined as a core subject in the new regulations was seriously at odds with a Catholic position that it was *the* core subject.[8] Both of these developments in effect undermined the relative autonomy of the

Catholic school system and, in the view of the bishops, had the potential to weaken the mission integrity of the system. Attempts by the Catholic bishops to persuade the government to allow their schools exemption from the requirements of the National Curriculum (as had been granted to independent schools) were unsuccessful. The strong Conservative state in education simply overruled the Catholic bishops on these issues and demonstrated quite clearly that the new strategy against 'intermediate institutions' in education policy included not only the local education authorities but also the Catholic hierarchy and its diocesan administrations. The partnership status accorded to the Church from the 1940s to the 1970s in educational policymaking had also been significantly weakened.[9]

The most direct challenge to the authority of the Catholic bishops in education policy occurred in relation to the government's strategy to 'increase choice and diversity' by establishing and developing a new category of school, to be called grant-maintained (GM). The concept of the GM school was introduced in the 1988 Education Act and ideologically promoted in the 1993 Act. GM schools could 'opt out' of the jurisdiction of local education authorities (and of diocesan authorities) and become relatively autonomous institutions directly funded by central government. To encourage headteachers, governors and parents to take the grant-maintained option, considerable financial incentives were associated with GM status. As Simon and Chitty (1993, p. 44) noted:

> The most decisive of the financial inducements so far offered lies in capital grants (for new buildings). . . . Several years' experience have now make it abundantly clear that schools becoming GMS have been treated far more generously than county schools. In 1991 for instance GMS schools got an average four times as much in the way of capital grants than mainstream county schools . . .

The introduction of grant-maintained schools with privileged funding in the 1980s and 1990s was not only part of a government strategy to weaken the influence of local education authorities in England *vis-à-vis* the central state, it was also part of a strategy to increase 'customer choice' in schooling.[10] Edwards and Whitty (1997, p. 39) have argued that the introduction of GM schools and the intended marketisation of education were closely linked:

> Potentially the largest move towards a market of autonomous and differentiated schools has been the creation of grant-maintained schools 'freed' from LEA control by the exercise of a collective consumer voice in favour of self-government.

The grant-maintained schooling strategy ideologically promoted by a strong central state in education presented serious challenges to the mission integrity of Catholic schooling in England as understood by the Catholic bishops. There were, in the view of the bishops, objections based upon Catholic moral and social teaching to a policy which gave particular advantages on an individualistic basis to certain schools at the expense of other schools. Such a policy violated Catholic commitments to the advancement of the common good in education. These objections were expressed in the formal response given by the Catholic bishops to the government White Paper of 1992:

> We do not in principle oppose increased independence and self-management for schools. However the GM option is more than this. It intensifies financial and curricular inequalities between schools and creates new inequalities. It also supposes that schools derive their strength from their own autonomy, without any sense of having a wider responsibility (the common good). Moreover there is no reason to believe that the growth of the GM sector will do other than undermine the financial viability and reputation of those schools which remain outside the GM sector.[11]

Against a strongly endorsed government policy of greater individualisation and of 'autonomous freedom' in schooling, the Catholic bishops were presenting a counter-cultural argument based upon the moral principles of the common good. However, as both Arthur (1995) and Chadwick (1997) point out, the opposition of the Catholic hierarchy was based not only upon moral questions raised by the GM option but also upon questions of governance and control. In effect, the decision to obtain GM status was a decision to be taken by the school governors and a majority of the parents[12]. Once a school obtained GM status the governors and the parents were the empowered agency to determine matters such as pupil admissions, the character of the school and other questions relating to the distinctive ethos of the school. In essence, episcopal jurisdiction over Catholic GM schools would be set aside in favour of the parent/consumer.

This was, in the view of the bishops, a violation of two crucial and distinctive features of Catholic schooling as established in previous decades, i.e. religious management integrity and the authority of episcopal jurisdiction. Cardinal Hume and Bishop Konstant (Chairman of the Catholic Education Service) attempted to resist these developments by political lobbying and negotiation and by disseminating within the Catholic community a clear understanding that the grant-maintained option was not favoured by the bishops. Despite such episcopal leadership (which had been effective in the past), the parents at over 100 Catholic schools voted in favour of the GM option. As Arthur (1994, 1995) has demonstrated, some Catholic parents and school governors in England were not prepared to accept the voice of the hierarchy as the definitive voice on this issue.

Although the GM episode in English schooling ended with the abolition of this status in 1997/98 by a newly-elected Labour government, its significance in any analysis of Church–State relations in education is considerable. At one stage in the GM struggle, a group of Catholic parents were prepared to take Cardinal Hume to court for his continued resistance to GM status at one school and the Cardinal threatened to place himself in contempt of the courts on this issue.[13] There could hardly have been a more dramatic manifestation of changed social and political relations within the Catholic community in England. From one perspective there were those who applauded this evidence of a more confident, educated and assertive laity, showing 'active citizenship' in educational policy decisions. From another perspective it seemed that secular values of self-interest and of market advantage in education had started to undermine the religious and moral integrity of Catholic schooling and to threaten its distinctive values and ethos.

By the 1990s the Catholic hierarchy in England and Wales had come to the view that, faced with a strong central state intent upon propagating the values of individual advantage and market competition in all social institutions including education, it had a responsibility to remind all Catholics (and others) about the nature of the Catholic Church's teaching on the common good in general and within educational provision and practice in particular. Faced with the unprecedented phenomenon of a strong interventionist state in educational policy which propagated an individualistic and market competitive ideology in schooling, the Catholic bishops took the unprecedented step of publishing a counter-cultural position which celebrated the virtues of the common good in social and educational policy. While very clear that their declarations had no party political bias and that they respected the right of an elected government to advance its programmes (i.e. the stance of 'the King's good servant'), they nevertheless argued that they had a responsibility to assert Catholic values and principles articulated since the time of St Thomas Aquinas (the stance of – 'but God's first'). It would be for the citizens of England and Wales (and not just the parents) to adjudicate between these two sets of principles for educational policy and practice.

In the first publication, *The Common Good and the Catholic Church's Social Teaching* (1996), a judicious statement sought to distinguish between sectors in which market values were appropriate and those where they were inappropriate:

> The Catholic Church has remained cautious and on guard towards free market economics for more than a hundred years, and we think it is time to re-emphasise in our society the concept of the common good. It provides the criteria by which public authorities can distinguish between those economic activities that can safely be left to market forces, and those that require regulation, state intervention or full provision by the public sector . . . Catholic Social Teaching, while it recognises that there

are at times merits in the market principle, resists the conclusion that
that principle should be extended wherever possible.

(Catholic Bishops' Conference of England
and Wales, 1995, pp. 19–20)

In a subsequent publication, *The Common Good in Education* (1997) the
Catholic hierarchy gave a decisive rejection of state-sponsored policies of
marketisation in education:

> Education is not a commodity to be offered for sale. The distribution of
> funding solely according to the dictates of market forces is contrary to
> the Catholic doctrine of the common good. Teachers and their pupils are
> not economic units whose value is seen merely as a cost element on the
> school's balance sheet. To consider them in this way threatens human
> dignity. Education is a service provided by society for the benefit of all
> its young people, in particular for the benefit of the most vulnerable
> and the most disadvantaged – those whom we have a sacred duty to
> serve. Education is about the service of others rather than the service of
> self . . . It is a noble and ennobling vocation which is diminished both
> by the constraints and the language of the market place.

(Catholic Bishops' Conference of England
and Wales, 1997, p. 13)

It is clear from the 1997 publication that the Catholic hierarchy saw the
attempted extension of market values into the realm of education as a serious threat to the mission integrity of the Catholic schooling system. If a
market culture in education encourages the pursuit of material interests,
what would become of a Catholic school's prime commitment to religious,
spiritual and moral interests? If calculation of personal advantage is necessary for survival in the market, how can Catholic schools remain faithful to
values of solidarity, community and the common good?

Contemporary Catholic schooling in England and Wales is in many ways
a success story. Catholic schools are strongly represented in the top sections
of published academic league tables and of test score results.[14] An increasing number of Catholic schools are oversubscribed by parents anxious to
obtain admission for their children and young people to schools frequently
described in the mass media as 'star performers'. The fact that the British
Prime Minister and his wife have committed their own children to the Catholic schooling system has brought added status to the whole enterprise.[15]
The contemporary British state wants 'top quality performance' from its
schools and Catholic schools are clearly making a significant contribution
to 'performance' and are publicly and politically applauded for doing so.
However, St Thomas More would have recognised the dangers inherent in
this most recent phase of State–Church relations in education. While the

contemporary 'success' of Catholic schooling in England and Wales is a cause for celebration among Catholic educators, they understand, at the same time, that the distinctive religious mission of Catholic schooling requires them to reflect constantly upon the verse in St Matthew's Gospel which says 'what shall it profit a man to gain the whole world and yet lose his own soul?' The challenge for Catholic schools in the 21st century (as in earlier centuries) is to remain 'the King's good servant, but God's first'.[16]

Acknowledgements

Valuable comments on the first draft of this paper were received from Professor Geoff Whitty, two anonymous referees and also from Archbishop Vincent Nichols, Chairman of the Catholic Education Service in England and Wales. Where I have taken their advice it has improved the analysis. The responsibility for the final version is mine.

Notes

1 Reynolds (1953, p. 359).
2 Mission integrity, in this case, may be regarded as fidelity in practice and not just in doctrine to the distinctive and authentic principles of Roman Catholic education. For further discussion, see Grace (2002a) forthcoming.
3 'Educational settlements' are resolutions of contested situations in which a particular balance of power relations, ideologies and interest groups has been achieved in a policy outcome. For more detailed accounts, see Grace (1987) and (1990).
4 Quoted in Arthur (1995, p. 34).
5 See Norman (1985). It should be noted, however, that with the influx of a large number of Irish Catholics into Britain in the mid-19th century, the English State looked to the Catholic Church and a system of Catholic schooling as an important means of social control. See Hickman (1995).
6 Quoted in Arthur (1995, p. 15).
7 For a detailed discussion see Dale (1989) on 'Thatcherism and Education'.
8 The Catholic bishops issued a strong statement in opposition to the proposals relating to Religious Education: 'Catholics believe that Religious Education is not one subject among many but the foundation of the entire educational process.' Quoted in Chadwick (1997, p. 91).
9 While the Catholic bishops did experience many set-backs in their negotiations with the government, they were able to secure some important rights in the 1993 Act regarding the inspection of Religious Education. This Act also, for the first time in history, made reference in primary legislation to Roman Catholic Church Schools, to Roman Catholic Bishops and their powers and to Diocesan Authorities in education. I am grateful to Archbishop Vincent Nichols for drawing my attention to this point.
10 See Fitz, Halpin & Power (1993).
11 Catholic Education Service (1992, p. 7).
12 For examples of the dilemmas which the grant-maintained option presented for Catholic headteachers, see Grace (1995). For a discussion of the tensions between the common good and individual self-interest see Grace (1998).

13 Arthur (1995) p. 153.
14 See Morris (1994) and (1998).
15 The Catholic school system in England and Wales serves about 10% of the school population. There are 1830 primary schools and 395 secondary schools within the maintained system of free schooling. In addition, there are 160 fee-paying independent schools. Within the maintained system, 75% of the pupils are Catholic and almost 70% of the teachers are Catholic (Source: Catholic Education Service, May 2001).
16 For an account of how these challenges are perceived and responded to by Catholic headteachers in England, see Grace (2002b) forthcoming.

References

Arthur, J. (1994) Parental participation in Catholic schooling: a case of increasing conflict, *British Journal of Educational Studies*, 42, 2, pp. 174–190.

Arthur, J. (1995) Government education policy and Catholic voluntary-aided schools 1979–1994, *Oxford Review of Education*, 21, 4, pp. 447–456.

Arthur, J. (1995) *The Ebbing Tide: policy and principles of Catholic education* (Leominster, Gracewing).

Catholic Bishops' Conference of England and Wales (1995) *The Common Good and the Catholic Church's Social Teaching* (London, CBC).

Catholic Bishops' Conference of England and Wales (1997) *The Common Good in Education* (London, CES).

Catholic Education Service (1992) *A Response to the White Paper 1992* (London, CES).

Chadwick, P. (1997) *Shifting Alliances: Church and state in English education* (London, Cassell).

Dale, R. (1989) *The State and Education Policy* (Milton Keynes, Open University Press).

Dawson, C. (1935) *Religion and the Modern State* (London, Sheed & Ward).

Edwards, T. & Whitty, G. (1997) Marketing quality: traditional and modern versions of educational excellence, in: R. Glatter, P. Woods & C. Bagley (Eds) *Choice and Diversity in Schooling* (London, Routledge).

Fitz, J., Halpin, D. & Power, S. (1993) *Grant Maintained Schools: education in the market place* (London, Kogan Page).

Gamble, A. (1988) *The Free Economy and the Strong State* (London, Macmillan).

Grace, G. (1987) Teachers and the state: a changing relation, in: M. Lawn & G. Grace (Eds) *Teachers: the culture and politics of work* (London, Falmer Press).

Grace, G. (1990) Labour and education: the crisis and settlements of education policy, in: M. Holland & J. Boston (Eds) *The Fourth Labour Government: politics and policy in New Zealand* (Auckland, Oxford University Press).

Grace, G. (1995) *School Leadership: beyond education management* (London, Falmer Press).

Grace, G. (1998) The future of the Catholic school; an English perspective, in: J. M. Feheney (Ed.) *From Ideal to Action: the inner nature of a Catholic school today* (Dublin, Veritas).

Grace, G. (2002a forthcoming) Mission integrity: contemporary challenges for Catholic school leaders, in: K. Leithwood & P. Hallinger (Eds) *Second International*

Handbook of Educational Leadership and Administration (Dordrecht, Kluwer Academic Press).

Grace, G. (2002b forthcoming) *Catholic Schools: mission, markets and morality* (London, Routledge Falmer).

Green, A. (1990) *Education and State Formation: the rise of education systems in England, France and the USA* (London, Macmillan).

Hickman, M. (1995) *Religion, Class and Identity: the state, the Catholic Church and the education of the Irish in Britain* (Guildford, Avebury).

Hornsby-Smith, M. (1999) (Ed.) *Catholics in England 1950–2000: historical and sociological perspectives* (London, Cassell).

Morris, A. (1994) The academic performance of Catholic schools, *School Organisation*, 14, 1, pp. 81–89.

Morris, A. (1998) Catholic and other secondary schools: an analysis of OFSTED inspection reports 1993–1995, *Educational Research*, 40, 2, pp. 181–190.

Norman, E. (1985) *Roman Catholicism in England* (Oxford, Oxford University Press).

O'Keeffe, B. (1999) Reordering perspectives in Catholic schools, in: M. Hornsby-Smith (Ed.) *Catholics in England 1950–2000* (London, Cassell).

Reynolds, E. (1953) *Saint Thomas More* (London, Burns Oates).

Simon, B. & Chitty, C. (1993) *SOS: Save Our Schools* (London, Lawrence & Wishart).

Whitty, G. (1989) The New Right and the National Curriculum: state control or market forces? *Journal of Education Policy*, 4, 4, pp. 329–341.

Whitty, G., Power, S. & Halpin, D. (1998) *Devoloution and Choice in Education: the school, the state and the market* (Buckingham, Open University Press).

Mission integrity

Contemporary challenges for Catholic school leaders[*]: beyond the stereotypes of Catholic schooling

Second International Handbook of Educational Leadership and Administration, Part 1. 2002, (Eds). K. Leithwood and P. Hallinger, 427–440, Kluwer.

It is often assumed that issues to do with Catholic school leadership are relevant only to Catholics and are therefore marginal to mainstream research and literature in the field of educational leadership. This misconception probably arises because of two pervasive and stereotypical views of the nature of Catholic schooling.

The first is the idea that Catholic schools are in fact 'private schools' whose cultures and leadership challenges are of a very different kind from those which characterise state or publicly provided schooling. From this perspective, Catholic schools are perceived as a somewhat privileged sector of any schooling system. The second is that Catholic schools serve only Catholic students (practising or nominal). From this perspective, Catholic schools appear to have an exclusive and autonomous relation to local communities and to local education administrative agencies. These two assumptions generally lead to the conclusion that the challenges and dilemmas facing Catholic school leaders cannot have much relevance for research, policy and practice in mainstream educational leadership.

From an international perspective, both of these assumptions can be seen to be serious oversimplifications of the actual complexity and diversity of Catholic schooling across the world and of its leadership cultures. While the first assumption has an understandable currency within the USA, there are a number of countries e.g., Belgium, The Netherlands, Germany, England, Scotland, Wales, Ireland and New Zealand, where Catholic schools receive significant support from public funds and as a consequence are an integrated (although distinctive) sector of publicly provided education.

The Catholic secondary schools in London, Liverpool and Birmingham in which the present writer's research has been undertaken are not private schools. Their formal status in England is that of 'voluntary-aided' schools, which means in practice that they are non-fee-paying institutions and part of the universal free secondary education system. Such Catholic schools, especially those located in inner-city areas, frequently have student populations registering high levels of poverty as indicated by entitlements to free school meals (FSM). They have arisen out of a tradition of Catholic working class schooling in England and they remain largely in the service of that class, albeit with greater ethnic and cultural diversity than in the past. Catholic schools in England are front-line providers of quality education in many working class and ethnically mixed communities. It is also quite often the case that the men and women who constitute its contemporary school leadership are themselves from Catholic working class origins and have achieved upward social mobility as a result of educational success within the Catholic school system.

Such Catholic schools in England serve Catholic communities, but not exclusively so. In the research inquiry to be reported later, of 60 participating secondary schools in three major cities, only 12 schools reported a 100 per cent Catholic student enrolment. In varying proportions, other Catholic schools admitted students from a pluralistic range of religious cultures, and in five of the schools non-Catholic students constituted 50 per cent of the enrolments. Catholic schools, especially in inner-city locations, are serving multi-faith and multi-ethnic populations and the leadership of these schools shares many of the challenges faced by state and public school leaders in urban education, although realised within a distinctive schooling culture.

The Secretary of the Congregation for Catholic Education (Pittau, 2000) has recently pointed to the extensive nature of Catholic school provision worldwide, including as it does 150,000 primary/elementary schools and 34,000 secondary/high schools internationally which serve almost 50 million students. While the administrative jurisdictions and local cultures in which these schools operate vary greatly, it seems likely that the leadership challenges and dilemmas faced by this large constituency of school leaders will generate valuable data to illuminate the field of educational leadership studies.

Foundation principles of Catholic schooling and concepts of mission integrity

The Catholic school system internationally claims that its presence in the network of educational services provided by every society is necessary because of the distinctive educational mission which it proclaims and because of the significant contribution which Catholic schools can make to the common good of any society. The first is an argument which stresses parental and citizens' rights to choose a particular faith-based educational experience for their children. The second is an argument which stresses the Catholic school system's ethic of service to the whole society and not simply to the Catholic community. The modern mission of the Catholic school (following the reforms of the Second Vatican Council) was formally articulated by the Sacred Congregation for Catholic Education in its 1977 publication, *The Catholic School*. This may be regarded as the foundation charter and modern mission statement for Catholic schools everywhere. However, the Congregation recognised that the realisation of the ideals and precepts contained in this document would be mediated by the specific local conditions in which Catholic schools were situated. In other words the Sacred Congregation sought to clarify 'the Catholic school's fundamental reason for existing and the basis for its genuine apostolate . . .' (p. 8) while at the same time recognising situational challenges to those principles:

> The Sacred Congregation for Catholic Education is aware of the serious problems which are an integral part of Christian education in a pluralistic society. It regards as a prime duty therefore the focusing of any attention on the nature and distinctive characteristics of a school which would present itself as Catholic. Yet the diverse situations and legal systems in which the Catholic school has to function in Christian and non-Christian countries demand that local problems be faced and solved by each Church within its own social-cultural context.
>
> (pp. 7–8)

While recognising that local and situational adjustments would have to be made by Catholic schools operating internationally (affected by cultural, ideological and economic circumstances), it is clear that the intention of the 1977 *Catholic School* document was to express conceptions of the authentic and distinctive Catholic educational mission to which all systems of Catholic schooling ought to aspire. This authentic mission was constituted by the following regulative principles:

Education in the faith

'The Catholic school forms part of the saving mission of the Church . . . Mindful of the fact that man (sic) has been redeemed by Christ, the Catholic school aims at forming in the Christian those particular virtues which will enable him to live a new life in Christ' (pp. 13–33).

Here Catholic schools are expected to give primacy to the formation of a spiritual and moral life as realised in Catholic religious culture and practice ie the enhancement of Catholicity among their students and its development relative to contemporary conditions. The faith imperative, as would be expected, is given as the foundation cause and rationale for the work of Catholic schools. However, closely coupled with this imperative is a special sense of mission to various categories of 'the poor'.

Preferential option for the poor

'First and foremost the Church offers its educational service to the poor, or those who are deprived of family help and affection or those who are far from the faith' (pp. 44–45).

Catholic educators have interpreted this section of the text to mean that Catholic schools should be at the service of the economically poor and powerless in deprived urban and rural locations. As the founder of the Sisters of Notre Dame expressed it, 'to educate the poor in the most abandoned places'.[1] However, in addition to the economic poor are those who are poor in terms of family stability and support and those who experience a poverty of religious and spiritual culture in their homes. The realisation of these aspects of the educational mission has been mediated, and in some cases compromised, by historical and political circumstances, financial constraints and the differing charisms of religious orders prominent in the Catholic educational missions. Some religious orders in education have been more obviously in the service of the poor than others.

Education as solidarity and community

'The Catholic school community is an irreplaceable source of service, not only to the pupils and its other members but also to society. Today . . . one sees a world which clamours for solidarity and yet experiences the rise of new forms of individualism. . . . They are to overcome their individualism and discover, in the light of faith, their specific vocation to live responsibly in a community with others. The very pattern of the Christian life draws them to commit themselves to serve God in their brethren and to make the world a better place to live in' (pp. 37–47).

When the 1977 document referred to 'the rise of new forms of individualism' in various parts of the world it was making a perceptive observation about the influence of certain social, political and economic ideologies which were rising to power at this time. New Right ideologies of competitive individualism, free market economics, a reduced social and economic role for the state and the extension of market values and practices into all forms of institutional life were beginning to influence political thought in a number of countries. The rise of new forms of individualism in socio-political and economic thinking was at odds with Catholic social teaching and in particular with Catholic conceptions of the common good. In the *Catholic School* publication of 1977 it can be argued that the Church was proclaiming a countercultural mission of solidarity and community for its schools precisely at the time when competitive individualism and market values were beginning to affect educational, social and economic 'reforms' or at least agendas for 'reform'.

Education and the common good

'Cooperation is between brothers and sisters in Christ. A policy of working for the common good is undertaken seriously as working for the building up of the kingdom of God. . . . Society can take note from the Catholic school that it is possible to create true communities out of a common effort for the common good' (pp. 46–47).

In re-emphasising the links between Catholic education and conceptions of the common good, the Sacred Congregation was reminding the world (and many Catholics) that from the time of St Thomas Aquinas in the thirteenth century, the social institutions of the Catholic Church were intended to be agencies for the common good and not simply for the particular good of Catholic communities.

Academic education as a means and not an end

'This is the basis of a Catholic school's educational work. Education is not given for the purposes of gaining power but as an aid towards a fuller understanding of and communion with man (sic), events and things. Knowledge is not to be considered for material prosperity and success, but as a call to serve and to responsible for others' (p. 43).

Once again a traditional Catholic educational position was rearticulated in modern terms and once again the basis for this position can be found in the writings of St Thomas Aquinas.[2] It is not sufficient simply to develop the intelligence, talents and skills of young people on an individual or 'self-fulfilment' basis. This could lead to the creation of talented and clever but also self-centred and materially acquisitive individuals with no regard for any conception of a common good. The Catholic position, as articulated by the 1977 document is that intelligence, talents and skills and command of knowledge are to be developed to the highest possible degree but always with a religious and moral understanding that such personal empowerment is to be used for the benefit of others. Academic education cannot be an end in itself.

These principles may be called the *formal or textual mission* for the contemporary Catholic schooling system internationally. But some fundamental questions for research investigation and discussion are 'to what extent are Catholic school leaders actually realising these principles in their policies and day-to-day practices?' and 'what are some of the major challenges to these principles in contemporary cultural, social and ideological conditions?'

In investigating these questions it is argued that concepts of mission integrity linked to different conceptions of educational leadership have valuable analytical potential.

Mission integrity and Catholic school leadership

The mission statements of contemporary Catholic schools are not simply reproductions of the formal mission as articulated by the Vatican. Local mission statements tend in practice to be adaptations of the formal mission mediated by a whole variety of agencies in the local context. The process whereby mission statements for schools are shaped and formed is itself of great research interest and of considerable institutional significance in understanding the culture and effectiveness of a particular school. As I have argued elsewhere (Grace 1998a), mission statements were being articulated in Catholic educational culture long before the concept was appropriated and generalised in modern institutional practice. Mission statements have many Catholic virtues. They constitute a principled and comprehensive charter of what a school claims to be its distinctive educational, spiritual, moral and social purposes. Such statements characteristically specify a range of desired educational outcomes and in their modern forms they are often the results of consultation exercises involving school boards, teachers and parents and, at their best, school students and members of the wider community. They are published to the community as a statement saying 'this is what the school is about' and implicitly saying 'this is the basis upon which you can judge us'. A serious and distinctive Catholic approach to school effectiveness research necessarily involves using mission statements as a fundamental evaluative framework against which to assess the outcomes of a schooling programme. Given that Catholic educational culture can claim to have been one of the originators of the very concept of a mission statement in education it seems entirely appropriate that modern Catholic educational practice should be assessed and evaluated in terms of conceptions of mission integrity.

Mission integrity is defined here as *fidelity in practice and not just in public rhetoric to the distinctive and authentic principles of a Catholic education*. However, it is clear from the start that mission integrity is a contested concept because different interpretations will exist, both internationally and in local contexts, as to what the distinctive principles are and as to what order of priority should be assigned to the relevant principles. Contrary to simplistic popular views of Catholic education as monolithic it is, in practice, internally differentiated to a significant degree and mediated by historical power relations and by the specificities of culture, class, race and gender relations. Within the international world of Catholic education this means that different conceptions of mission and of mission integrity will co-exist in various locations.

In recognition of this internal complexity of Catholic schooling any definition of mission integrity becomes more problematic. Nevertheless most Catholic educators would agree that mission integrity in education means not only fidelity to local statements but also significant fidelity to Vatican statements such as that contained in *The Catholic School* (1977). In other words, any school which claimed the title of 'Catholic' could not be seriously at odds with the guidance offered by the Sacred Congregation for Catholic Education as to what the distinctive principles of a Catholic education can be said to be.

I have argued in a number of places (Grace, 1995, 1996, 1997) that the responsibilities of educational and school leadership are qualitatively different from those of educational and school management. Such leadership has to be vision-related, mission-related, values-related and concerned with not losing sight of the larger questions about the purposes of educational activity which can be marginalised in the press of managerial and technical busyness. As Hodgkinson (1983 p. 207) has put it in *The Philosophy of Leadership*:

> For the leader in the praxis situation there is an obligation, a philosophical obligation, to conduct where necessary a value audit. This is an analysis of the value aspects of the problem he (sic) is facing. . . . It is careful reflection upon such questions . . . prior to administrative action, which is the hallmark and warrant of leadership responsibility.

To Hodgkinson's argument that school leaders have a responsibility to undertake a continuing value audit of the educational enterprise, I would add the more specific argument that school leaders have a prime responsibility to guard and enhance the mission integrity of the school. This means that school leaders (as opposed to simply school managers) are necessarily concerned with issues of principle and authenticity, ethical and moral conduct, values in practice and the formation of youth in concepts of the good life. While mission integrity must be a prime concern for leaders of every category of school, it has a particular resonance for the leaders of faith-based schools where conceptions of educational mission are especially salient. Mission integrity goes beyond the performance indicators of various kinds and technical measures of efficiency, effectiveness and value for money calculations. It focuses on the question, what purposes are served by all this activity?

International challenges to Catholic school leadership: challenges of a new millennium

Whereas the *Catholic School* document of 1977 was marked by an optimistic spirit which seemed to reflect the new thinking arising from the Second Vatican Council, the latest publication from the Vatican, *The Catholic School on the Threshold of the Third Millennium* (1998) presents the international challenges to Catholic school leaders in more sombre terms. Challenges are seen to arise from loss of faith, moral relativism, consumer materialism, growing polarisation of rich and poor and a general breakdown in the quality of community and of family life. These challenges to Catholic schooling are expressed in stark formulations:

> First and foremost we have a crisis of values . . . of subjectivism, moral relativism and nihilism. The extreme pluralism pervading contemporary society leads to behaviour patterns which . . . undermine any idea of community identity. . . . the globalization of the economy affects human

life more and more throughout the world. . . . We witness the widening of the gap between rich and poor. . . . To this we must add . . . a growing marginalisation of the Christian faith as a reference point and a source of light. . . .

(p. 35)

The Catholic school is thus confronted with children and young people who experience the difficulties of the present time. Pupils who shun effort are incapable of self-sacrifice and perseverance and who lack authentic models to guide them, often even in their own families. In an increasing number of instances they are not only indifferent and non-practising, but also totally lacking in religious or moral formation. To this we must add – on the part of numerous pupils and families – a profound apathy where ethical and religious formation is concerned. . . . What is in fact required of the Catholic school is a certificate of studies or . . . quality instruction and training for employment.

(pp. 37–38)

In these circumstances, the Sacred Congregation for Catholic Education is warning Catholic school leaders everywhere that the distinctive mission of Catholic education is actually becoming more difficult than it was in the past and that their responsibilities for the quality of mission integrity in the schooling system had become more demanding. Complicating this situation is a recognition (already expressed in an earlier publication, *Lay Catholics in Schools* [1982]) that the decline in the numbers of religious and teaching orders had profound consequences for Catholic schooling and its leadership.

The Challenge of faith leadership

The Catholic schooling system internationally has relied to a significant degree upon religious sisters, brothers and priests to provide much of its leadership personnel. This has been true in both developed and in developing countries. In the USA, for instance, Bryk, et al. (1993 p. 157) noted that:

'The majority of principalships in Catholic high schools (61 per cent in 1988) still come from religious orders, an arrangement that provides schools some distinct benefits'. Bryk's research and other studies[3] have demonstrated that the Catholic schooling system can no longer rely upon the 'strategic subsidy' of religious and teaching orders in its educational mission. The situation in the USA provides an indicator of world-wide developments in this respect. In 1967, religious sisters, brothers and priests constituted 58 per cent of all the teachers in Catholic elementary and secondary schools. By 1990 this proportion had dropped to less than 15 per cent or in absolute numbers from 94,000 in 1967 to 20,000 religious in 1990.[4] The Vatican document,

The Catholic School on the Threshold of the Third Millennium (1998) refers to 'the alarming decrease in numbers' among religious working in Catholic schools as teachers and as school leaders. From a Vatican perspective it also points out that for the maintenance of a distinctive Catholic identity in schools:

'the presence of consecrated religious within the educating community is indispensable. . . . They are an example of the unreserved and gratuitous gift of self to the service of others in the spirit of their religious consecration. The presence of men and women religious, side by side with priests and lay teachers, affords pupils a vivid image of the Church and makes recognition of its riches easier.' (p. 42)

The fact however that the 'vivid image' of Catholic religious faith, commitment and spiritual leadership as provided by consecrated religious is declining as a world-wide phenomenon in the Catholic schooling system means that much contemporary attention is now being given to what is called 'transmission of the charism'. Transmission of the charism is the key issue for Catholic school leadership internationally. It refers to the processes whereby the special qualities of pedagogical and pastoral commitment, of willingness to work in challenging and deprived educational settings and the capacity to give inspiring professional and faith leadership can be recontextualised from a clerical to a lay leadership. It is the passing on of a distinctive sense of Catholic school leadership as a 'call' or vocation to serve the young. The vocation which animated religious leaders of Catholic schools now has to be reconstituted in their lay successors. Wallace (2000 p. 191), viewing the issue from a United States perspective, expresses it in dramatic terms:

'There is a major identity crisis occurring in Catholic schools. The dramatic shift from religious to lay personnel raises the question of whether or not some Catholic schools are becoming private schools with a religious memory but a secular presence'. For Wallace the key issue is the quality of contemporary faith leadership in Catholic schools and the provision of effective professional, theological and spiritual formation courses for the new lay leadership. However, crucially interwoven with these issues are other challenges for Catholic school leaders in the arena of mission integrity.

The Challenge of academic success

It seems ironic and contradictory that academic success, a universally desired outcome for all school systems, should constitute a challenge and a dilemma for Catholic school leaders and yet, in contemporary conditions, this is the case. Catholic schools in many societies have an established and even growing reputation for achieving relatively high levels of academic success for their students. But if academically 'failing' schools have their problems, it must also be recognised that so do academically 'successful' schools, at least within Catholic culture. The problem facing many Catholic schools and school leaders worldwide is that just because they are so academically and socially effective, this very success may threaten the integrity of other aspects of their educational mission. This potential danger was noted in the Vatican Congregation's (1998) publication when it observed:

> What is in fact required of the Catholic school is a certificate of studies or . . . quality of instruction and training for employment.

With the growth of stronger accountability and quality assurance procedures for schools worldwide and with a stronger emphasis upon public and visible academic monitoring and performance indicators, a hegemony or ideological dominance of academic success in the evaluation of schooling has emerged. In many cases academic success has moved from being a very important part of the matrix of school outcomes to being its chief and dominating characteristic. To the extent that this is true of Catholic schools, the danger is that a successful pursuit of 'a certificate of studies' or a 'training for employment' will displace or marginalise religious, moral and social formation as part of the programme of a school. In addition to this Catholic schools might become increasingly populated by students and teachers for whom the achievement of academic success has become an end in itself, divorced from its traditional Catholic connection with ideas of service to the common good. In other words a utilitarian academic success culture might gradually displace a distinctive Catholic school culture in which knowledge and faith are kept in a balanced relation[5] and in which intellectual empowerment for public service is the animating spirit or ethos. It is widely recognised that the responsibility for trying to prevent this utilitarian academic incorporation of the Catholic school and its transformation into a 'results factory' lies with school leaders and principals. It is seen to be their duty to safeguard mission integrity and to maintain a Catholic and comprehensive sense of what the proper ends of schooling are in this sector.

Market values in education versus Catholic values in education

The attempted colonisation of institutions of education in the 1980s by market ideologies, values, practices and discourse has presented Catholic school leaders in some countries with sharp challenges to traditional conceptions of the educational mission. Catholic schools, with other schools, have been caught up in a global ideological struggle between those who claim that the application of competitive market forces and values within education will be a revitalising reform for schooling, making it more efficient, effective and responsive to education 'consumers' and those who argue that it will be a distortion and corruption of what education is about. While writers such as Chubb and Moe

(1990, 1992) have celebrated the potential of market disciplines and market competition to enhance educational effectiveness everywhere:

> 'the whole world is being swept by a realization that (education) markets have tremendous advantages over central control and bureaucracy',[6] others have pointed to their less attractive features. Ranson (1993 p. 336) for instance has argued that:

> 'Action in the market is driven by a single, common currency: the pursuit of material interests. The only effective means upon which to base action is the calculation of personal advantage: clout in the market derives from the power of superior resources to subordinate others in competitive exchange.'

Thus expressed, market values and practices in education appear to be at odds with some of the foundational values of the Catholic educational mission. If a market culture in education encourages the pursuit of material interests what becomes of a Catholic school's prime commitment to religious and moral interests? If calculation of personal advantage is necessary for survival in the market how can Catholic schools remain faithful to values of solidarity and community? If schools in a market economy in education must show good 'company' results in academic success and social status outcomes what becomes of the Catholic school principle of 'preferential option for the poor'? In a situation in which socially approved and measurable outcomes become critical to the survival of schools and in which a bright and up-market image is also essential, schools which serve deprived and fragmented communities have few market assets. The temptation in a market economy for schooling is to try by manipulation of admissions policies and exclusion policies to maximise the number of potentially 'profitable' students and to reduce the number of challenging pupils. In other words, a more calculative and selective policy on student recruitment and retention may begin to displace an earlier policy of more open community service.

Bryk, et al. (1993) have argued that Catholic schools in the USA have long been engaged in a cultural struggle to balance market concerns (critical to survival) with Catholic values (critical to mission). The sensitivity of American Catholic schools to market values has been the inevitable result of receiving no financial support from public funds, unlike Catholic schools in a number of other societies.[7] However, attempts by market advocates in education to incorporate Catholic schools as significant examples of effective schools within a marketised culture of education have been dismissed as simplistic by these researchers. Bryk, et al. (1993 p. 300) concluded their inquiry in these terms:

> 'The control of Catholic school operations involves considerably more than market responsiveness to clients. Many important observations

about these schools cannot be reconciled in these terms. Market forces cannot explain the broadly shared institutional purpose of advancing social equity or account for the efforts of Catholic educators to maintain inner-city schools (with large non-Catholic enrolments) while facing mounting financial woes.'

The detailed research reported in *Catholic Schools and the Common Good* (1993), while it celebrates the balance achieved between market and mission in the USA, concludes in sombre terms. Contemporary conditions in America are beginning to demonstrate that market forces, market values and the inexorable circumstances of institutional survival and financial solvency are in fact threatening the integrity of the Catholic educational mission, in particular with regard to service to deprived urban communities. The urgency of this development has been underlined from subsequent research by O'Keefe (1996, O'Keefe and Murphy 2000), a Jesuit professor at Boston College. Examining the pattern and the pace of Catholic school closures in poor urban communities in Boston, New York, Philadelphia and Chicago, O'Keefe concluded that:

'At the outset of the 1990s many schools closed precisely in those areas where they were needed most.'[8]

As competitive market conditions in education intensify in a number of societies and as the 'strategic subsidy'[9] provided by the religious orders in education weakens, the traditional Catholic mission to the poor becomes more problematic. Complicating the position in many inner-city localities are demographic changes, resulting in an increase of ethnic populations which are not Catholic and a reduction in the numbers of the local Catholic community. This raises the disputed question of whether Catholic schools in such locations are at the service of more pluralistic poor communities or only of the Catholic poor and of Catholic ethnic groups. Catholic school leaders have to work out and defend their conceptions of mission integrity in these rapidly changing social and economic contexts. They have to try to hold the balance between market and mission, 'success' and service, individual advantage and community solidarity and also to construct new relationships between Catholic schools and poor populations which are in some locations increasingly either non-Catholic or, if Catholic, non-practising.

The challenges of Catholicity

All leaders of faith-based schools are expected to transmit that faith or at least to create the most favourable educational environment for the faith to be renewed in the youth of the community. This is after all the prime purpose for the existence of such schools. This applies to Jewish, Islamic and Sikh schools as well as to the various Christian schools which operate internationally. In the case of Catholic schools, this responsibility is known as the renewal of Catholicity. Catholicity may be defined as the realisation of the doctrines and practice of the Christian faith as expressed in the teachings, liturgies and ecclesial practice of the Roman Catholic Church. Whatever else Catholic schools are expected to do, their foundation purpose is to enhance the spiritual and moral formation of young Catholic Christians who will be active in the world as witnesses of Christ and as workers for justice and peace. Catholic schools in many contemporary contexts may be increasingly successful in terms of academic achievement, popularity with the parents and employers, sporting and social reputation and market effectiveness but, as I have argued elsewhere:

> Catholic schools, by reason of their spiritual mission, have to pay particular attention to the verse in St Matthew's Gospel which asks: "What shall it profit a man to gain the whole world and to lose his own soul?"[10]

In other words, Catholic school leaders everywhere when reviewing the effectiveness of their schools in educating the young have to constantly review the question of the nature and vitality of the Catholicity which is being realised within the school. In that sense Catholic school leaders are responsible for the 'soul' of the school. Taken seriously, this is a very challenging responsibility especially in those societies where the Christian faith is becoming marginalised and where religious practice among adults is in decline. It is also a problematic responsibility because within Catholic communities there are different conceptions of what a satisfactory realisation of Catholicity in a school would be. Catholic school leaders therefore face an external culture which is largely indifferent to the issue of Catholicity and an internal culture which is divided on the issue.

At least two contrasting formulations of Catholicity in schools try to influence the policies and practices of school leaders. The first may be called *Traditional Catholicity* because many of its expectations and prescriptions are realisations of Catholic religious culture which existed before the reforms of the Second Vatican Council (1962–1965). The second may be called *Reformed Catholicity* because its practice represents in many ways the outcome of the reforms of the Second Vatican Council. Advocates of both these positions currently seek to influence Catholic school leaders internationally in order to influence the crucial question of how the Catholic ethos of a school is in practice constituted.

For traditionalists, a Catholic school should be judged on its relative success in encouraging young people to be regular attenders at Sunday Mass and to have a good understanding of Catholic doctrine, liturgy and sacred symbolism. Desirably a 'good' Catholic school will be an environment which encourages some of its students to realise a vocation for the priesthood or for religious life.

For others, this is a 'golden age' view of Catholicity which is unlikely to be recovered in contemporary conditions. Those more influenced by the reforming spirit of the 1960s look for a Catholicity among the young which is realised in active participation in school-based Masses and liturgies, designed and enacted by school students. Commitment to social and community service and to voluntary service overseas are take to be important forms whereby lay vocations are expressed in the modern age.

As guardians of the mission integrity of Catholic schools in this foundational area of Catholicity, school leaders may be exposed to considerable pressures. These pressures may come from local bishops and priests, from religious orders responsible for schools, from local interest groups in the Catholic community or from groups of parents. The issue is not simply, as it might appear, a rather esoteric theological question. It manifests itself in very real and concrete issues of policy and practice which school leaders have to grapple with. Insofar as the Catholic ethos of a school is affected by the proportion of Catholic students (practising or nominal), should there be a minimum proportion below which a school could not be said to be 'Catholic'? What should be the policy towards Christians from other churches or towards parents and students of other faiths? Should the school principal and members of the senior professional team always be practising Catholics? What should be the policy for the recruitment of teachers who are not Catholic and should there be any limit upon the proportion who are not Catholic? Should there be an attempt to maintain a distinctively Catholic curriculum[11] and pedagogic environment involving a Catholic framing for curriculum subjects, a privileged place for religious education and catechesis and requirements to attend school Masses and liturgies?

The possible answers to these questions have to be worked out by Catholic school leaders operating in different socio-political, economic and cultural contexts across the world.

Notes

* The use of the term 'school leaders' throughout this chapter refers in the main to school principals and headteachers. However, it must be remembered that school leadership is also represented by governors, trustees, school board members and the Catholic hierarchy itself.
1 As quoted to the present writer by a Notre Dame sister, headteacher of a secondary school in inner-London.
2 For sources on St Thomas Aquinas and education, see Corbishley (1943), Donohue (1968), MacIntyre (1999) and Arthur, Walters and Gaine (1999).
3 See Carr (2000) and Jacobs (2000).
4 Bryk, et al. (1993 pp. 33–34).
5 The necessity for the balanced relation of faith, knowledge and culture is strongly argued in *The Religious Dimension of Education in a Catholic School* (1988).
6 Chubb and Moe (1992 pp. 45–46).
7 Catholic schools receive significant support from public funds in the UK and Ireland, in Belgium and the Netherlands, and in Germany. This is also the case in Australia and New Zealand and some provinces of Canada. For a review of the current financial problems of Catholic schools in the USA see Harris (2000).

8 O'Keefe (1996 p. 193).
9 I have used the concept of 'strategic subsidy' to refer to the crucial underwriting of the Catholic educational mission especially in deprived locations by members of religious and teaching orders. Strategic subsidy refers to the provision by these orders of personnel and economic, cultural and spiritual capital for the schooling system. The weakening of this subsidy poses major problems for the future of Catholic schooling and Catholic school leadership in many areas.
10 Grace (1998b p. 202).
11 See, for instance, Davis (1999).

References

Arthur, J. (1994). Parental participation in Catholic schooling: A case of increasing conflict. *British Journal of Educational Studies, 42(2),* 74–190.

Arthur, J. (1995). *The ebbing tide: Policy and principles of Catholic education.* Leominster, UK: Gracewing.

Arthur, J., Walters, H., & Gaine, S. (1999). *Earthen vessels: the Thomistic tradition in education.* Leominster, UK: Gracewing.

Birmingham Catholic Partnership (1998). *The Catholic secondary guarantee.* Birmingham: Catholic Partnership Office.

Bourdieu, P. (1986). Three forms of capital. In J. Richardson (Ed.), *Handbook of theory and research for the sociology of education.* New York: Greenwood Press.

Bryk, A., Lee, V., & Holland, P. (1993). *Catholic schools and the common good.* Cambridge, MA: Harvard University Press.

Carr, K. (2000). Leadership given to the religious mission of Catholic schools. In J. Youniss, J. Convey & J. McLellan (Eds.), *The Catholic character of Catholic schools* (pp. 62–81). Notre Dame, IN: University of Notre Dame Press.

Catholic Bishops' Conference of England and Wales (1996). *The common good and the Catholic church's social teaching.* London: Catholic Education Service.

Catholic Bishops' Conference of England and Wales (1997). *The common good in education.* London: Catholic Education Service.

Chubb, J., & Moe, T. (1990). *Politics, markets and America's schools.* Washington, DC: Brookings Institute.

Chubb, J., & Moe, T. (1992). *A lesson in school reform from Great Britain.* Washington, DC: Brookings Institute.

Congregation for Catholic Education (1998). *The Catholic school on the threshold of the third millennium.* Vatican City: Libreria Editrice Vaticana.

Corbishley, T. (1943). St. Thomas and educational theory. *Dublin Review, 212(42).*

Davis, R. (1999). Can there be a Catholic curriculum? In J. Conroy (Ed.), *Catholic education: Inside out/outside in* (pp. 207–229). Dublin: Lindisfarne Books.

Donohue, J. (1968). *St. Thomas and education.* New York: Random House.

Grace, G. (1995.) *School leadership: Beyond educational management.* London: Falmer Press.

Grace, G. (1996). Catholic school leadership. In T. McLaughlin, J. O'Keefe & B. O'Keeffe (Eds.), *The contemporary Catholic school* (pp. 70–88). London: Falmer Press.

Grace, G. (1997). Critical leadership studies. In M. Crawford, L. Kydd & C. Riches (Eds.), *Leadership and teams in educational management.* Buckingham, UK: Open University Press.

Grace, G. (1998a). Realising the mission: Catholic approaches to school effective-ness. In R. Slee, G. Weiner & S. Tomlinson (Eds.), *School effectiveness for whom?* (pp. 117–127). London: Falmer Press.

Grace, G. (1998b). The future of the Catholic school: An English perspective. In J. Feheney (Ed.), *From ideal to action: The inner nature of a Catholic school* (pp. 190–202). Dublin: Veritas.

Grace, G. (2002). *Catholic schools: Mission, markets and morality.* London: Routledge Falmer.

Harris, J. (2000). The funding dilemma facing Catholic elementary and secondary schools. In J. Youniss & J. Convey (Eds.), *Catholic schools at the crossroads.* New York: Teachers College Press.

Hodgkinson, C. (1983). *The philosophy of leadership.* Oxford: Basil Blackwell.

Hunt, T., Oldenski, T., & Wallace, T. (Eds.) (2000). *Catholic school leadership.* London: Falmer Press.

Jacobs, R. (2000). Contributions of religious to US Catholic schooling. In J. Youniss, J. Convey & J. McLellan (Eds.), *The Catholic character of Catholic schools* (pp. 82–102). New York: Teachers College Press.

Macintyre, A. (1999). Aquinas's critique of education: Against his own age, against ours. In A. Rorty (Ed.), *Philosophers of education: New historical perspectives.* London: Routledge.

O'Keefe, J. (1996). No margin, no mission. In T. McLaughlin, J. O'Keefe & B. O'Keeffe (Eds.), *The contemporary Catholic school* (pp. 177–197). London: Falmer Press.

O'Keefe, J., & Murphy, J. (2000). Ethnically diverse Catholic schools: School struc-ture, students, staffing and finance. In J. Youniss & J. Convey (Eds.), *Catholic schools at the crossroads* (pp. 117–136). New York: Teachers College Press.

Pittau, G. (2000). Education on the threshold of the third millennium: Challenge, mission and adventure. *Catholic Education, 4(2),* 39–152

Pope Paul VI. (1975). *Apostolic exhortation: Evangelii nuntiandi.* Vatican City: Libreria Editrice Vaticana.

Ranson, S. (1993). Markets or democracy for education. *British Journal of Educa-tion Studies, 41(4),* 333–352.

Sacred Congregation for Catholic Education (1977). *The Catholic school.* Vatican City: Libreria Editrice Vaticana.

Sacred Congregation for Catholic Education (1982). *Lay Catholics in schools: Wit-nesses to faith.* Vatican City: Libreria Editrace Vaticana.

Thrupp, M. (1999). *Schools making a difference: Let's be realistic.* Buckingham, UK: Open University Press.

Vatican Congregation for Catholic Education (1988). *The religious dimension of education in a Catholic school.* Vatican City: Libreria Editrice Vaticana.

Wallace, T. (2000). We are called: The principal as faith leader in the Catholic school. In T. Hunt, T. Oldenski & T. Wallace (Eds.), *Catholic school leadership* (pp. 191–203). London: Falmer Press.

Youniss, J., & Convey, J. (Eds.) (2000). *Catholic schools at the crossroads: Survival and transformation.* New York: Teachers College Press.

Youniss, J., Convey, J., & McLellan, J. (Eds.) (2000). *The Catholic character of Catholic schools.* Notre Dame, IN: University of Notre Dame Press.

Part 6

Catholic values, Catholic curriculum and education policy

Catholic social teaching should permeate the Catholic secondary school curriculum

An agenda for reform

International Studies in Catholic Education, 2013, 5(1), 99–109.

International research shows that the curricula of Catholic secondary schools are increasingly becoming dominated by the pressures of conforming to the requirements of nation states. These requirements are generally expressed in economic and utilitarian terms and evaluated by criteria of measurable outputs. As a result of these pressures, Catholic secondary schools are in danger of losing a distinctive religious and educational cultural programme expressed in a distinctive Catholic school curriculum. It is suggested in this article that a serious permeation of Catholic social teaching is crucial, not only for the intrinsic importance of its subject matter but also as a means to resist total cultural incorporation into state-mandated curricula. Particular attention is given to the educational potential contained in Pope Benedict XVI's encyclical, *Caritas in Veritate* (2009).

Introduction

In their publication, *Our Best Kept Secret: The Rich Heritage of Catholic Social Teaching* (1988), Michael Schultheis et al. argue that such teaching, 'seems to have been forgotten, or never known, by a majority of the Roman Catholic community' (3).

Reviewing the situation in 1988, the authors detailed this rich (but relatively unknown) heritage as including the Papal encyclicals of Leo XIII (1891), Pius XI (1931), Paul VI (1967) and John Paul II (1981, 1988). To this can now be added the ground-breaking encyclical of Benedict XVI, *Caritas in Veritate* (2009).

Michael Schultheis and his co-authors saw the major problem to be the lack of access by the majority of the Catholic population to the formal discourse in which Papal encyclicals are expressed. While it is undoubtedly true that the language used in the encyclicals has been an impediment, it is also true that Catholic educational institutions at all levels have failed to provide curriculum mediations of this teaching as a crucial part of the formation of Catholic youth. A great opportunity for the dissemination of the counter-cultural social messages of the Church has thereby been lost despite the existence of valuable sources such as Dorr (1983/2003) and Walsh and Davies (1991).

This article argues that Pope Benedict's encyclical, *Caritas in Veritate*, on integral human development in charity and truth, by reason of its radical observations and its timely application to contemporary world conditions, could provide the material for Catholic educators to use in a wide range of secondary school curricular subjects.

In addition to the intrinsic value of the Pope's teaching, the use of this encyclical throughout the curriculum will provide a distinctive religious, cultural and educational message which will not be found in local state secular schools.

How can the teachings of *Caritas in Veritate* permeate the curricula of Catholic schools and colleges?

From a close reading of *Caritas in Veritate* (CV), at least three major themes can be discerned: (1) religious, moral and cultural issues; (2) economic, business and enterprise issues; and (3) social, environmental and political issues.

Insofar as Catholic schools and colleges, internationally, have curricula constituted by Theology and Religious Education, Philosophy and Ethics, Personal and Moral Education, Mathematics, Business and Enterprise Studies, Economic and Social Sciences, Politics, Environmental and Physical Sciences and Humane subjects (Literature, History, Languages, Geography, etc.), the potential for permeation of Catholic social teaching is considerable across many subjects.

Religious, moral and cultural issues

In this sector of the school curriculum, study sessions for senior students could be constructed as discussion topics related to specific CV extracts, with assignment questions designed to elicit personal, critical responses from the students. Some examples would be:

- 'Charity demands justice: recognition and respect for the legitimate rights of individuals and peoples. It strives to build the earthly city according to law and justice. On the other hand, charity transcends justice and completes it in the logic of giving and forgiving' (para. 6, 7).[1]

  In what ways does charity 'transcend' justice?

- 'Underdevelopment is the lack of brotherhood among individuals and peoples. As society becomes ever more globalised it makes us neighbours but does not make us brothers. Reason can establish civic equalities but it cannot establish fraternity' (para. 19, 20).

Outline your understanding of the Christian doctrine of fraternity and indicate how it could be applied to international development.

- 'Today, people frequently kill in the holy name of God . . . This applies especially to terrorism motivated by fundamentalism which generates grief, destruction and death and obstructs dialogue between nations' (para. 29, 33).

How would you answer the arguments of Professor Richard Dawkins that this is the inevitable outcome of religious belief?

- 'When he is far away from God, man is unsettled and ill at ease. Social and psychological alienation and the many neuroses that afflict affluent societies are attributable, in part, to spiritual factors' (para. 76, 88).

To what extent do you agree with this statement?

- 'The greatest service to development then, is a Christian humanism . . . Openness to God makes us open towards our brothers and sisters and towards an understanding of life as a joyful task to be accomplished in a spirit of solidarity' (para. 78, 91).

Does the record of Christian social action in the world support, in your view, this assertion?

Clearly, a study programme based upon this section of *Caritas in Veritate* must be based upon a resource book of readings covering issues such as conceptual distinctions of forms of charity, developing ideas of social justice, interpretations of fraternity, study of the various types of religious fundamentalism, engagement with the work of the 'new atheists', e.g. Dawkins (2006), and historical study of Christian social action. While this will be demanding for both teachers and students, it can be suggested that senior students in Catholic schools are likely to engage with these issues with interest and vigour. In other words it should contribute powerfully to a renewed and better-informed Catholic social conscience among the young.[2]

Economic, business and enterprise issues

The development of curriculum subjects and curriculum materials related to the study of Economics, Finance, Business Administration and Enterprise is a growing feature of Catholic schools and colleges internationally. This reflects, in part, the expectations of government, parents and senior students that these subjects are a necessary preparation for an increasingly competitive, mobile and globalised world of international corporate business, finance and trade. The utilitarian appeal of these subjects is high.

A challenge for Catholic schools and colleges is that the addition of these subjects to the curriculum may represent an entirely secular and utilitarian cultural implant in their programmes unless these subjects are brought into an organic relation with the religious, moral and social teachings of the Church. However, is this happening? There is little evidence that this organic relation is being developed in the schools. The cultural problem here is that many writers on Economics and related subjects have kept religious and moral issues outside the boundaries of their subject content and analysis. In a recent publication, *The Credit Crunch: Making Moral Sense of the Financial Crisis* (2009), Edward Hadas has argued: 'In addition to greed itself and bad ideas about human nature, one other factor may have played a role in the pre-crisis abdication of responsibility in finance. This is the refusal to take morality seriously in any economic discussions' (42).[3] It must also be admitted that the 'rich heritage' of Catholic social and moral teaching relevant to these subjects has, in general,[4] been ignored in many Catholic schools internationally. That is why this present situation, marked by a global economic and financial crisis (salient in the thoughts of contemporary students) and the publication of *Caritas in Veritate* which addresses these issues from a Catholic perspective, provides an opportunity for all Catholic schools and colleges to focus upon the relevance of Catholic social teaching to contemporary conditions.

Caritas in Veritate presents an agenda of issues for discussion and reflection which all senior students in Catholic education should encounter in their studies. The following are some examples of what Pope Benedict offers for their consideration:

- 'The world's wealth is growing in absolute terms but inequalities are on the increase. The scandal of glaring inequalities continues' (para. 22, 25).
- 'The conviction that the economy must be autonomous, that it must be shielded from the influences of a moral character, has led man to abuse the economic process in a thoroughly destructive way' (para. 34, 39).
- 'The market can be a negative force, not because it is so by nature, but because a certain ideology can make it so' (para. 36, 42).
- 'John Paul II taught that investment always has moral as well as economic significance' (para. 40, 47).
- 'Financiers must rediscover the ethical foundations of their activity so as not to abuse the sophisticated instruments what can serve to betray the interests of savers' (para. 65, 77).

Catholic schools and college teachers have the potential to be significant innovators in bringing together the study of Economics, Finance, Business Administration and Enterprise with an in-depth understanding of Catholic religious, moral and social teaching, so that a higher-order level of knowledge and understanding can be achieved in these crucial contemporary subjects.

Caritas in Veritate could be the catalyst for this necessary cultural transformation.[5]

Social, environmental and political issues

The intrinsic appeal of social, environmental and political issues to senior students in Catholic schools and colleges is considerable.[6] They are, after all, the inheritors of a world which many of them believe is in a dysfunctional state on all three dimensions. As a generation, they are probably possessed of more information and consciousness of the nature and extent of social, environmental and political dysfunctions in the world than any previous generation. It is entirely likely that they expect their school and college programmes to engage seriously with these issues, not only in knowledge terms but also in suggesting what Catholic social action is needed to help a process of change and development.

In meeting these expectations, *Caritas in Veritate* has much to offer because Pope Benedict XVI shares their concerns and provides profound guidance for action and transformation:

> The crisis thus becomes an opportunity for discernment in which to shape a new vision for the future.
>
> (24)

The Pope's discernment and vision is developed in a number of strong statements which have the potential to animate the consciousness and action of Catholic youth in their subsequent vocations and roles in adult life.

Such statements as:

- 'The processes of globalization . . . open up the unprecedented possibility of large-scale redistribution of wealth on a world – wide scale; if badly directed however, they can lead to an increase in poverty and inequality' (para. 42, 50).
- 'Today the material resources available for rescuing peoples from poverty are potentially greater than ever before, but they have ended up largely in the hands of people from developed countries who have benefited more from the liberalisation that has occurred in the mobility of capital and labour' (para. 42, 51).
- 'The way humanity treats the environment influences the way it treats itself . . . This invites contemporary society to a serious review of its life-style, which, in many parts of the world is prone to hedonism and consumerism, regardless of their harmful consequences' (para. 51, 63).
- 'Every migrant is a human person who, as such, possesses fundamental inalienable rights that must be respected by everyone and in every circumstance' (para. 62, 75).

- 'There is urgent need of a true world political authority . . . vested with the effective power to ensure security for all, regard for justice, and respect for rights' (para. 67, 79–80).[7]

It is sometimes the case that senior students in Catholic schools and colleges begin to distance themselves from the practice and discourse of the Faith because they perceive it to be disconnected from the many challenges of the 'real world'[8] in which they live.

Detailed study of *Caritas in Veritate* has the potential to show that, on the contrary, the Christian religion in the Catholic tradition is integral to an understanding of these challenges and a valuable source of guidance in ways of responding to them. There is a Heavenly City to which all believers aspire, but there is also an Earthly City which believers are called upon to perfect by social action. As Pope Benedict expresses it:

- 'Development requires attention to the spiritual life . . . trust in God, spiritual fellowship in Christ, reliance upon God's providence and mercy, love and forgiveness, self-denial, acceptance of others, justice and peace. All this is essential if "hearts of stone" are to be transformed into "hearts of flesh" (Ezk. 36:26), rendering life on earth "divine" and thus more worthy of humanity' (para. 79, 92).

In other words, what is projected to contemporary youth as the 'real world' is in fact a construct of globalised materialism from which religious faith is either marginalised or represented by the media in its distorted and funda-mentalist extremes. Catholic social teaching, and in particular the teachings of *Caritas in Veritate* show to the young the authentic face of religion and show a 'real world' that can be attained by social action inspired by faith.

Catholic social teaching and the Catholic school curriculum

In 1999, Robert Davis wrote a ground-breaking chapter with the title, 'Can there be a Catholic curriculum?' His purpose was to generate a debate[9] among Catholic educators about this crucial issue at a time when both gov-ernment and economic agencies internationally appeared to be dominating the content, assessment and purposes of curricula. Davis' argument was that discussion of this issue had virtually disappeared from the considerations of Catholic educators.

His thesis was that:

the price Catholic schools have had to pay for their accreditation as appropriate centres for the 'delivery' of the modern curriculum is a restriction of their Catholicity to those features of school life where secular society is prepared to permit the manifestation of Catholic ideas – mainly worship, ethos and Religious education.

(221–222)

While worship, ethos and religious education are clearly central to the maintenance of a distinctive Catholic educational mission, Davis was raising the question of whether this was sufficient in itself if the major part of the curriculum and discourse in the school was, in essence, secular, utilitarian and shaped by government and economic requirements.

In as far as Davis' analysis is correct, in many societies, it points to an urgent need to strengthen the Catholic cultural content of the curriculum in general to prevent a process of incorporation into a secularised and technicist educational culture.

It has been the argument of this article that the rich heritage of Catholic social teaching, with its implications for the teaching of many subjects in the curriculum, could provide such distinctive and counter-cultural material. While *Caritas in Veritate* provides the immediate stimulus to do this, the encyclical itself is built upon the insights of earlier work, especially from Pope Paul VI and Pope John Paul II. Taken together, this is a rich resource which innovative teachers can use to illuminate a range of subjects in ways which are distinctively different to those used in state secular schools. In this way, the Catholicity of the school will be strengthened not only by its worship, ethos and formal religious education, but by a total curriculum experience which integrates faith and learning through the agency of Catholic social teaching.

To bring about such a transformation will require school authorities to struggle for more relative autonomy in curriculum provision; it will require changes in professional preparation and continuing professional development programmes for Catholic teachers and it will require school leaders to be innovative agents of change. However, if the mission integrity[10] of Catholic schools and colleges in an increasingly secular, globalised and technicist world is to be maintained, such cultural action is essential.

Education and the formation of the Catholic social conscience

Speaking of education in *Caritas in Veritate,* Benedict XVI reminds his readers that, 'the term "education" refers not only to classroom teaching and vocational training . . . but to the complete formation of the person' (para. 61, 73).

As educational discourse in contemporary society becomes increasingly dominated by the language of 'training', a Catholic educational discourse which emphasises 'formation of the person' is not only counter-cultural, but more humane. It insists that the ultimate goal of the educational process is the formation of good persons equipped with knowledge and skills to serve the common good motivated by faith and a Catholic social conscience.

But what is this conscience and how is it formed?

In his essays *On Conscience* (1984/reprinted 2006) Cardinal Joseph Ratzinger argued that:

> conscience signifies the perceptible and demanding presence of the voice of truth in the subject himself. It is the overcoming of mere subjectivity in the encounter . . . with the truth from God.
>
> (p. 25, 2006 edition)

At the same time:

> included in the concept of conscience is an obligation, namely the obligation to care for it, to form it and educate it.
>
> (63, 2006 edition)

In addition to the direct teaching received by the young from their parents and attendance at Mass, Catholic schools and colleges clearly represent crucial arena for the forming and informing of conscience. The Catholic social conscience of the young will not simply result from the acquisition of knowledge about Catholic social teaching, although that is the necessary foundation. It will require the nurture of their spirituality and Christian faith by a constant interaction between such social teaching and the teaching, practice and mission of Jesus Christ and the saints. To be truly animated, such students need opportunities to be involved in Catholic social action projects in their communities and beyond. The *International Handbook of Catholic Education* (2007) records examples of such formative and practical action by Catholic schools and colleges in different parts of the world.[11] The challenge is not that such formation and expression of the Catholic social conscience is absent in Catholic education but rather that it is in danger of being marginalised in the contemporary pursuit of better academic and test results. The history of Catholicism is rich in the heritage of the martyrs of conscience who have shown 'obedience to the truth which must stand higher than any human tribunal'[12] (26, 2006 edition). Catholic schools and colleges are not lacking in role models with which to inspire contemporary students to think and act beyond a culture of acquisitive and competitive individualism. In writing *Caritas in Veritate*, Pope Benedict XVI has given them a better vision for the future and has emphasised that love of God must always be shown in love of neighbour.

Conclusion: Catholic social teaching: a major theological and cultural resource for Catholic education

This article has argued that Catholic education internationally could be renewed and reanimated by a systematic permeation of Catholic social teaching across all subjects of the curriculum. This strategy would have many advantages. It would, first and foremost, have the potential to engage the interest and involvement of senior students at a time when many of them begin to question the relevance of their faith to contemporary challenges. It would help to inform and strengthen their Catholic social conscience as they came to understand that the teachings of Jesus Christ and the saints as mediated by the Catholic tradition of social analysis makes an organic relation between faith and action in the world. At the same time, it would help to prevent both students and schools from becoming incorporated into a global culture in which 'the only criterion is practical utility and the only value is economic and technological progress'.[13]

While *Caritas in Veritate* provides the immediate stimulus for making such a cultural transformation in Catholic education, and is strongly founded upon earlier Papal encyclicals which need to be rediscovered, the corpus of Catholic social teaching is more extensive than that provided by the Magisterium. An appendix to this article suggests a supplementary range of other sources which can be used by Catholic educators. However, it has to be recognised that serious cultural transformations in educational practice are not easy, especially in contemporary conditions where academic 'productivity', public accountability, market competition and value for money calculations are dominating educational institutions. As many hard-pressed school leaders and teachers will observe, measurements of Catholic social conscience are not included in school accountability processes by public agencies. So, while Catholic social teaching may be a valuable resource for Catholic school curricula, it may not 'count' in the public mechanisms for school evaluations and judgements of 'success'.

It is in situations such as this that a distinctive quality of Catholic school and college leadership must assert itself. Catholic school leaders have to 'render to Caesar', but they also have to 'render to God'. They are the guardian of the mission integrity of the schools. However, public accountability requirements are not the only impediments: there are workload and time pressures which block the path to religious, cultural and curriculum change. It is one thing to list the sources for the serious study of Catholic social teaching; it is another thing for already pressurised educators to find easy access to such sources for classroom stimulus material. A survey of the available literature, prior to the publication of *Caritas in Veritate* suggests that one of the most useful mediating text for school leaders and teachers is the Fourth Edition of *Catholic Social Teaching*, published by the Center of Concern in Washington in 2003. Here is, in effect, a valuable teacher's handbook which gives access to Catholic social teaching in classroom-related format.

To supplement and to background the profound insights of *Caritas in Veritate,* teachers and students can construct a term's programme focused on seven core principles of Catholic social teaching as outlined in this text: (1) The Dignity of the Human Person; (2) The Dignity of Work; (3) The Person in Community; (4) Rights and Responsibilities; (5) Option for those in Poverty; (6) Solidarity; and (7) Care for Creation. Contained within these principles are discussion and analysis topics of great potential interest, e.g. the common good, 'structures of sin', liberation theology, human rights, resisting market idolatry, subsidiarity, peace-making, the just war.[14]

In 1996, the Catholic Bishops' Conference of England and Wales published a ground-breaking document, *The Common Good and the Catholic Church's Social Teaching*, in which they called for:

> more participation in the future development of Catholic Social Teaching so that it is properly owned by all Catholics.
>
> (para. 31)

The way to ensure this ownership and the formation of a maturely developed Catholic social conscience in all members of the Church is to permeate the curriculum and the pedagogy of Catholic schools and colleges, with the rich heritage of Catholic social teaching. Catholic Bishops Conferences across the world could now give leadership in this crucial area to strengthen the religious and cultural distinctiveness of Catholic school curricula at a time when such curricula are under threat from utilitarian and secular national priorities.

Acknowledgements

This is a revised version of a chapter which originally appeared in the book *Catholic Social Conscience* (2011), published by Gracewing Publications. The author and the publishers of this journal thank Gracewing for permission to publish this revised version.

Notes

1 All quotations are taken from the 2009 edition of *Caritas in Veritate* published by The Catholic Truth Society, London and reproduced with permission.
2 It also has to be accepted that some young people will disagree with the stance taken by the Pope and the Catholic Church on these issues as part of their own individual critical development.
3 There have been some attempts to bring the Christian religion and the world of economic enterprise into dialogue, e.g. *Morality and the Market Place: Christian Alternatives to Capitalism and Socialism* (Griffiths 1982); *God and the Marketplace: Essays on the Morality of Wealth Creation* (Davies 1993); *Managing as if Faith Mattered* (Alford and Naughton 2001); *Globalisation for the Common Good* (Mofid 2002). However, this literature does not seem to have affected school curricula in general.
4 This situation varies internationally. Catholic schools and colleges in the USA, especially Jesuit schools, have engaged seriously with Catholic social teaching in their curricula and in social action.
5 *Caritas in Veritate* could be the catalyst for this, but it could also help in the rediscovery of other Papal encyclicals of Catholic social teaching. It is clear that Pope

Benedict XVI was deeply influenced by Pope Paul VI's encyclical, *Populorum Progressio* (1967). See pp. 11–21 of *Caritas in Veritate*.

6 See *Young Adult Catholics* (Hoge et al. 2001).

7 This is a clear criticism of the present effectiveness of the United Nations Organisation.

8 'Real world' is a contemporary ideological device used to suggest that proposed alternatives to the status quo are impractical theory or naive utopias.

9 For one response to this debate, see *Can There be a Catholic School Curriculum?* published by the Centre for Research and Development in Catholic Education in 2007.

10 In first using the concept of mission integrity in 2002, I stressed the importance of the mission to the poor. However, mission integrity involves not only service to a particular category of students, but also a distinctive Catholic curriculum content.

11 See *International Handbook of Catholic Education* (Grace and O'Keefe 2007) chapters 6, 10, 22, 24, 33, 37 and 39.

12 See also the earlier statement of Father Joseph Ratzinger, when acting as theological adviser to the Second Vatican Council: 'Over the Pope as expression of the binding claim of ecclesiastical authority, there stands one's own conscience, which must be obeyed before all else, even if necessary against the requirements of ecclesiastical authority. This emphasis on the individual whose conscience confronts him with a supreme and ultimate tribunal, and one which in the last resort is beyond the claim of external social groups, even the official church, also establishes a principle in opposition to increasing totalitarianism' (Vorgrimler, 1967, 134).

13 Congregation for Catholic Education (1988, para. 10).

14 *Catholic Social Teaching: Our Best Kept Secret* (De Berri et al. 2003, 18–34).

References

Alford, H. (OP), and M. Naughton. 2001. *Managing as if Faith Mattered: Christian Social Principles in the Modern Organisation.* Notre Dame: University of Notre Dame Press.

Arthur, J., P. Boylan, G. Grace, and P. Walsh. 2007. *Can There be a Catholic School Curriculum?: Renewing the Debate.* London: CRDCE.

Benedict XVI. 2009. *Caritas in Veritate: Encyclical Letter on Integral Human Development in Charity and Truth.* London: Catholic Truth Society.

Catholic Bishops' Conference of England and Wales. 1996. *The Common Good and the Catholic Church's Social Teaching.* London: CBC.

Congregation for Catholic Education. 1988. *The Religious Dimension of Education in a Catholic School.* London: Catholic Truth Society.

Davies, J., ed. 1993. *God and the Marketplace: Essays on the Morality of Wealth Creation.* London: Institute of Economic Affairs.

Davis, R. 1999. "Can There be a Catholic Curriculum?." In *Catholic Education: Inside Out/Outside in,* edited by J. Conroy, 207–230. Dublin: Lindisfarne Books.

Dawkins, R. 2006. *The God Delusion.* London: Bantam Books.

De, Berri E. (SJ), J. Hug (SJ), P. Henriot (SJ), and M. Schultheis (SJ). 2003. *Catholic Social Teaching: Our Best Kept Secret.* 4th ed. New York: Orbis Books.

Dorr, D. 1983/2003. *Option for the Poor: A Hundred Years of Catholic Social Teaching.* 2003 rev ed. New York: Orbis Books.

Grace, G. 2002. "'Mission integrity': Contemporary Challenges for Catholic School Leaders." In *Second International Handbook of Educational Leadership and Administration*, edited by K. Leithwood and P. Hallinger. Dordrecht/Boston: Kluwer Academic Press.

Grace, G., and J. O'Keefe, (SJ), ed., 2007. *International Handbook of Catholic Education* (2 Volumes). Dordrecht: Springer.

Griffiths, B. 1982. *Morality and the Market Place: Christian Alternatives to Capitalism and Socialism*. London: Hodder and Stoughton.

Hadas, E. 2009. *The Credit Crunch: Making Moral Sense of the Financial Crisis*. London: Catholic Truth Society.

Hoge, D., W. Dinges, M. Johnson, and J. Gonzales. 2001. *Young Adult Catholics: Religion in the Culture of Choice*. Notre Dame: University of Notre Dame Press.

John Paul II. 1981. *Laborem Exercens* [On human work] *encyclical letter*. Vatican City, Rome.

John Paul II. 1988. *Sollicitudo Rei Socialis* [The social concern of the church] *encyclical letter*. Vatican City, Rome.

John Paul II. 1991. *Centesimus Annus* [One hundred years] *encyclical letter*. Vatican City, Rome.

Leo XIII. 1891. *Rerum Novarum* [On the condition of labour] *encyclical letter*. Vatican City, Rome.

Mofid, K. 2002. *Globalisation for the Common Good*. London: Shepheard-Walwyn.

Paul VI. 1967. *Populorum Progressio* [The development of peoples] *encyclical letter*. Vatican City, Rome.

Pius XI. 1931. *Quadragesimo Anno* [The reconstruction of the social order] *encyclical letter*. Vatican City, Rome.

Ratzinger, J. 2006. *On Conscience*. San Francisco, CA: Ignatius Press.

Schultheis, M., (SJ), Berri, (SJ)E. De, and P. Henriot, (SJ). 1988. *Our Best Kept Secret: The Rich Heritage of Catholic Social Teaching*. London: Catholic Fund for Overseas Development.

Vorgrimler, H, ed., 1967. *Commentary on the Documents of Vatican II Vol V*. New York: Herder and Herder.

Walsh, M., and B. Davies. 1991. *Proclaiming Justice and Peace: Papal Documents from Rerum Novarum Through Centesimus Annus, North American Edition*. Mystic, CT: Twenty-Third.

Further sources for the study of Catholic social teaching

Booth, P., ed. 2007. *Catholic Social Teaching and the Market Economy*. London: Institute of Economic Affairs.

Caldecott, S. 2009. *Catholic Social Teaching: A Way In*. London: Catholic Truth Society.

Charles, R SJ. 1998. *Christian Social Witness and Teaching* (2 Volumes). Leominster: Gracewing.

Clark, C., and H. Alford. 2009. *Rich and Poor: Rebalancing the Economy*. London: Catholic Truth Society.

Coleman, J., and W. Ryan. 2005. *Globalization and Catholic Social Thought*. Ottawa: Novalis.

Cullen, P., B. Hoose, and G. Mannion, eds., 2007. *Catholic Social Justice: Theological and Practical Explorations*. London: Continuum.

Gutierrez, G. 1983. *A Theology of Liberation: History, Politics and Salvation*. London, SCM Press.

Hollenbach, D. 2003. *The Common Good and Christian Ethics*. Cambridge: Cambridge University Press.

Hornsby-Smith, M. 2006. *An Introduction to Catholic Social Thought*. Cambridge: Cambridge University Press.

McDonough, S. (SSC) 1990. *The Greening of the Church*. London: SCM Press.

Pontifical Council for Justice and Peace. 2004. *Compendium of the Social Doctrine of the Church Vatican City*. Rome: Libreria Editrice Vaticana.

Rowland, C., ed., 1999. *The Cambridge Companion to Liberation Theology*. Cambridge: Cambridge University Press.

Chapter 15

Christianity, modernities and knowledge

International Handbook of Comparative Education, Part 2. 2009, (Eds). R. Cowen, A. Kazamias, E. Unterhalter, 907–922, Springer.

From sacred Christian knowledge to secular market knowledge

In *Pedagogy, Symbolic Control and Identity* (1996), Basil Bernstein reflected theoretically on the significance of these issues and it is clear that his insights provide a valuable starting point for a 'comparative education of the future'.

Bernstein outlines a major cultural transformation which can be discerned in Europe (and internationally), from a faith-based conception of knowledge and pedagogy to a secular, market-based conception of education. Historically, official knowledge and the curriculum and pedagogy derived from it in Europe were realisations of Christian religious culture in pursuit of a greater understanding of God:

> The Christian God was a god you had to think about. It was a god that not only was to be loved, but to be thought about. And this attitude created an abstract modality to the discourse.
>
> (Bernstein, 1996, p. 83)

Educational discourse in the medieval university or 'school' involved exploration of the Word and exploration of the world, 'Word and world held together by the unity of Christianity' (ibid).

The fundamental Christian regulative principle of school knowledge and pedagogy was the existence of God and the incarnation of Jesus Christ, whose natures could be partly apprehended by the study of sacred text and partly by exploration of the created universe. Culture, knowledge and pedagogy were strongly framed within the Christian revelation and world view as mediated by the Catholic Church as the dominant Christian institution.

This religious regulative principle was, in Bernstein's view, progressively replaced during the Renaissance and the Enlightenment by a 'humanizing secular principle', representing the stage of early modernity, but this principle is now being replaced by a 'dehumanizing principle' of market commodification of knowledge and pedagogy in late modernity. The argument is elaborated in these terms:

> Today, throughout Europe . . . there is a new principle guiding the latest transition of capitalism. The principles of the market and its managers are more and more the principles of the policy and practices of education. Market relevance is becoming the key orientating criterion for the selection of discourses. . . . This movement has profound implications from the primary school to the university.
>
> There is a new concept of knowledge and of its relation to those who create it and use it. This new concept is a truly secular concept. Knowledge should flow like money to wherever it can create advantage and profit. Indeed, knowledge is no longer like money, it *is* money.
>
> (Bernstein, 1996 p. 87)

Accompanying this secularisation, commodification and marketisation of knowledge in contemporary settings, there are comparable transformations in pedagogic discourse and communication. Pedagogy is not simply a means for the transmission of knowledge, it is also a powerful regulator of consciousness and a formative influence upon personal identity.[1] Pedagogy in the secularised market curriculum has itself become dominated by output measures of specific competences and skills, by performance models of comparative achievement levels and by efficiency and effectiveness criteria relating to the 'delivery' of the required objectives of prescribed curricula. It follows from this analysis that student consciousness and sense of identity and personal worth will be affected in particular ways by what Bernstein has described as 'a virtually secular pedagogic discourse' (p. 80).

Faced with these profound changes in the framing of culture, knowledge and pedagogy in early and late modernity it is important to examine the educational responses which have been made by both Catholic and Reformed Christianity.[2] The development of secularisation in the modern world from the Enlightenment to the present day presents agencies of sacred culture with a powerful challenge. Secularisation represents the denial of the validity of the sacred and of its associated educational cultures and its attempted replacement by logical, rational, empirical and scientific intellectual cultures in which the notion of the transcendent has no place. Secularisation involves a significant change in the cultural power relations of any society. While secularisation changes intellectual and cultural power relations it also operates to affect the world view of many individuals so that religious concepts, religious discourse and religious sensitivities are simply irrelevant to the everyday business of life. This is what Berger (1973) has called 'a secularization of consciousness'.

Reformation and counter-reformation in education

Giddens (1991) in *The Consequences of Modernity* argued that secularisation had significant consequences for an understanding of what constituted knowledge:

> Religious cosmology is supplanted by reflexively organised knowledge, governed by empirical observation and logical thought and focused upon material technology and socially applied codes.
>
> (p. 109)

What his analysis overlooks is, that while there has been (in the West) what could be called a secular reformation in the culture of knowledge, pedagogy and educational processes there has, at the same time, been a religious counter-reformation in which Catholic Christianity has been prominent.

Commenting on the nature of the current secular reformation (the second reformation), Bauman (2000) argues that its central idea is that of 'human rights', especially as expressed in freedom of choice regarding beliefs, values and actions. A strong form of autonomous individualism marks this stage of late modernity or early postmodernism. A powerful idea is that the identity of the person can be constructed from whatever cultural elements the individual chooses – a construct which Gellner (1996) calls 'modular man' (and woman).

Christian educational agencies (and those of other faiths) exist as part of a counter-reformation in modernity which relates the formation of human persons to religiously given beliefs, values and principles and not to an entirely self-determined modular process.

In terms of identity formation the Enlightenment sought to replace the concept of religious believer and church member with that of rational citizen and civic participant. In late modernity, according to Bernstein, the attempted ideological transformation is from that of citizen to that of consumer and 'market player'.

Whatever else globalisation represents, it seems clear that it involves an attempted marketisation of cultures and societies worldwide, with challenging implications for educational systems. These challenges are especially sharp for faith-based as opposed to secular schooling systems.

The challenges of early modernity: the educational responses of Catholic Christianity

The challenges of early modernity were constituted for the Catholic Church by the Protestant reformations of the sixteenth and seventeenth centuries and by the cultural effects of the Enlightenment in the eighteenth and nineteenth centuries. The Protestant reformations threatened the Church's control of culture, knowledge and pedagogy and its hegemony in the religious and spiritual domain. The Enlightenment and its consequences more radically threatened the very idea of the Christian God and of the culture of the sacred.

In his classic study, *The Evolution of Educational Thought* (1938) Emile Durkheim characterised the Society of Jesus as the leading Catholic agency in countering the challenges of both Protestantism and secularism in the early modern period. For this reason he assigned three chapters of his book to a close examination of Jesuit educational culture – its curriculum, pedagogy and assessment. Durkheim recognised the remarkable significance of the Jesuits in shaping and forming Catholic curricula and pedagogy in Europe. Their intention was to create an intellectually stimulating Christian engagement with classics, theology, philosophy, history, literature, music, art and drama. An emphasis upon rhetoric, disputation and debate was designed to produce the ideal Jesuit student who would become a confident apologist for the Faith. The humane studies of a Jesuit education were intended to form Catholic intellectuals and men of public affairs whose scholarship confirmed the truths of the Catholic faith and who could confidently articulate these in exchanges with Protestants, secularists and atheists. While Jesuit pupils, in the words of Durkheim, 'lived amidst a flurry of written assignments' (p. 255), the ultimate purpose of these assignments, whatever the subject, was to illuminate God's design for the created world and to form in the pupil a sense of service in relation to this grand design. This was an education intended to generate a vocation to serve others – at its best, by commitment to the clerical or religious life or in various lay professions for the general good.

The year 1999 marked the 400th anniversary of the publication of the *Ratio Studiorum* or 'The Plan and Methodology of Jesuit Education'. In a commemorative volume published in 2000, various Jesuit scholars reflected upon its significance, its impact and future in the face of new challenges.[3] It was understood that the influence of the *Ratio* and its educational culture had spread far beyond Jesuit schools and colleges. Many subsequent religious orders with missions in education had been influenced to a greater or lesser extent by Jesuit educational experience. The Institute of the Blessed Virgin Mary, The Society of the Sacred Heart, and other religious orders were directly affected by Jesuit educational methodology.[4] However, probably the greatest impact of the Jesuits is to be found in the example they provided of an active religious order with an educational mission. This set the pattern for the Catholic Church's response to the challenges of early modernity. The following centuries witnessed a multiplication of new religious orders and teaching brotherhoods and sisterhoods dedicated to the vocation of education. The Catholic response to the challenges of early modernity was to generate specially trained men and women in organised formations dedicated to the work of Catholic education. The prime knowledge to be transmitted was the truths and doctrines of the Catholic faith and the pedagogy of the catechism was the dominant form. At the same time great emphasis was placed on traditional forms of academic achievement, moral formation and a strict disciplinary regime. The Catholic religious orders founded in early modernity were, in effect, missionaries of education against the twin dangers of Protestantism and secularisation. Their educational regimes were designed to work at all levels of society, from governing elites to the urban and rural masses. The range of their operations extended across the whole world as they followed the injunction of their Founder to 'go and teach all nations'.[5]

At the heart of this great Catholic educational response to the challenges of early modernity were concepts of doctrinal certainty and vocational calling. Against the questioning of secularism, the existence of God was to be asserted and in various ways 'proved'. Against the innovations of Protestantism, the eternal validity of Catholicism and of the Catholic Church was reasserted. Permeating the whole system was the regulative principle of 'finding your vocation'. Catholic education was the means by which youth could find their calling from God – their vocational destiny in the service of God.

This destiny might be that of Catholic parenthood and lay occupations of various kinds (with public service professions strongly favoured) or the ultimate vocation of service to the Church in clerical or religious life. While so many Catholic teachers of this era were themselves members of religious orders the concept of a vocation in the service of God was a daily incarnation in the classroom lives of the pupils and students. The vocational word was, in this sense, 'made flesh' in the presence and the conduct of their teachers. Everything else in the system, the academic curriculum, the moral formation, the social and community bonding was there to facilitate the student in finding his or her approved vocation in the service of God (and the Catholic Church). This is the essence of a Christian faith-based schooling system, that is, the search for the nature of God especially as revealed in the Person of Christ and the search for God's purposes in vocation for the individual student. This system, as Bernstein (1996) has argued, was faced with considerable challenges in the cultural transformations of late modernity.

The challenges of late modernity: the educational responses of Catholic Christianity

In late modernity the Catholic Church faced a world situation characterised by a more pervasive culture of secularism and materialism than it had ever before encountered. In particular it faced an international cult of perpetual consumerism propagated by the many agencies of global capitalism and an international situation marked by sharper divisions between rich and poor nations.

The Catholic Church, under the inspiration of Pope John XXIII, had itself undergone an attempted spiritual, religious, moral and social transformation in the proceedings of the Second Vatican Council (1962–1965). As Adrian Hastings (1991, p. 525) has argued:

> [T]here can be no question that the Vatican Council was the most important ecclesiastical event of the century . . . It so greatly changed the character of by far the largest communion of Christendom.

The new spirit of Vatican II had considerable radical potential. This potential involved attempts to develop a new conception of the Church as not simply clerical but constituted as 'the people of God'; a move away from papal fiat towards greater collegial authority; a new principle of openness and dialogue with the world, other Christian denominations, other religious faiths and with 'all people of good will' regardless of faith; a renewed corpus of Catholic social teaching centred upon 'a preferential option for the poor' and a new conception of sin, as not merely individual failings but also social and structural failings. A changed socio-political stance in international relations involved a move from the traditional denunciations of Marxism and of communist regimes (as atheistic and oppressive) to a more extensive criticism of structures of oppression and exploitation – 'structures of sin', constituted in global capitalism, in race relations (apartheid in South Africa) and discernible in various parts of the world, for example, Latin America.

In 1977, the Sacred Congregation for Catholic Education issued from Rome a foundational document, *The Catholic School,* which powerfully expressed the new spirit which it was hoped would characterise Catholic education internationally. This document inaugurated a post-Vatican II conception of what a Catholic Christian education should be in the era of late modernity. Any attempt in a 'comparative education of the future' to evaluate Catholic school systems from the standpoint of values, knowledge, pedagogy, identity and social relations, must use as its theoretical framework this 'foundation charter' for contemporary Catholic education. As there is little understanding of these principles in the secular academic world, they need to be stated here in some detail.

Foundation principles for Catholic education in the era of late modernity

On the distinctive and necessary role of the Catholic school

There is a 'pressing need to ensure the presence of a Christian mentality in the society of the present day, marked, among other things, by cultural pluralism. For it is Christian thought which constitutes a sound criterion of judgement in the midst of conflicting concepts and behaviour: reference to Jesus Christ . . . teaches the values which ennoble from those which degrade.

'Cultural pluralism leads the Church to reaffirm her mission of education to ensure strong character formation. Her children then will be capable of both resisting the debilitating influence of relativism and of living up to their baptism. For this reason, the Church is prompted to mobilise her educational resources in the face of the materialism, fragmentation and technocracy of contemporary society' (pp. 15–16).[6]

This section of the charter stressed the importance of the critical role of Catholic schooling in late modernity. The role of the Catholic School was counter-cultural.

Later statements from Rome suggested that modernity has become associated with the unrestrained pursuit of profit and of technological innovation to the detriment of the spiritual and moral formation of persons. Catholic schools internationally have been called upon to be counter-cultural to these tendencies.

Catholic schools and human formation

'A school is not only a place where one is given a choice of intellectual values, but a place where one is presented with an array of values which are actually lived. . . . Christ is the foundation of the whole educational enterprise in a Catholic school . . . the Catholic school aims at forming in the Christian those particular virtues which will enable him[7] to live a new life in Christ' (pp. 29–33).

Catholic educators are to resist the reductionism of education as academic achievement only. The formation of values and virtues is crucial to human development in the contemporary world.

Against the many dramatic and glamorous role models provided by a modern media culture permeating the world, Catholic schools are encouraged to continue to project to Catholic youth, the Person of Christ as the most perfect guide for living and human formation.

Integration of faith and life

'The Catholic school has, as its specific duty, the complete Christian formation of its pupils and this task is of special significance today because of the inadequacy of the family and society . . . Young people have to be taught to overcome their individualism and discover, in the light of faith, their specific vocation. The very pattern of the Christian life draws them to commit themselves to serve God . . . and to make the world a better place to live in' (p. 37).

The important role of the Catholic school in assisting young people to find their God-given vocation is again reasserted. Generating a culture of vocation is seen to have heightened significance because of contemporary tendencies to think in terms of 'good jobs' only, to the detriment of notions of a 'calling' or a 'vocation'.

Catholic schools are expected to develop educational cultures in which faith, reason and life are brought into an integrated relationship as a holistic educational experience. From this perspective, the understanding of particular academic subjects and of particular vocational possibilities should be strongly framed within the perspective of the Faith.

On knowledge

'Education is not given for the purpose of gaining power but as an aid towards the fuller understanding of and communion with man, events and things. Knowledge is not to be considered as a means of material prosperity and success, but as a call to serve and to be responsible for others' (p. 43).

The authors of *The Catholic School* saw an external world in which knowledge itself was being transformed into a market commodity associated with power, wealth and personal status. Their argument in this section was that Catholic educational knowledge was not to be seen only in terms of individual personal empowerment but rather as empowerment for social purposes. The commodification of knowledge in late modernity was to be resisted.

Catholic schools were called upon to resist an individualistic 'success' culture and a market conception of knowledge by holding to traditional conceptions that knowledge entails service to a larger good.

On teachers as witnesses

'The Catholic school depends not so much on subject matter or methodology as on the people who work there. The extent to which the Christian message is transmitted through education depends to a very great extent on the teachers . . . The nobility of the task to which teachers are called demands that, in imitation of Christ . . . they reveal the Christian message not only by word but also by every gesture of their behaviour.[8] This is what makes the difference between a school whose education is permeated by the Christian spirit and one in which religion is only regarded as an academic subject like any other' (p. 36).

Lay teachers were encouraged to follow the example of their predecessors, the religious, in being witnesses for Christ. The transmission of the charisms of religious congregation to their lay successors would be essential to preserving the distinctive roles of Catholic schools in society.

In effect, the Church was attempting to encourage Catholic lay teachers and school leaders, who now constituted the majority of the personnel in schools, to become inheritors and models of the charisms of the declining religious orders in education.

Catholic schools and social justice

'Since it is motivated by the Christian ideal, the Catholic school is particularly sensitive to the call from every part of the world for a more just society . . . In some countries, because of local laws and economic conditions, the Catholic school runs the risk of giving counterwitness by admitting a majority of children from wealthier families . . . This situation is of great concern to those responsible for Catholic education, because first and foremost the Church offers its educational service to the poor to those who are deprived of family help and affection or those who are far from the faith' (pp. 44–45).[9]

There is evidence here of concern that too many Catholic schools internationally were in the service of the rich rather than the poor. A danger for Catholic schooling in late modernity was that despite a rhetoric of service to the poor, it might in practice not be realising this foundation principle.

Catholic school service to elite students had historically been premised on the belief that the future leaders of society could be 'converted' to the service of the poor by religious and moral teaching.

The Second Vatican Council called for more direct engagement with the education of the deprived and the powerless, by a commitment to 'a preferential option for the poor' in schooling.

Catholic schools and the common good

'The Catholic school community is an irreplaceable source of service . . . Today, one sees a world which clamours for solidarity and yet experiences the rise of new forms of individualism. Society can take note from the Catholic school that it is possible to create true communities out of a common effort for the common good' (p. 47).[10]

The authors of *The Catholic School* saw a late modernity marked by the growth of acquisitive and competitive individualism, encouraged by global capitalism. This was an attempt to keep Catholic schools in the service of social solidarity and the common good.

The ideological influence of the New Right in politics and economics was becoming evident to Church leaders and it was seen to be necessary to rearticulate and to re-emphasise Catholic social teaching about the common good and its relationship to education.

Catholic schools and openness

'In the certainty that the spirit is at work in every person, the Catholic school offers itself to all, non-Christians included, with all its distinctive aims and means' (p. 66).[11]

Against widely held views that Catholic schools served Catholics only, the Congregation for Catholic Education made it explicit that Catholic schools were (subject to available places) at the service of all who wished to enter. The concept of the ghetto school was replaced by a school at the service of the world.

The roles of Catholic schools in late modernity

This new 'openness to the world' was very much in the spirit of the Second Vatican Council. However, conservative Catholics feared the potential of such universal open access to dilute the Catholic ethos and culture of the schools.

This radical and explicit agenda for the transformation of Catholic schooling worldwide was offered for the consideration of Episcopal Conferences, that is, the Conference of Catholic Bishops in various parts of the world who are responsible for the administration, policy and practice of their particular educational systems:

> We appeal to each Episcopal conference to consider and to develop these principles which should inspire the Catholic school and to translate them into concrete programs which will meet the real needs of the educational systems operating in their countries.
>
> (pp. 71–72)

It seems likely that the reforming principles of *The Catholic School* document may have been taken up with enthusiasm in some societies, with caution in others, and in conservative settings, virtually ignored.

At its best, the post-Vatican II version of Catholic Christian education will be characterised by its counter-cultural stance to the features of late modernity. Against a confusion of role models for the young, the schools will offer the Person of Christ; against the hegemonic consumerism of global capitalism, the schools will attempt to form a spirituality of service and of God-given vocations; against a reductionist view of knowledge as commodity and of pedagogy as technical delivery, the schools will attempt to hold to humane educational values and a dialogic learning experience for the students. The ideal post-Vatican II Catholic school will be an agency for the advancement of social justice and the common good and it will make its services available to the poor and disadvantaged and to those who are 'far from the Faith'.[12]

That is the new vision for the role of Catholic education system arising from the deliberation of the Second Vatican Council. However, the question for large-scale comparative education research in the future is to what extent does this ideal conception of Catholic schooling exist in practice, as opposed to only in the documents and formal discourse of the Church?

To what extent have the Conferences of Bishops throughout the world taken this radical vision seriously and sought to transform their educational systems to meet the challenges of late modernity using the principles of the 1977 foundation charter?

Given that the Catholic educational system is the largest faith-based schooling system in the world with 120,000 schools serving almost 50 million students (Pittau, 2000), it is remarkable how little research and scholarly attention it has received from the various branches of Education studies, including comparative education studies.[13] This seems to be the result of what Gallagher (1997, p. 23) has referred to as 'secular marginalisation' in the intellectual culture of late modernity:

> especially in the academic and media worlds, a secular culture reigns with the result that religion is subtly ignored as unimportant.

As the editors of this volume assert, one of the paradoxes or contradictions of the present juncture is that education is becoming more powerfully linked to the economics of global capitalism on the one hand, but also to resurgent forms of religion on the other.[14] The study of how these profound contradictions in the cultures of schooling are realised in the future becomes a major research project for comparative education. The fate of post-Vatican II Catholic schooling provides a rich field for investigation as part of that larger project.

Notes

1 For a detailed discussion, see Bernstein (1996, pp. 75–81).
2 Reformed Christianity here refers to all those churches and religious groups which have developed since the Reformation in the sixteenth and seventeenth centuries, and which are broadly described as Protestant.
3 See Duminuco (2000), especially Appendix A: 'The characteristics of Jesuit education', and Appendix B: 'Ignatian pedgogy: A practical approach' (pp. 162–275). See also Appendix 2 (pp. 276–1291), 'Ignatian pedagogy today', which includes the statement, 'the goal of Jesuit education is the formation of men and women for others, people of competence, conscience and compassionate commitment' (p. 277).
4 For a detailed discussion, see Rosemary DeJulio, 'The response of Mary Ward and Madeleine Sophie Barat to the Ratio Studiorum', in Duminuco (2000, pp. 107–126).
5 For one major study of this great educational missionary enterprise, see Murphy (2000).
6 This has been a constant theme in subsequent Vatican pronouncements on Catholic education in late modernity: 'Many young people find themselves in a condition of radical instability . . . They live in a one-dimensional universe in which the only criterion is practical utility and the only value is economic and technological progress . . . Not a few young people . . . trying to find an escape from loneliness, turn to alcohol, drugs, the erotic, the exotic. Christian education is faced with the huge challenge of helping these young people discover something of value in their lives' (*The Religious Dimension of Education in a Catholic School*, 1988, pp. 8–10).
7 The spirit of Vatican II did not, unfortunately, lead to the use of gender-inclusive language in the documents of the Church.
8 This emphasis upon the importance of 'witness' in Catholic educational formation, was strengthened further by Pope Paul VI's much quoted (in Catholic contexts) statement: 'Today, students do not listen seriously to teachers but to witnesses; and if they do listen to teachers, it is because they are witnesses' (Evangelii Nuntiandi, 1975), quoted in Duminuco (2000, p. 285).
9 For further discussion of this, see Grace (2003).
10 The Catholic Bishops' Conference of England and Wales reiterated the common good objectives of Catholic social and educational teaching in two publications in 1996 and 1997.

11 Catholic schools in 'missionary' contexts such as Africa, the Middle and Far East, India, etc. had always been open to those of other faiths. This radical development in 1977 extended this openness to all contexts internationally.

12 For some research studies which have attempted to assess the impact of Vatican II reforms upon the practice of Catholic schooling, see Arthur (1995), Bryk et al. (1993), Flynn (1993), Grace (2002), Greeley (1998), McLaughlin et al. (1996), O'Keefe (2000), Sullivan (2000) and Youniss et al. (2000 a,b).

13 Some attempt to remedy this situation will be made in a forthcoming publication, *International Handbook of Catholic Education*, edited by Gerald Grace and Joseph O'Keefe, S.J., to be published in 2007.

14 This was also recognised by Bernstein (1996, p. 80): 'We have produced for the first time a virtually secular pedagogic discourse and culture, and at the same time, a revival of the sacred.'

Bibliography

Apple, M. (2001). *Educating the 'right' way: Markets, standards, God and equality.* New York and London: Routledge Falmer.

Armstrong, K. (2001a). *Islam: A short history.* London: Phoenix Press.

Armstrong, K. (2001b). *The battle for God: A history of fundamentalism.* New York: Ballantine Books.

Arthur, J. (1995). *The ebbing tide: Policy and principles of Catholic education.* Leominster: Gracewing Publications.

Bauman, Z. (2000). *In search of politics.* Oxford: Polity Press.

Berg, M., & Pretiz, P. (1994). *Five waves of Protestant Evangelization.* In G. Cook (Ed.). *New face of the Church in Latin America.* Maryknoll, NY: Orbis Books.

Berger, P. (1973). *The social reality of Religion.* London: Penguin.

Bernstein, B. (1996). *Pedagogy, symbolic control and identity: Theory, research and critique.* London: Taylor & Francis.

Bonino, J. (1994). *The condition and prospects of Christianity in Latin America. In* G. Cook (Ed.) *New face of the Church in Latin America.* Maryknoll, NY: Orbis Books.

Brouwer, S. Gifford, P., & Rose, S. (1996). *Exporting the American gospel: Global Christian fundamentalism.* New York: Routledge.

Bryk, A., Lee, V. & Holland, P. (1993). *Catholic schools and the common good.* Cambridge, MA: Harvard University Press.

Casanova, J. (1994). *Public religions in the modern age.* Chicago, IL: University of Chicago Press.

Catholic Bishops' Conference of England and Wales (1996). *The common good and the Catholic Church's social teaching.* London: CBC.

Catholic Education Service of England and Wales (1996). *The common good in education.* London: CES.

Cook, G. (Ed.) (1994). *New face of the Church in Latin America.* Maryknoll, NY: Orbis Books.

DeJulio, R. (2000). Women's ways of knowing and learning: The response of Mary Ward and Madeleine Sophie Barat to the Ratio Studiorum. Chapter 5 in Duminuco (2000).

Duminuco, V. (Ed.) (2000). *The Jesuit Ratio Studiorum: 400th anniversary perspectives.* New York: Fordham University Press.

Durkheim, E. (1977). *The evolution of educational thought.* London: Routledge and Kegan Paul (first published by Presses Universitaires de France, 1938).

Flynn, M. (1993). *The culture of Catholic schools*. Homebush, NSW: St. Paul Publications.

Gallagher, M. (1997). New forms of cultural unbelief. *In* P. Hogan & K. Williams (Eds.), *The future of religion in Irish education*. Dublin: Veritas.

Gellner, E. (1996). *Conditions of liberty: Civil society and its rivals*. London: Penguin.

Giddens, A. (1991). *The consequences of modernity*. Cambridge: Polity Press.

Grace, G. (2002). *Catholic schools: Mission, markets and morality*. London and New York: Routledge Falmer.

Grace, G. (2003). First and foremost the Church offers its educational service to the Poor: Class, inequality and Catholic schooling in contemporary contexts. *International Studies in Sociology of Education, 13*(1), 35–53.

Grace, G. (2004). Making connections for future directions: Taking religion seriously in the sociology of education. *International Studies in Sociology of Education, 14*(1), 47–56.

Grace, G., & O'Keefe, J. (Eds) (2007). *International handbook of Catholic education,* 2 volumes. Dordrecht, Springer.

Greeley, A. (1998). Catholic schools at the crossroads: An American perspective. In J. M. Feheney (Ed.), *From ideal to action: The inner nature of a Catholic school today*. Dublin: Veritas.

Hastings, A. (1991). *A history of English Christianity, 1920–1990.*, London: SCM Press.

Martin, D. (1999). The Evangelical upsurge and its political implications. *In* P. Berger (Ed.), *The desedcularisation of the world: Resurgent religion and world politics*. Grand Rapids: W. Eermans Publishing.

McLaughlin, T., O'Keefe, J., & O'Keeffe, B. (Eds.) (1996). *The contemporary Catholic school: Context, identity and diversity*. London and Washington: Falmer Press.

Murphy, D. (2000). *A history of Irish emigrant and missionary education*. Dublin: Four Courts Press.

O'Keefe, J. (2000). The challenge of pluralism: Articulating a rationale for religiously diverse urban Roman Catholic schools in the United States. *International Journal of Education and Religion, 1,* 64–88.

Pittau, G. (2000). Education on the threshold of the Third Millenium, challenge, mission and adventure. *Catholic Education, 4*(2), 139–152.

Sacred Congregation for Catholic Education (1977). *The Catholic School*. Homebush, NSW: St. Paul Publications.

Sacred Congregation for Catholic Education (1982). *Lay Catholics in schools witnesses to faith*. London: Catholic Truth Society.

Sullivan, J. (2000). *Catholic schools in contention*. Dublin: Veritas.

Vatican Congregation for Catholic Education (1988). *The religious dimension of education in a Catholic school*. Dublin: Veritas.

Walford, G. (2001). *Evangelical Christian schools in England and the Netherlands Oxford Review of Education, 27*(4) 529–541.

Youniss, J., & Convey, J. (Eds) (2000a). *Catholic schools at the crossroads: Survival and transformation*. New York: Teachers College Press.

Youniss, J., Convey, J. and McLellan, J. (Eds) (2000b). *The Catholic character of Catholic schools*. Notre Dame, IN: University of Notre Dame Press.

Chapter 16

Catholic values and education policy

Routledge International Handbook of Education, Religion and Values, 2013, (Eds). J. Arthur and T. Levat, 84–99, Routledge.

Introduction

In his magnum opus, *Catholicism* (1994), Richard McBrien approaches the question of Catholic values in these terms:

> There is no authoritative guidebook by which Christians can determine in almost every conceivable circumstance what is consistent with the Gospel and what is not . . . The challenge of moral education therefore is not the teaching of moral rules but the development of Christian character . . .
>
> It is the ability to discern, the capacity to make wise and responsible decisions and to act on them.
>
> McBrien, 1994: 965

This chapter will attempt to elaborate that definition by analysing the various ways in which Catholic values and their relation to education policy in the secular world have been discerned and expressed at various levels within the Catholic Church and in various locations.

An analysis will be made of the Catholic values and education policy relation, as discerned and expressed by the central hierarchical authority of the Church, represented by the Congregation for Catholic Education in Rome. This will be followed by a study of policy documents issued by national Bishops' Conferences in certain countries that are responses to particular challenges, discerned by the bishops in those locations. Finally, the discernment of Catholic school leaders in England on the Catholic values and education policy relation will be reported based upon a research study undertaken by the author in 2002 and supplemented by wider research reported in the *International Handbook of Catholic Education* (2007) and the journal, *International Studies in Catholic Education* (2009–2012).

Catholic values and education policy: Perspectives from Rome

There is a general consensus among writers that the Second Vatican Council of the 1960s marked a major religious and cultural transformation within Catholicism. As Adrian Hastings (1991: 525) has argued:

> There can be no question that the Vatican Council (1962–1965) was the most important ecclesiastical event of this century, not just for the Roman Catholics, but for all Christians. It so greatly changed the character of by far, the largest communion of Christendom.

It inaugurated new approaches to the liturgy, to conceptions of the Church (with a new emphasis upon 'the people of God'), to relations with other Christians and other faiths, and to relations with the secular world.[1] Principles of openness, dialogue and partnership became more salient, as did principles of commitment to the common good and social justice.

These transformations can be discerned in the sphere of Catholic education post-1960s, especially as expressed in the important document *The Catholic School* (TCS), published by the Congregation for Catholic Education in 1977. The Congregation produced what can be regarded as the foundation charter for Catholic education in the contemporary world by outlining in a succinct and accessible form, Catholic values and principles in education and (by implication) how these should relate to education policies in various parts of the world.

A close reading of this charter reveals seven regulative principles and values commitments for the guidance of Church and school leaders in their negotiations with state and secular agencies on matters of educational policy. In other words, the Congregation argued that if the mission integrity of Catholic education was to be maintained, these value positions should ideally be respected in educational practice and in educational policy outcomes. These principles may be stated in summary form as follows:

A civic and an apostolic service

The Congregation recognised that Catholic educational institutions have a duty to serve the legitimate interests of the State, while at the same time realising their apostolic mission in religious and spiritual terms. Such a mandate had been given in the words of Jesus Christ, 'render to Caesar that which is Caesar's, and to God that which is God's'.[2] Thus the TCS charter stated that the Church fosters 'truly Christian living and apostolic communities, equipped to make their own positive contribution, in a spirit of cooperation, to the building up of the secular society' (Congregation for Catholic Education, 1977: n. 12).

As the TCS document was disseminated on an international scale it could not be expected to elaborate the ways in which this regulative principle might, or might not, articulate with national education policies in various parts of the world. But the implications of the statement are very clear. Catholic educators would be prepared to cooperate with the legitimate interests of the State (and the Church would be adjudicator of 'legitimacy'), and education policy developments must respect the dual mission of Catholic institutions to be civic and apostolic. This fundamental value position articulated in 1977 was destined to come under massive pressure in the future as many States in a competitive globalised world increased their demands for economically related educational 'production' from the schools. As more service to Caesar was required, the international challenge for Catholic schools was to try to ensure that their service to God did not diminish as a result.

Catholic education: a process of character formation

The Congregation was aware that the expectations of governments for education were becoming more utilitarian and so against this development it was necessary to emphasise the priority objective of character formation in Catholic education and the importance of values education. This is a strong permeating theme throughout the TCS charter and is variously expressed as:

> it is Christian thought which constitutes a sound criterion of judgement in the midst of conflicting concepts and behaviour: reference to Jesus Christ teaches man to discern the values which enoble from those which degrade him.
> Congregation for Catholic Education, 1977: n. 11

> a school is not only a place where one is given a choice of intellectual values, but a place where one has presented an array of values which are actively lived.
> Ibid.: n. 32

> Catholic schools must be seen as meeting places for those who wish to express Christian values in education. The Catholic school . . . must be a community whose aim is the transmission of values for living.
> Ibid.: n. 53

In other words, it had to be emphasised to the secular authorities that Catholic schools did not exist primarily to form compliant and competent workers for the marketplace but rather Christian citizens of character and integrity, possessed of values and virtues acquired during their Catholic education and whose contribution to society (and the economy) would be influenced by those values and virtues.

Secular authorities also needed to understand that processes of values education and character formation in Catholic schools might involve the development of a counter-cultural stance to wider social developments in the globalised world. Post-Vatican II education could be a powerful source of criticism of political, economic and educational policies, in some circumstances, and not simply a reliable and conservative ally, as had often been the case in the past.

This counter-cultural stance is referred to in these terms:

> Cultural pluralism, therefore, leads the Church to reaffirm her mission of education to ensure character formation . . . (pupils) who will be capable of resisting the debilitating influence of relativism . . . For this reason the Church is prompted to mobilise her educational resources in the face of the materialism, pragmatism and technocracy of contemporary society.
>
> Ibid.: n. 12

In a research study of character education, James Arthur and his research team observed that with growing pressures upon schools to provide the economy with functionally competent persons, character education was being marginalised. What was needed was: 'A reinvigorated conscious focus upon character education in school; if a proper balance is to be restored to the educational process' (Arthur et al., 2006: 3).

It can be said that the Congregation for Catholic Education in Rome has emphasised the priority of character formation in Catholic education not only in the 1977 document but also in its subsequent publications in 1982, 1988, 1998, 2002 and 2007.[3]

To what extent these statements of guiding principles and values have impacted upon educational practice and education policy developments internationally is in urgent need of more research inquiry.

Presence of the church in the educational field: a requirement of cultural pluralism

The Congregation for Catholic Education in 1977 was fully aware of wider social and political changes in the globalised world, involving the increased mobility of peoples and a growing cultural pluralism in many societies. More and more societies were characterised by a variety of cultures of different faiths and also of cultures that were increasingly secularist and hostile to the existence of religious faiths as an irrelevance in the modern scientific era. At the same time many national States were taking stronger control of their educational systems. In these circumstances it was necessary for the Church to assert as Catholic values and principles, the duty of a State (especially when claiming the status of a democracy) to provide a variety of schools, representing different cultures of education in societies that were culturally pluralist. This position was expressed as follows:

> [The Church] encourages the co-existence and, if possible, the coop-eration of diverse educational institutions which will allow young peo-ple to be formed by value judgements based on a specific view of the world . . . to promote that freedom of teaching which champions and guarantees freedom of conscience and the parental right to choose the school best suited to parents 'educational purposes.'
> Congregation for Catholic Education, 1977: nn. 13–14

> as the State increasingly takes control of education and establishes its own so-called neutral and monolithic system, the survival of those nat-ural communities based on a shared conception of life is threatened. Faced with this situation, the Catholic school offers an alternative.
> Ibid.: n. 20

The educational policy implications of this principled position are clear. In every socio-political and cultural context internationally, the Church would seek to negotiate with the State to establish Catholic schools for those citi-zens who wanted a faith-based education for their children. It would also attempt to obtain a degree of relative autonomy from State directives about curriculum, pedagogy and assessment in those schools.[4]

The Catholic school: a truly educative school

One of the valuable features of the document (Congregation for Catholic Edu-cation, 1977) is that those responsible for its production, Gabriel-Marie, Car-dinal Garrone (Prefect) and Antonio Javierre, Archbishop of Meta (Secretary) understood that it was necessary to address many of the existing criticisms of Catholic schools and to clarify some new developments resulting from the deliberations of the Second Vatican Council. This section of the TCS charter (ibid.: nn. 16–32), was designed to present to secular authorities and to secu-lar educators a new understanding of Catholic education in the post-Vatican II era. There would be no change, of course, in the fundamental mission:

> It is precisely in the gospel of Christ, taking root in the minds and lives of the faithful, that the Catholic school finds its definition as it comes to terms with the cultural conditions of the times.
> Ibid.: n. 9

However, the means by which this fundamental mission was to be under-taken would have different emphases following the Second Vatican Council. These different emphases are expressed, as would be expected, in careful and nuanced language, but the intention is to show that Catholic schooling was in a process of change. One of the strongest criticisms of Catholic schools in the past, was that they were not centres for true education but rather centres for the indoctrination of the young into the doctrines and the practices of the Roman Catholic faith. Their purpose was proselytism, rather than the cultivation of critical intelligence.

The TCS document sought to argue that this claim was no longer valid because Catholic schools in the modern age would be 'truly educative' in these ways:

> Christian education can sometimes run into the danger of so-called proselytism, of imparting a one-sided outlook. This can happen only when Christian educators misunderstand the nature and methods of Christian education.
>
> Ibid.: n. 19

> It must never be forgotten that the purpose of instruction at school is education, that is, the development of man from within, freeing him from that conditioning which would prevent him from becoming a fully integrated human being.
>
> Ibid.: n. 29

> [The Catholic school] must develop persons who are responsible and inner-directed, capable of choosing freely in conformity with their conscience.
>
> Ibid.: n. 31

For post-Vatican II Catholic education the ideal, as stated by the Congregation, was a move from the pedagogy of the catechism to the pedagogy of dialogue and encounter. This would mean not only a more truly educative experience for young people but also a means to legitimate Catholic education as part of any national system of education. In education policy terms, hostile critics could no longer argue (at least in evidence-based terms; see Grace, 2003a), that Catholic schools, as indoctrination centres, should not qualify for public funding.

If young people in Catholic schools came to embrace 'the gospel of Christ', they would be doing so on the basis of their faith experiences and their personal reasoning and not as the result of a conditioning process. A new form of dialogic Catholic education was in place.

Commitment to social justice and the common good

Charity, as a concept and as a practice has a long and honourable history in Catholic culture and Catholic schools and colleges today are deeply involved in charitable giving to those in need in the wider world. Social justice, on the other hand, is a modern concept that only entered the formal discourse of the Catholic Church when it was first used by Pope Pius XI in his encyclical, *Quadragesimo Anno* (1931). As Calvez and Perrin argue, Pius XI made distinctions between social charity and social justice in the strongest possible terms:

> A charity which defrauds the worker of his just wage, is no true charity but a hollow name and a pretence . . . Doles given out of pity will not exempt a man from his obligations of justice . . . True charity, on the contrary, is the virtue which makes men try to improve the distribution of goods as justice requires.
>
> Calvez and Perrin, 1961: 164

By the Second Vatican Council, the commitment of the Church to working for social justice in the world had become more salient and active and this can be discerned in the education policy of the Church as expressed in the *Catholic School* document (1977). This commitment can be found in a section of the TCS charter (Congregation for Catholic Education, 1977: 58–62):

> first and foremost the Church offers its educational services to the poor, or those who are deprived of family help and affection, or those who are far from the faith.
>
> Ibid.: n. 58

> if the Catholic school were to turn its attention exclusively or predominantly to those from the wealthier social classes, it could be contributing towards maintaining their privileged position, and could thereby continue to favour a society which is unjust.
>
> Ibid.: n. 58

Commitment to a Catholic value position of working for social justice through the agency of Catholic education was made very clear:

> the Catholic school is particularly sensitive to the call from every part of the world for a more just society, and it tries to make its own contribution towards it.
>
> Ibid.: n. 58

The authentic apostolate of Catholic education was declared to the world as a mission involving Catholic schools and colleges in struggles for social justice and the common good, deriving from an education 'motivated by the Christian ideal' (see Grace, 2003b).

Historically, the Church had been able to extend its services to the poorest of the poor through the agency of its many religious Congregations with missions in education. These Congregations provided a strategic subsidy for the mission, in the form of spiritual, cultural, physical and financial resources and a supply of teachers requiring minimal remuneration. However, the decline in vocations for these Congregations, already evident in the 1970s, presented a major challenge for the future provision of educational services for the poor at the lowest possible cost. In educational policy terms it was apparent that the Church would not be able to maintain its mission integrity of service to the poor without significant financial support from governments internationally.

The Congregation drew the attention of state authorities to these developing problems in its comments on 'the economic situation of Catholic Schools' (ibid.: nn. 81–2). Expressed in very nuanced terms, as an aspiration that Catholic schools internationally would receive 'an economic and juridical status similar to State Schools' (ibid.: n. 81), it was unlikely to make much impact on the policies of secular governments. Later research, as reported in the *International Handbook of Catholic Education* (Grace and O'Keefe, 2007) has demonstrated that if significant state financial support for Catholic schools is not available (for constitutional or ideological reasons), the mission of a 'preferential option for the poor' in Catholic education is deeply compromised.[5]

Developing openness while maintaining Catholicity

In one of the most radical sections of the TCS charter, the Congregation committed itself to a policy of openness in relation to admissions to Catholic schools:

> In the certainty that the Spirit is at work in every person, the Catholic school offers itself to all, non-Christians included . . . The only condition it would make, as is its right, would be remaining faithful to the educational aims of the Catholic schools.
>
> Congregation for Catholic Education, 1977: nn. 85–6

Historically, many Catholic schools in locations known as 'mission territories' had admitted non-Christian students and it was the case that schools in the Middle East, India, Asia and Africa had school populations in which students from Muslim, Hindu and Buddhist faith traditions were predominant. What was radical about the 1977 statements was that this principle was now extended on a worldwide basis. It also resonated with the earlier statement (ibid.: n. 58), that Catholic schools were available to 'those who are far from the faith'.[6]

However, the Congregation for Catholic Education understood that a greater openness to those of other faiths might produce challenges for maintaining a distinctive Catholic Christian ethos in the schools. The goal of being 'distinctive and inclusive'[7] required a judicious balance to be achieved between openness to others, on the one hand, and preserving a distinctive Catholic religious and educational ethos, known as Catholicity or Catholic identity in the schools.

In the section (ibid.: nn. 73–8) the TCS document addressed the challenge of 'ensuring the distinctive Catholic character of the school' in changed circumstances. In a situation of greater openness to others, the responsibility for the maintenance of Catholicity was seen to be that of the local bishop in partnership with Catholic parents and teachers. The Congregation expressed alarm that some religious Congregations were abandoning work in schools for other forms of community apostolate. A clear implication was that the presence of vowed religious as leaders and teachers in Catholic schools was, in the view of the Congregation, crucial to the maintenance of the Catholic ethos of the schools.[8]

In developments since 1977, dilemmas relating to maintaining a distinctive Catholic ethos in the schools have become sharper and more complicated arising from a conjunction of many factors. These include a serious reduction in the number of religious working in schools; an increase in the employment of teachers who are not Catholics; the pressures of secular governments for more utilitarian and visible educational 'production'; and the assertion by some parent groups of educational priorities at variance with Catholic values in education as defined by local bishops.[9]

The apostolic value of Catholic education: beyond the culture of measurement

In its constant insistence that the apostolic value of Catholic education was to be found in the formation of virtuous persons and responsible citizens, inspired by their faith in the gospel of Christ, the Congregation for Catholic Education took a distinctive stance on what constituted an 'effective' or 'successful' educational outcome. Whereas in mainstream secular education internationally, the cult of educational measurement (by performance tests, standard achievement tests and academic results ranking) was becoming more influential, Catholic education was encouraged to take a more profound and holistic approach to the effectiveness of schooling. A Catholic conception of school effectiveness[10] would be the extent to which a Catholic education helped to form good persons and good citizens, who had come to accept (through an open and dialogic educational experience) that the gospel of Jesus Christ was the hope for the world. This more comprehensive and holistic goal for education would only become apparent in the longer term, i.e. in the lives and actions of the adult alumni of Catholic schooling. Thus the Congregation was clear that policies of educational assessment based upon measured test and academic results achieved during the years of schooling were only part of a larger project for determining the effectiveness of schools. The longer term assessment would involve the lives of adult persons,[11] i.e. 'the layman is at the same time a believer and a citizen and should be constantly led by Christian conscience alone' (Congregation for Catholic Education, 1977: n. 79). In stating in categorical form, 'the validity of the educational results of a Catholic school cannot be measured by immediate efficiency' (ibid.: n. 84), the TCS document provided an important critique of State educational policies for assessment which were based solely on government criteria for efficiency and immediate measurable results.

The seven principles and Catholic education internationally

The purpose of the Catholic school document of 1977 was to make available to Catholic school leaders and teachers some 'principles for discernment' that could then be applied to educational policy development in various parts of the world.

These value commitments and principles were regarded by the Congregation as expressing the nature of an authentic Catholic education in the international context. It was understood that the responsibility for applying these principles for discernment in actual policy negotiations with secular governments rested with the local bishops in each country. In its concluding observations, the Congregation commended its guidance to local bishops in these terms:

> The Catholic school is in a unique position to offer a most valuable and necessary service. With the principles of the gospel as its abiding point of reference, it offers its collaboration to those who are building a new world – one which is freed from a hedonistic mentality and from the efficiency syndrome of modern consumer society.
>
> We appeal to each Episcopal conference to consider and to develop these principles which should inspire the Catholic school and to translate them into concrete programmes.
>
> Ibid.: nn. 91–2

We will now examine the extent to which these principles for discernment were responded to by Episcopal conferences and religious Congregations in various parts of the world.

Responses of Episcopal conferences and religious Congregations in education

In seeking to explain the influence of the *Catholic School* document of 1977 on Catholic educational policy and practice in various locations, as discerned and activated by national Conferences of Bishops and religious Congregations, it has to be understood that TCS was only one element in a large post-Vatican II literature that could influence those Conferences. Predating TCS, two Vatican documents, *Populorum Progressio* (1967), encyclical letter of Pope Paul VI and *Justice in the World* (1971) a report of the Roman Synod of Bishops had strongly developed Catholic commitments to social justice and the common good. The value of the TCS (1977) publication was that it applied many of these general commitments to policies and practices in Catholic education internationally.

South Africa

In examining Catholic responses to the apartheid policy in South Africa of racially segregated schooling, Pam Christie (Christie, 1990: 16) notes that 'the South African Catholic hierarchy was initially slow to move against apartheid.' However, as a result of the impact of Vatican II teachings and also the initiatives of religious Sisters directly involved in schooling, the Bishops issued in 1971 a strongly worded statement entitled *Declaration of Commitment on Social Justice and Race Relations within the Church*. In the period 1977 to 1986 Catholic education policy in South Africa moved in the direction of open or integrated schools available to both black and white students. This policy was pursued against threats of government punitive action. However, the South African case, as shown by the research of Christie (1990) and Kelly and Higgs (2012), demonstrates that religious Congregations working in education were crucial in activating the South African Bishops' Conference to make its public statements.[12]

Post-Vatican II Catholic values applied to educational policy and practice were activated by the religious Congregations in an explicit way: 'The teaching Congregations wished to establish and maintain schools that were "open" to the People of God, irrespective of race, as they are of creed' (Christie, 1990: 24).

Here was Catholic education, in its counter-cultural stance, made manifest in a dramatic way against government policy in South Africa.

England and Wales

In the 1990s, the Catholic Bishops of England and Wales were involved in proclaiming a countercultural stance to another dominant ideology in education policy. This ideology, advocated by writers such as Chubb and Moe (1990) and taken up enthusiastically by Conservative governments in the UK in the 1990s, argued for the application of market culture, market discipline and market competition to enhance educational effectiveness and productivity. In an early critique of this position, Ranson highlighted the consequences of such an approach:

> Action in the market is driven by a single common currency – the pursuit of material interests. The only effective means upon which to base

> action is the calculation of personal advantage: clout in the market derives from the power of superior resources to subordinate others in competitive exchange.
>
> Ranson, 1993: 336

This expressed well the challenge that a marketised and commodified approach to education posed to the foundational values of Catholic education. If a market culture in education encourages the pursuit of material interests what effect will this have on a Catholic school's prime commitment to religious, spiritual and moral interests? If calculation of personal advantage is necessary for survival in the market, how can Catholic schools remain faithful to the common good? If schools in a market economy in education must show good 'company' results (in academic and social status terms) will this not compromise the principle of 'preferential option for the poor'?

Faced with this strong ideological challenge to Catholic values in education the Catholic bishops, in the document *The Common Good in Education* (1997) issued a counter-cultural response for the guidance of Catholic educators:

> Education is not a commodity to be offered for sale. The distribution of funding solely according to the dictates of market forces is contrary to the Catholic doctrine of the common good. Teachers and pupils are not economic units whose value is seen merely as a cost element on the school's balance sheet. To consider them in this way threatens human dignity. Education is a service provided by society for the benefit of all its young people, in particular for the benefit of the most vulnerable and the most disadvantaged – those whom we have a sacred duty to serve. Education is about the service of others, rather than the service of self.
>
> Catholic Education Service, 1997: 13

The Catholic bishops went on to suggest that all Catholic schools should show a commitment to the common good in education and that this would involve demonstrating partnership and solidarity with other schools (rather than individual competition) and, where possible, the sharing of specialist resources.

Once again, Catholic values in education policy and practice were shown to be distinctively different from those currently dominant in secular government policy.

Latin America

The Latin America context provides a more difficult and complex cultural location for analysing the relation between Catholic values and education policy. This arises partly because of the number of nation states included in the category 'Latin America', each having their own distinctive cultural and political characteristics, and partly because ideological struggles in the relation of Catholic values to education policy and practice became polarised following the Second Vatican Council.

Reviewing the situation in 1993, Gustavo Gutiérrez, Francis McDonogh, Candido Padin, OSB and Jon Sobrino, SJ have argued that the Conference of Latin American Bishops at Medellín, Colombia in 1968 marked a strong commitment by the Church 'to work for justice and to changing social, economic and political structures as well as seeking to change hearts' (p. 1). By the Third Conference at Puebla, Mexico in 1979, the principle of 'the preferential option for the poor' had been ratified and liberation theology was becoming influential in Church policy. In parallel with these developments, the publications of Paulo Freire, *Cultural Action for Freedom* (1970), *Pedagogy of the Oppressed* (1972) and *Education for Critical Consciousness* (1974) were suggesting to Catholic educators how these values and principles might be applied in educational practice. New ways of 'being school' were advanced including 'cultural circles', and community focused Base Education Movements. The Latin American Confederation of Religious[13] were closely involved in a variety of new approaches to Catholic education.

In the 1980s and 1990s a strong conservative reaction against these developments became apparent, supported by a section of the Catholic hierarchy in Latin America and by negative reactions to liberation theology and liberation education from the Vatican. Catholic education was caught up in these ideological struggles. These effects can be seen in the more muted expression of Catholic values in the education sector at the Fourth General Conference of Latin America Bishops at Santo Domingo in 1992 (reported in English in 1993). Published as *Santo Domingo Conclusions* (1993) references to the preferential option for the poor in education were made in a qualified form, as were references to critical consciousness that focused on the influence of mass media.

Reviewing the situation of Catholic education, specifically in Brazil, Streck and Segala (2007) suggest that all forms of Catholic education are now involved in a struggle to maintain mission integrity in the face of the growing influence of market forces and competition in society:

> the sponsoring institutions are forced to manage the schools like companies in order to survive . . . On the one hand, they try to maintain the autonomy, the confessional character and the public character of the educational institutions; on the other hand, they are placed within a competitive market that regards education as a commodity.
>
> Streck and Segala, 2007: 175[14]

India

In 2007, Cardinal Telesphore Toppo, President of the Catholic Bishops' Conference of India contributed a chapter to the *International Handbook of Catholic Education*, which consisted of an analysis of the guiding principles and values of Catholic education in that country. The Cardinal was able to demonstrate that Catholic education in India exemplified two important principles arising from the Second Vatican Council, i.e. 'the preferential option for the poor' and openness to those 'far from the faith'. Although under 2 per cent of the population, the Catholic community provided 20,000 educational institutions, including 9,000 primary schools, 4,800 secondary schools, 500 teacher colleges and 900 technical schools. The mission of Catholic education had been extended especially to the most marginalised people of India, the Dalits,[15] the Tribals and poor women in rural areas. Catholic educational institutions served a population of over ten million students consisting of 23 per cent Catholic, 5 per cent other Christians, 53 per cent Hindus, 8 per cent Muslims and the remainder from other categories. 54 per cent of the students were girls and women (Telesphore Toppo, 2007: 655). In 2006, the Conference of Catholic Bishops renewed their commitment to 'Catholic education and the Church's concern for the marginalised', while warning that: 'Commercialization of education isolated the institutions' vision from the Catholic vision of education and is a counter witness to the mission of Jesus Christ' (ibid.: 662).

In commenting on this challenge to Catholic values, and other challenges in contemporary India, Father Nicholas Tete, SJ in chapter 35 of the *International Handbook of Catholic Education* (2007) has argued:

> Catholic education will also focus on combating the fast dehumanizing culture of individualism, materialistic consumerism, capitalism, cut-throat competition, politics of communalism, corruption, gender discrimination, casteism and all types of violence. It will work less for the privileged few and more for the marginalised masses.
>
> Tete, 2007: 691

In these terms, the counter-cultural stance of Catholic education is strongly asserted. Tete concludes: 'A new Vatican II inspired Catholic educational mission is in the process of developing in India' (ibid.: 693).

The bishops and the religious Congregations: variations in responses to Vatican II

The four case studies reported in this chapter are examples where, by and large, the new relation of Catholic values and education policy and practice developed by the TCS document (Congregation for Catholic Education,

1977) and subsequent statements from Rome, has been taken seriously and attempts have been made to renew the Catholic education mission, especially in its counter-cultural stance to some features of the globalised world. However, as was the case in Latin America, such responses have not been universal. The situation has been, and is now, complex and contested. There has been opposition to change by conservative interests within the Church and some religious Congregations or, in some cases, strategies of institutional inertia[16] in which transformative ideas have simply been ignored. As I argued in earlier writing:

> more analytical attention needs to be given to the socio-cultural and political role of the contemporary Catholic Church in its internal conflicts and the attempted transformations of its theology, cultural and social teaching.
>
> Grace, 2003b: 37

The Catholic Church is not a monolithic institution as secular observers believe but rather a community of the People of God. As with any community, it is united on core beliefs and values but experiences some internal differences in discernments about how these beliefs and values relate to specific policies in the secular world.

The discernments of Catholic school leaders

The Vatican Council's first statement, the *Declaration on Christian Education (Gravissimum Educationsis)* in 1965 had emphasised that: 'Teachers must remember that it depends chiefly on them whether the Catholic school achieves its purpose' (Flannery, 1998: 733).

It could have added that, within the category 'teachers', school leaders in the form of headteachers and principals, had a particular responsibility to be faith leaders as well as professional leaders and also guardians of the mission integrity of Catholic schools and colleges internationally.

Such school leaders held positions where Catholic values in education met concretely the implications of various education policies enacted by secular governments. They are, so to speak, in the front-line of practical action and decision-making in Catholic education and therefore the discernments that they make on particular issues are crucial to an understanding of the values–policy relation in practice.

While the research evidence on these discernments is still not extensive, this section of the analysis will report some illustrative examples, drawn from research by the author on Catholic schools in England.

In England in the 1980s and 1990s, Catholic headteachers were faced by massive challenges in the field of educational policy, arising from Conservative governments' commitments to the application of market forces in schooling, the generation of competition in a sharper form and public accountability procedures, e.g. 'league tables' of academic 'productivity' in test scores and examination results. A new culture of education was being imposed upon all state-funded schools,[17] which specified what they should teach (the National Curriculum) and how they would be publicly assessed and evaluated. Financial incentives were available for those schools that cooperated with government policies and a public policy of 'naming and shaming those schools that failed to meet government targets in education was inaugurated.

Many of these ideological and policy developments were in conflict with Catholic values in education, especially since they undermined principles of the common good in education through the application of market principles of intense competition and the commodification of schooling as academic productivity in essence.

Faced with this conflict situation, Catholic headteachers in England had to try to resolve the dilemma of a challenge to Catholic values, issues of school survival and strong state intervention in education policy that had dramatically reduced their previous status of relative autonomy. In research undertaken in the period 1997–2000 I explored the discernment made by 60 headteachers in Catholic secondary schools in London, Birmingham and Liverpool to probe how they dealt with these values dilemmas and what strategic policies they formulated in these difficult circumstances (Grace, 2002a).

In focused interviews with these 60 Catholic school leaders, three patterns of discernment and action became apparent, which were styled as: 'market regulators' (30); 'pragmatic survivors' (25); 'pro-marketeers' (5).

The 'market regulators' had a strong consciousness of the dissonance between Catholic values in education and the new ideology of education promoted by the government. The strategic actions taken by this group involved counter-cultural policies manifested in two ways. For some of these school leaders, the way to try to resist, what they saw as the corrupting effects of a competitive market-place in education was to create informal professional networks. These networks used exchange of information and informal agreements about admissions policies, relations with parents and attempts to honour local 'catchment areas' for recruitment, despite the official existence of an open free market.

A second response was to form an organised partnership of Catholic schools which were committed to work together on the principle of common good educational support. The Birmingham Catholic Secondary School partnership[18] (established in 1988) was a pioneer in establishing a counter-cultural form of educational organisation and practice to that officially promoted by the government. As one of the leading members of the partnership argued:

> I do believe that if there is to be a real attempt to deliver the objectives set out in *The Common Good in Education*, then it will only be achieved

by the development of genuine partnerships of schools on a much greater scale and in a much more profound way than we have seen so far.

Grace, 2002a: 199

While 50 per cent of the sample sought in various ways to regulate the impact of market forces in education by these strategic actions, almost the same number adopted a strategy of pragmatic survival. This group of school leaders took the view that if the school was to survive (and to continue its service to the community) it would have to adopt the 'strategies for survival' dictated by the new educational market place that had been created. This was expressed most explicitly by one school leader (but it represented, in essence, the stance of the group):

> Clearly there is a defined market and your budget is attached to pupil numbers. You've got to maximise your numbers . . . Market forces are operating . . . and you can't ignore them . . . If you don't survive, the end result is that you don't provide a Catholic education for the young in your area.

Ibid.: 193

Some of the pragmatic survivors expressed an appropriate amount of Catholic guilt in acknowledging that their stance was a long way from the Catholic values as expressed by the bishops in *The Common Good and Education* (Catholic Education Service, 1997) but, placed as they were in the 'frontline', they could see no alternative to compliance with state policy.

The pro-marketeers, although small in number, were often robust in their defence of more individual competition in Catholic education. Their position was that 'the competitive edge works wonders' and that it would bring benefits for the pupils in driving up higher standards.

As Catholic schools were committed to academic excellence, these schools leaders had no consciousness that government policy was in conflict with Catholic values in education.

This empirical analysis illuminates the argument already made, that there is no unitary discernment of the relation between Catholic values and educational policy. Different perspectives exist within the Church about the nature and priority of these values and about the nature of a school's mission integrity in changing circumstances. Subsequent international research and scholarly analysis[19] demonstrates the wider existence of such differences in Catholic education internationally.

Conclusion

This analysis has sought to show the relation between Catholic values and education policy internationally as discerned and expressed at three different levels within the Catholic Church: that of the Congregation for Catholic Education in Rome; that of bishops and religious Congregations in specific locations and that of Catholic school leaders at the frontline of values commitments and policy realities.

What the analysis demonstrates overall is that Catholic values in education are, in some significant areas, counter-cultural to many developments in a globalised world increasingly dominated by a market culture of materialism, consumerism and individualistic competitive relations. At the same time, Catholic schools, following the teaching of the Parable of the Talents, take seriously the fulfilment of the talents of their students and thereby have an international reputation for academic high standards.[20] This conjunction of counter-culturalism on the one hand and of academic quality on the other produces an interesting and potentially contradictory relation with secular states and their education policies.

Many states in the contemporary globalised world want to benefit from the academic quality of Catholic schools but their counter-cultural tendencies can be politically problematic, because they constitute a religious, moral and social critique of the policies that governments are pursuing. It is therefore in the interests of the State to maximise and reward the former, while seeking to ignore or marginalise the latter. The Catholic Church, at various levels, has to resist these strategies to compromise the mission integrity of its schools, colleges and universities.[21] It has to hold fast to the teaching of Jesus Christ, 'Render to Caesar that which is Caesar's, and to God that which is God's'.

Notes

1 Pope John XXIII was a pioneer in developing this more open approach to the secular world, when he addressed his 1963 encyclical, *Pacem in Terris,* not only to the Catholic faithful but also to 'all men of good will'.

2 Matthew 22 v. 21. *The Revised Standard Version,* Catholic edition (1966). Ignatius Press.

3 The 2007 document from the Congregation continues to emphasise this theme:

> the formational experience of the Catholic school constitutes an impressive barrier against the influence of a widespread mentality that leads young people especially to consider themselves and their lives as a series of sensations to be experienced rather than as a work to be accomplished.
>
> (*Educating Together in Catholic Schools* n. 42)

4 For various accounts of these attempts, see the *International Handbook of Catholic Education* (Grace and O'Keefe 2007) Chapters 9 (Brazil) 14 (England and Wales), 16 (Spain), 18 (France), 25 (Germany), 28 (Zambia), 31 (Kenya), 40 (China/Hong Kong). See also, for Nigeria, the article by R. Omolade in *International Studies in Catholic Education* (2009).

5 For a review of the situation in the US, see O'Keefe and Scheopner (2007).

6 In practice, Catholic bishops and the leaders of Catholic schools have claimed a first priority in admissions for baptised Catholics, with any further available

places being open to non-Catholics. In some contexts however national govern-ments may require Catholic schools to take students assigned by the State.

7 See Sullivan's (2001) book for a detailed discussion of the issues.

8 See Archbishop Michael Miller, CSB, Secretary of the Congregation for Catholic Education in his contribution to the *International Handbook of Catholic Education* (2007): 'Religious are needed in schools because they bear radical witness to evangelical values and so inspire a Gospel spirit in lay teachers and in their pupils' (Miller, 2007: 476).

9 For one account of the growing assertion of parent groups against the education policies of the Catholic hierarchy, see Arthur (1995: 148–60).

10 For an extended discussion of this, see Grace (1998).

11 There is a great need for more research into the long term effects of a Catholic education, especially in terms of the involvement of Catholic school alumni in the mission of the Church and in public service for the common good. For one account, using life history analysis, see Grace (2002a: 62–79).

12 It is clear, from the evidence, that religious women working in education gave the leadership in resistance to apartheid in South Africa.

13 There are interesting parallels here with the situation in South Africa i.e. religious working in education as the pioneers of change. However, in the case of LACR, the Vatican suspended this organisation in disapproval of its radical approach.

14 Despite these constraints, some religious congregations, especially the Jesuits have pioneered new forms of education for the poor. See Klaiber's account of Fe y Alegría schools established in Venezuela, Peru and other Latin America nations (Klaiber, 2007: 187–8).

15 An oppressed class in the Indian caste system, previously called 'untouchables'.

16 Corrado de Robertis, MCCJ and Keith Morrison (2009) suggest that this has been the case in their critical study of Catholic education in Macau/China.

17 Most Catholic schools in England are designated as 'Voluntary Aided' and receive substantial State funding and therefore are an integral part of the free State schooling system.

18 See, for instance, see Grace (2002a: 197–201) and Foley and Grace (2001).

19 See, for instance, differences about 'openness' and 'Catholicity' in Malta in Mifsud (2010). See also Bruguès (2009) for issues in France.

20 This statement is validated in most of the 45 research accounts reported in the *International Handbook of Catholic Education* (Grace and O'Keefe, 2007).

21 For a recent statement on universities, see Conway (2011).

References

Arthur, J. (1995) *The Ebbing Tide: Policy and Principles of Catholic education.* Leominster: Gracewing Books.

Arthur, J., Crick, R., Samuel, E., Wilson, K. and McGettrick, B. (2006) *Character Education: The formative virtues and dispositions in 16–19 year olds, with partic-ular reference to the religious and spiritual.* London: John Templeton Foundation.

Bruguès, J.-L. (Archbishop) (2009) 'De quelques défis lances aujourd'hui à l'école', *International Studies in Catholic Education,* 1(1), 73–84.

Calvez, J.-Y. and Perrin, J. (1961) *The Church and Social Justice.* London: Burns and Oates.

Catholic Bishops' Conference of England and Wales (1996) *The Common Good and the Catholic Church's Social Teaching.* London: CBC.

Catholic Education Service (1997) *The Common Good in Education.* London: CES.

Catholic Institute for International Relations (1993) *Santo Domingo Conclusions: New evangelization: human development and Christian culture.* London: CIIR.

Christie, P. (1990) *Open Schools: Racially mixed Catholic schools in South Africa 1976–1986.* Johannesburg: Raven Press.

Chubb, J. and Moe, T. (1990) *Politics, Markets and America's Schools.* Washington, DC: The Brookings Institute.

Congregation for Catholic Education (1977) *The Catholic School.* Vatican City: Libreria Editrice Vaticana.

Congregation for Catholic Education (1982) *Lay Catholics in Schools: Witness to faith.* Vatican City: Libreria Editrice Vaticana.

Congregation for Catholic Education (1988) *The Religious Dimension of Education in a Catholic School.* Vatican City: Libreria Editrice Vaticana.

Congregation for Catholic Education (1998) *The Catholic School on the Threshold of the Third Millennium.* Vatican City: Libreria Editrice Vaticana.

Congregation for Catholic Education (2002) *Consecrated Persons and Their Mission in Schools.* Vatican City: Libreria Editrice Vaticana.

Congregation for Catholic Education (2007) *Educating Together in Catholic Schools: A shared mission.* Vatican City: Libreria Editrice Vaticana.

Conway, E. (2011) 'The future of Catholic higher education in Ireland', *International Studies in Catholic Education,* 3(2), 158–69.

De Robertis, C. and Morrison, K. (2009) 'Catholic schooling, identity and social justice in Macau', *International Studies in Catholic Education,* 1(2), 152–69.

Flannery, A. (1998) *Vatican Council II: The Conciliar and Post Conciliar Documents Vol 1.* Dublin and New York: Dominican Publications and Costello Publications.

Foley, J. and Grace, G. (2001) *The Birmingham Catholic School Partnership: Holding to common good values in a market competitive age.* London: CRDCE.

Freire, P. (1970) *Cultural Action for Freedom.* New York: Harvard University Press.

Freire, P. (1972) *Pedagogy of the Oppressed.* Harmondsworth: Penguin.

Friere, P. (1974) *Education for Critical Consciousness.* New York: Bloomsbury Publishing.

Grace, G. (1998) 'Realising the mission: Catholic approaches to school effectiveness' in Slee, R., Weiner, G. and Tomlinson, S. (eds) *School Effective for whom?* London: Falmer Press, pp. 117–27.

Grace, G. (2002a) *Catholic Schools: Mission, markets and morality.* London and New York: Routledge Falmer.

Grace, G. (2002b) 'Mission integrity: Contemporary challenges for Catholic school leaders' in Leithwood, K. and Hallinger, P. (eds) *Second International Handbook of Educational Leadership and Administration.* Dordrecht: Kluwer Academic Publishers, pp. 427–49.

Grace, G. (2003a) 'Educational studies and faith-based schooling: Moving from prejudice to evidence-based argument', *British Journal of Educational Studies,* 51(2), 149–67.

Grace, G. (2003b) 'First and foremost the Church offers its educational services to the poor: Class, inequality and Catholic schooling in contemporary contexts', *International Studies in Sociology of Education,* 13(1), 35–53.

Grace, G. and O'Keefe, J. (2007) (eds) *International Handbook of Catholic Education* (2 Vols). Dordrecht: Springer.

Gutiérrez, G., McDonagh, F., Padin, C. and Sobrino, J. (1993) *Santo Domingo and After: the challenges for the Latin American Church*. London: CIIR.

Hastings, A. (1991) *A History of English Christianity 1920–1990*. London: SCM Press.

Kelly, M. and Higgs, C. (2012) 'The Cabra Dominican sisters and the "open schools" movement in apartheid South Africa', *International Studies in Catholic Education*, 4(1), 4–15.

Klaiber, J. (2007) 'Catholic schools in Peru: Elites, the poor and the challenges of neo-liberalism', in Grace, G. and O'Keefe, S.J. (eds) *International Handbook of Catholic Education*. London: Springer, pp. 181–93.

McBrien, R. (1994) *Catholicism*. New York: HarperCollins.

Mifsud, F. (2010) 'Other faith students in Maltese Catholic schools: responses of school leaders', *International Studies in Catholic Education*, 2(1), 50–63.

Miller, M. (Archbishop) (2007) 'Challenges facing Catholic schools: A view from Rome', in Grace, G. and O'Keefe, S.J. (eds) *International Handbook of Catholic Education*. London: Springer, pp. 449–80.

O'Keefe, J. and Scheopner, A. (2007) 'No margin, no mission: Challenges for Catholic urban schools in the USA', in Grace, G. and O'Keefe, S.J. (eds) *International Handbook of Catholic Education*. London: Springer, pp. 15–35.

Omolade, R. (2009) 'Challenges for Catholic schools in Nigeria', *International Studies in Catholic Education*, 1(1), 30–41.

Pope John XXIII (1963) *Pacem in Terris*. Vatican City: LEV.

Pope Pius XI (1931) *Quodragesimo Anno*. Vatican City: LEV.

Pope Paul VI (1967) *Populorum Progressio*. Vatican City: LEV.

Ranson, S. (1993) 'Markets or democracy for education?', *British Journal of Educational Studies*, 41(4), 333–52.

Roman Synod of Bishops (1971) *Justice in the World in Proclaiming Justice and Peace*. Mystic, CT: Twenty-Third Publications.

Southern African Catholic Bishops' Conference (1977) *Declaration of Commitment on Social Justice and Race Relations within the Church*. Pretoria: SACBC.

Streck, D. and Segala, A. (2007) 'A theological-pedagogical turning point in Latin America: A new way of being school in Brazil', in Grace, G. and O'Keefe, S.J. (eds) *International Handbook of Catholic Education*. London: Springer, pp. 165–79.

Sullivan, J. (2001) *Catholic Education: Distinctive and inclusive*. London: Kluwer Academic Publishers.

Tete, N. (2007) 'Catholic education in India: Challenge, response and research', in Grace, G. and O'Keefe, S.J. (eds) *International Handbook of Catholic Education*. London: Springer, pp. 683–94.

Toppo, T. (Cardinal) (2007) 'Catholic education and the Church's concern for the marginalised: A view from India', in Grace, G. and O'Keefe, S.J. (eds) *International Handbook of Catholic Education*. London: Springer, pp. 653–63.

Index